*f*P

SELECTED PREVIOUS WORKS BY PETER GODMAN

Poetry of the Carolingian Renaissance

Alcuin: The Bishops, Kings and Saints of York

From Poliziano to Machiavelli

*The Silent Masters: Latin Literature and
Its Censors in the Twelfth Century*

*The Saint as Censor: Robert Bellarmine
Between Inquisition and Index*

Hitler

and

T H E

Vatican

Inside the Secret Archives

that Reveal the New Story

of the Nazis and the Church

PETER GODMAN

FREE PRESS

NEW YORK LONDON TORONTO SYDNEY

*f*P

FREE PRESS
A Division of Simon & Schuster, Inc.
1230 Avenue of the Americas
New York, NY 10020

For information about special discounts for bulk purchases,
please contact Simon & Schuster Special Sales:
1-800-456-6798 or business@simonandschuster.com

Designed by Joseph Rutt

Manufactured in the United States of America

1 3 5 7 9 10 8 6 4 2

Library of Congress Cataloging-in-Publication Data
Godman, Peter.
Hitler and the Vatican: inside the secret archives that reveal
the new story of the Nazis and the Church/Peter Godman.
p. cm.
Includes bibliographical references and index.
1. Catholic Church—Germany—History—1933–1945. 2. Pius XII, Pope, 1876–1958—
Relations with Germany. 3. Church and state—Germany—History—1933–1945.
4. World War, 1939–1945—Catholic Church. 5. National socialism and religion. I. Title.
D810.C6G63 2004
327.430456'34'09041—dc22   2003064359

ISBN 978-0-7432-4598-2

to
Candi and Peter

It is at times of crisis . . . that one can judge the hearts and characters of men, the brave and the poor of spirit. It is at these times that they give the measure of themselves and show whether they are equal to their vocation, their mission.

We are at a time of crisis.

Eugenio Cardinal Pacelli, July 13, 1937
(*Sa Sainteté Pie XII, Discours et panégyriques
1931–1938* [Paris, 1939], 383)

Contents

Introduction

"WITH THE CHURCH, or without it?" mused Adolf Hitler, during one of his more relaxed moments, on December 13, 1941.[1] Over the teacups, in the company of his Nazi intimates, the Führer's thoughts turned to the problem of religion. In his youth, he had believed that the solution was dynamite. Since then, he had taken a different line. That line he illustrated in subtle reflections on his six divisions of SS, who, without affiliation to any church but with serenity in their souls, went to their deaths; on Christ as an Aryan; and on the links of Saint Paul, that proto-Bolshevik, with the criminal underworld. It is not recorded whether, during a pause in Hitler's harangue, his fellow fanatics added sugar to their tea.

For them, his apostles, what he asserted was to be believed. They placed their faith in a conqueror who claimed to have stormed the state without yielding to the claims of the religious confessions. That had been Mussolini's mistake. The Duce, alleged the Führer, would have done better to follow his own revolutionary course. Then came the outburst: "I would march into the Vatican and turf the whole lot out! Then I'd say: 'Sorry, I've made a mistake!' But they'd be out!" Although that strategy had not yet, in 1941, matured in Hitler's mind, when allowance is made for the exaggerations of megalomania, such were his authentic attitudes.[2]

Authentic in their coarseness, brutality, and cynicism, Hitler's declarations to his circle differed from his statements to the outside world. Capable of professing respect, if it suited his purposes, for established religion in public, privately this baptized Catholic expressed calculating regard for the organization of the Roman Church. The Führer spoke in many voices, with the ventriloquism of a consummate liar.

The voices, public and private, of Adolf Hitler are well known. Less familiar are some of the pronouncements by the Roman Church during the same period. From its inmost citadel, the Vatican, only one figure seems now to be heard. Pius XII (1939–58) still monopolizes attention. To the statements and the silences of "Hitler's Pope," unique importance is attached.[3] It was he alone, we are told, who spoke in the name and with the authority of the Vatican, within the sinister confines of which lurked a cove of anti-Semites whose self-appointed prosecutor is Daniel Goldhagen.[4]

The prosecution's case, being symmetrical, is easy to understand. On one side of the dock cowers Hitler, guilty and condemned; on the other stands the Vatican, complicit in his crimes. But the symmetry is distorted and its foundations quake, because they are built on evidence cut to fit the easy simplifications of polemic.

Take, for example, "the Vatican." What did that term mean before and during the Second World War? The "monolithic institution" of John Cornwell's fantasy? Or a disparate array of departments and individuals, not always in agreement with one another and sometimes acting at odds? Such was the reality of the so-called totalitarian state in Germany and Italy—less a monolith than a mess of conflicting agencies and characters. No one today accepts at face value Nazi or fascist claims of complete control. Yet many appear to be willing to do just that in the case of the Vatican.

Why? If the Vatican is assumed to be similar to the mythical monolith of the totalitarian state, that assumption serves a purpose. Similarity insinuating sympathy, "Hitler's Pope" can then be presented as the leader of an organization like that of the Führer's or the Duce's. A motive thus seems to be offered for why the authoritarian Pius XII is supposed to have been on the dictators' side. This tactic has obvious advantages. Identify the Vatican with the person of one pope, and you are free to concentrate on a well-known individual to the exclusion of others, more obscure and difficult to research. This leaves you with leisure for denunciation, and spares you the drudgery of work.

Work in dusty archives is, to some, less appealing than the hot air of speculation and the warm glow of publicity. Not that they are defenseless when accused of misrepresenting the Vatican, because they have failed to examine the sources. They reply that this is the Vatican's own fault. By refusing to grant historians access to materials dating from the 1930s and 1940s, the Roman Church has proved that it has something to hide. Suspicions confirmed by this circular reasoning, grotesque conclusions are drawn. Reproached with his inadequate command of even published evidence, the most vehement of the Vatican's prosecutors answers that he is less a historian than a moralist.

Moralism operates with certainties that, in the present state of our knowledge, do not exist. Fundamental and difficult questions remain unanswered. How much, for example, do we know about the ideas and policies of the men who worked in the Vatican on the eve of the Second World War? Not enough to enable us to be confident about understanding them and their actions "from the inside." Rome during this period has been viewed almost exclusively from an outsider's perspective.

From the outside, 1939 has seemed the crucial date. In the year when war broke out, Eugenio Pacelli was elected pope. About him it is all too easy to speculate. Do his silences about the crimes of the Nazis not imply sympathy for them? Was that pope both an anti-Semite and an anti-Communist, blind to the suffering of the Jews but obsessed by the peril of the "Bolsheviks"? Confident judgments have been pronounced on these issues, but few of them are based on acquaintance with the context in which, at the Vatican, Pacelli and others worked.

That is what this book attempts to do. Its aim is to penetrate behind the scenes of what has seemed a closed world, to examine the thoughts and the motives of the men who formulated policy at the head of the Church, and to consider both the actions that they took and the courses that they chose not to follow. Negative decisions can be just as significant as positive ones. What was discussed, written, and debated inside the Vatican, but not stated publicly, offers us insight into the choices made by its leadership. That leadership drew on a wide range of opinions, some of them previously unknown.

Unknown and unknowable until recently, for example, were sources from the most secret department in the central administration of the Church. In the archives of the Inquisition—also called the Supreme Congregation of the Holy Office—were formulated ideas about Nazism and related phenomena that were considered so sensitive that, in 1940 (when Hitler's victory seemed possible), they were transported to the United States, out of concern that they might be seized in the event of a German occupation of Rome.

That concern was justified. The views contained in these documents would not have appealed to the Nazis. And because all of these documents were known to Pius XII before he became pope, they acquire a special piquancy. Drafted and revised during the reign of his predecessor, Pius XI (1922–39), by officials of the highest Catholic authority in matters of faith and morals, these sources enable us to reconstruct in detail the motives and the reactions of Rome.

Rome stands at the center of this book, as a stage on which figure a number of unfamiliar characters. Others play new or hidden roles in a drama carried out behind the scenes. That drama began earlier than is sometimes supposed; 1939 intensified a crisis that had been looming for years. To understand its origins and course, perhaps it is time to think afresh: to turn our attention from the well-worn themes of Pius XII's personal responsibility for the Holocaust and of the Church's "collective guilt," and begin to listen, inside the Vatican, to unheard voices.

Hitler

and

THE

Vatican

———∞———

Unanswered Questions

WHY DID THE CATHOLIC CHURCH not raise its voice against the cruelties of racism, the brutality of totalitarianism, the repression of liberties in the Third Reich? Did the notorious silences about the Nazis on Rome's part undermine its claims to moral authority? These questions have not been raised neutrally. Spiced by speculation, polemic has focused on "Hitler's Pope": Pius XII (1939–58). It has not been known that, long before he was crowned, during the 1930s, a condemnation of the moral and doctrinal errors of National Socialism was prepared by the Holy See. That condemnation was couched in terms intelligible to Adolf Hitler, such as the following:

> The Church condemns as heretical the opinion that human nature is not essentially the same in all people, but that mankind which now inhabits the earth is composed of races so different from one another that the lowest of them is even further from the highest race than it is from the highest kind of animal that resembles man.

Had this sentence been made public, it is certain that Hitler would have recognized the damned opinion because he had expressed it himself in his "victory speech" held before the congress of the National Socialist Party on November 3, 1933. The Führer would no doubt have reacted with rage to criticism by the Church, for racism was a cardinal doctrine in the Nazi creed.

The Vatican's plans were far-reaching. Aimed at views stated in

Mein Kampf and in Hitler's other writings or speeches, they struck at such fundamental elements in the ideology of National Socialism as "blood" and its "purity": "The Church condemns the view that any mixture of blood with a foreign and inferior race, in particular a mixture of the Arian with the Semitic race, is, by reason of that mixture alone, a most heinous crime against nature and marks a grave fault in the conscience."

Nor did the attack on Hitler stop there. His ideas and those of other Nazi leaders on subjects ranging from "eugenics" to sterilization, from education to leadership and individual rights, were damned by the Vatican in successive drafts:

> All people about whom there are grounds to fear that they may produce imperfect offspring may be prevented from contracting a marriage that could be fertile, even if they are otherwise capable of marriage, and they may be sterilized, even against their will. Children conceived by parents of this kind may be removed by the direct intervention of an abortion.

Or:

> The first and chief right to educate belongs to that institution which has the first and chief right to provide for the race, i.e.: the state, neither to the Church nor the parents . . .
>
> As to the education of young people, they should not, in first place, be imbued with religious sentiments or with love and fear of God but with a feeling of affection for the race so that they regard nothing on this earth with more respect than the race and the state built on the basis of racial character.

Or:

> Nothing but the absolute and unlimited leadership of one man is the form of government in the state that is in keeping with the lawful path which nature follows in selecting races and individuals.

Any other form of government is more or less a contravention of nature.

Or:

Single individuals and associations of people have no rights, either by divine or natural law, which are prior to the state or independent of it and not only is the exercise of rights decided upon by the state but even their origin and simple existence.

The program of National Socialism and its practice were being branded as incompatible with Christianity years before Pius XII mounted the throne of St. Peter in 1939. His predecessor Pius XI (1922–39) and other leading figures in the curial establishment believed that such statements would be interpreted, in Germany, as a declaration of spiritual war.

The story of how and why the Catholic Church planned to condemn the Nazis, and of what became of those plans, sheds new light on the inner workings of the Vatican on the eve of the Second World War. The sources, previously inaccessible, enable us to penetrate behind the scenes and understand the ways in which, after the Nazis came to power, Rome thought and operated.

The operations of the Roman authorities—not always a model of efficiency—were conducted through an ill-coordinated bureaucracy that followed procedures which had developed over centuries. Attentive to precedents set in the past, members of the Curia knew that history provided them with several possible forms of condemnation, at various levels of solemnity.

The forms in which Rome's statements were made, and the contexts in which they appeared, could convey messages subtler and more precise than the public declarations of a secular state. There was a significant difference, for example, between a papal pronouncement of disapproval reported in the Vatican's semiofficial newspaper,

Osservatore Romano, and an anathema leveled by the Pope as head of the Church's Supreme Tribunal. The first resembled a rumble of thunder, menacing but remote. The second was similar to a bolt of lightning, aimed to strike at an error, root and branch.

A decree from the Supreme Tribunal, signed by the Pope, had binding force on Catholics in matters of doctrine and morals. In these matters of fundamental importance, the judgment of the Supreme Pontiff was definitive. When he condemned an error with the weight of his unerring authority, it was announced by that papal tribunal known, since the sixteenth century, as the Roman Inquisition or Holy Office. One of its severest sentences, delivered as punishment, was ex-communication—exclusion from the community of the faithful, to which Adolf Hitler nominally belonged.

Less punitive in effect and more positive in purpose were the en-cyclicals, or papal letters, which expressed the *magisterium* ("teach-ing") of the Pope. Issued in his name, often on the basis of contributions made by members of the Vatican's bureaucracy, such documents represented declarations of principle by the head of the Roman Church. Beneath these two peaks of solemnity—the encycli-cal and the inquisitorial decree—lower levels of publicity could also signal the Vatican's view.

Works might be placed on the Index of Prohibited Books, indicat-ing that they were banned for Catholics; diplomatic notes of protest or clarification might be exchanged with foreign governments; in-structions might be imparted to orthodox institutions of learning, or-dering them to contest suspect ideas. During the 1930s, all of these possibilities were considered or implemented by Rome. When and why they were employed or discarded, and by whom, were questions that engaged Hitler's attention.

The Führer was sensitive to the nuances of the Vatican's official voice. Ambiguous in his alternations between respect and loathing for the Church, he hesitated to repudiate Christianity. Its language, its cate-gories, its images loom large in *Mein Kampf* and in his later writings and speeches.[1] Divine providence, Hitler claimed, guided National Socialism in its struggle for "racial purity." Jesus Christ, for him, was not only "the true God" but also "our greatest Aryan leader." [2] The next figure in the Führer's pantheon appears to have been himself.

Like Mussolini, he saw himself as a redeemer. Unlike the Duce, Hitler claimed that his movement had discovered the true meaning of the New Testament. The Old Testament was excluded because it was "Semitic"; God's law was to be identified with racism. Hitler portrayed himself as the prophet of this doctrine, which the Catholic Church had perverted; and the "positive Christianity" to which the program of the Nazi Party referred was meant to heal the confessional divisions between German Catholics and Protestants, and to unite the nation in its fight against the Jews. [3]

The Jews and the "Bolsheviks" played leading parts in Hitler's melodrama of hatred, and he dressed them in demonic costumes. Yet the confusion of roles produced by his misuse of religious language never led the Führer to forget that, on the world stage that he desired to dominate, the Vatican still occupied some of the limelight.

There opinions were divided from the beginning. Some in the Vatican saw Hitler as a perfidious enemy of Christianity, others as a Catholic conservative who might be taken at his word. That the Führer's words, public and private, changed as bewilderingly as Proteus made him difficult to pin down. That difficulty was compounded by the fact that the two sides spoke different languages and came from different cultures. Italian priests trained in the subtleties of theology or the rigors of law had little in common with an Austrian autodidact whose scant knowledge of both subjects was borrowed and whose ideas were all too often his own. [4]

Direct experience of the Nazis was a more reliable guide to their intentions than the confusing rant of their rhetoric. One of the few in the Vatican, during the 1930s, who commanded such experience was Eugenio Pacelli, the future Pius XII. As papal nuncio to Bavaria, he reported to the secretary of state, Cardinal Pietro Gasparri, [5] on November 14, 1923, about Hitler's failed attempt at a putsch in Munich five days earlier. The Nazis, Pacelli stated, had attempted to rouse the rabble against the Church, the Pope, and the Jesuits. [6] A "vulgar and violent campaign" in the popular press, directed by Hitler's followers against Catholics and Jews, was signaled on April 24, 1924.[7] No sympathy for National Socialism, as he encountered it in Germany, can be read into the dispatches of the diplomat who, in 1939, allegedly became "Hitler's Pope." Pacelli recognized the movement headed by the Führer for what it was. Yet it was he who, in 1933, concluded with the government of Nazi Germany a Concordat that would cast, throughout that decade, a shadow on the policy of the Vatican.

To follow Pacelli's own definition, "Concordats are agreements binding in international law which establish a link between states, and have the purpose of justly balancing and clarifying, in the form of a treaty, religious and ecclesiastical interests on the one hand and the interests of the state on the other, in such a way that complete reciprocity is guaranteed."[8] Nothing, for Hitler, was guaranteed by the Concordat except a boost to his international prestige. Gleeful at the Vatican's acknowledgment of his government's legitimacy, he ignored the concept of "reciprocity" from the outset. Violations of the treaty would be flagrant between the time of its signing (July 20) and its ratification (September 10) in 1933. And that raises the problem of Rome's motives in concluding such an agreement with a partner whom it had every reason to regard as treacherous.

Several of those motives are revealed, in a memorandum dated June 20, 1933, by Cardinal Gasparri, then Pacelli's predecessor as secretary of state:

> As long as Hitler does not declare war on the Holy See or the Catholic hierarchy in Germany:
> I.   The Holy See and the Catholic hierarchy in Germany should refrain from condemning Hitler's Party.
> II. If Hitler wants the Catholic Centre to be dissolved *as a political Party*, he should be obeyed without fuss.
> III. Catholics should be free to become members of Hitler's Party, just as Catholics in Italy are free to become members of the Fascist Party.
> IV. German Catholics should be equally free not to become members of Hitler's Party, providing that it is always within the limits of the law, as is the case with Italian Catholics with respect to the Fascist Party.

Gasparri added, in what was to become a leitmotiv of caution: "I am of the opinion that Hitler's Party corresponds to nationalist feeling in Germany. Therefore a politico-religious struggle in Germany over Hitlerism ["hitleranismo"] must be avoided at all costs, especially when the Eminent [Cardinal] Pacelli is secretary of state.[9]

As secretaries of state to Pius XI, Pacelli and Gasparri lived in the Fascist Italy which, in 1929, had signed and ratified a concordat with the Holy See.[10] That represented the model for them both. To Gasparri, it seemed worth buying at the price of excluding the clergy from party-political activities in Germany, as had been done in Italy. Pastoral concerns were to have priority, according to the Vatican. Mussolini welcomed this choice because it reinforced his hegemony over the state, and the Duce's admirers among the Nazis thought similarly. When they praised the Italian Concordat, they referred, above all, to its article prohibiting clerical involvement in politics.[11]

That involvement, as Hitler saw it, had been far too direct in the early 1930s, when the German bishops had condemned National Socialism as a "heresy incompatible with Christianity" and forbidden Catholics to become members of the Party.[12] That was what Gasparri, in June 1933, was anxious to prevent from recurring. By then the political situation had changed, and Hitler was effecting a revolution by what appeared to be legal means.

Eighteen days after the elections that had given the Nazis and their coalition partners (the Nationalists) a majority in the Reichstag, on March 23, 1933, the Führer declared, about the Enabling Act that conferred on his government comprehensive powers of legislation, that the Christian religion was to be "the basis of our complete morality." That declaration led the German bishops to withdraw their condemnation. Reconciliation, or at least an armed truce, became the order of the day. As long as Hitler avoided open war, so should the Catholic Church, its former secretary of state counseled his successor.

Gasparri's words exercised a lasting influence on Pacelli. They were recalled by him, in one of his first audiences with the German hierarchy, soon after his election to the papacy in 1939—despite *Kristallnacht* and a series of repressive measures against Catholics in the Third Reich.[13] Although the moral and doctrinal grounds for a condemnation had become more urgent and detailed, Pius XII hesitated to speak out. Not only Gasparri's admonitions contributed to sealing his lips but also experience of the German episcopate's dealings with the Führer and the lessons taught by Pius XI.

Patron and mentor of Pacelli, Pius XI had begun, in March 1933, to take a more positive view of Hitler than previously. Communism—the worst of threats, in the Vatican's eyes—was the reason. The Führer was the only figure on the international stage, apart from himself, to stand up to the "world-danger of Bolshevism," and earned the Pope's praise.[14] That praise implied no sympathy for Hitler's other goals or methods. In August of the same year, Pius XI, during a conversation with the British diplomat Ivone Kirkpatrick, criticized the Nazis' treatment of Austria as a "disgrace" and described the "German persecutions of the Jews" as "an offence not only against morality but against civilization."[15] Yet it was with Hitler's government that the Vatican ratified a Concordat one month later.

Only ratification could make it legally possible to move against those who wished to disturb the peace between the Vatican and Berlin,[16] Pacelli was assured by representatives of that government. They then gave the secretary of state a week to make up his mind. Blackmail, combined with pseudo-legal arguments, did not remove his doubts. But this trained jurist who, during the Weimar Republic, had negotiated, with much skill and little success, for terms less favorable than those being offered by Hitler, was at long last offered what he would refer to as a "legal basis" for relations between the Catholic Church and Germany. Faced with the prospect of increasing violence if the Concordat was not ratified, Pacelli embarked on his long and unhappy path down what has been rightly called a "one-way street."[17]

Believing that there was no going back, he negotiated its twists and turns warily. Just one month later, on October 19, 1933, he drafted (in Italian) a memorandum about violations of the Concordat: "Wishing to spare the government of the Reich the unpleasantness of a public discussion of the situation . . . the Holy See has preferred, up to now, to follow the course of confidential negotiations rather than have recourse to a public protest."[18]

Menace in moderation, protest softened by diplomacy: Much of

Eugenio Pacelli's subsequent strategy is foreshadowed in these phrases. When he wrote them, he was under pressure not only from the government of Nazi Germany but also from its Catholic hierarchy. Its senior member—the infinitely painstaking, incurably anxious, and utterly unimaginative Cardinal Adolf Bertram of Breslau[19]—had urged him, on September 2, 1933, to ratify the Concordat as soon as possible on the grounds (among others) that to fail to do so would worsen the position of the German episcopate.[20]

That position was never strong. Having condemned National Socialism as heretical, then withdrawn the condemnation, the bishops were rarely capable of facing the Nazi dilemma with unity or decisiveness. Divided among themselves about resistance or compromise, they were perplexed by Hitler's "revolution achieved by legal means." Patriotism mingled with reverence for his authority, which to them was divinely ordained; and when the Führer or his followers committed outrages, such as advocating the abolition of the "Jewish" Old Testament, the stands they took tended to be selective.

Cardinal Michael Faulhaber of Munich, a friend of Pacelli's and an enthusiast for the Concordat,[21] preached, during the Advent of 1933, four sermons on the delicate subject of "Judaism, Christianity, [and] Germanness."[22] The luster of this noble act was hardly enhanced by Faulhaber's later explanation that his purpose had been to defend the Old Testament, not the Jews. Nor was their persecution condemned by the bishop often hailed as a courageous opponent of the Nazis, the "lion of Münster" Clemens August von Galen, who denounced, in well-publicized sermons, abuses by the Gestapo and the judicial murders of "euthanasia," with no reference to the Holocaust.[23]

The "one-way street" that had led to the Concordat soon lengthened into a maze and, as the German bishops wandered in its recesses, they looked to Rome for guidance. Disoriented by the shakiness of their "legal basis" being undermined by Nazi attacks, few of them realized that, in the place from which they sought answers to the questions which they were incapable of resolving, there was not one Rome but two.

—⊶⊷⊶—

Two Romes

"ROME IS OUR STARTING POINT and our point of reference; it is our symbol or, if you prefer, our myth. We dream of Roman Italy—wise and strong, disciplined and imperial. Much of the immortal spirit of ancient Rome is reborn in Fascism!" declared Benito Mussolini, on April 21, 1922, a few months before the march on Rome.[1] The rhetoric of the future dictator had already acquired a mystical and messianic tone. Not "the Rome of the monuments and ruins" inspired his passion, but "the city of living souls" which he aimed to regenerate. The "new man" of the Fascists was to be fashioned by a redeemer who also saw himself as a prophet. Action and intuition were the Duce's methods; rigor and combat were his slogans. That is why, when Winston Churchill, in 1923, described him as "the greatest living legislator," the praise may have seemed faint to its recipient. Benito Mussolini wished to be regarded as a new Augustus, a second Caesar.

More than a city, the Rome that he envisaged was to become the center and the symbol of a political religion.[2] This anticlerical atheist, who had begun his career by attacking the Church and would end it by comparing his misfortunes with those of Jesus Christ, was well aware of the power of religious language and rituals. In the here and now of a Rome that he set out to shape in his image of totalitarian grandeur, a reformation of Italian society was to take place. The task demanded a superman. Against the paradise that Mussolini aimed to establish on earth were pitted the demonic forces of liberals, democrats, socialists, communists, and (later) Jews. Yet he would triumph against these foes of mankind, for he was not only Caesar Augustus, but also the Savior.

This claptrap served to exalt and legitimate the regime in the person of its Duce. Support for him was not confined to the Fascist foot soldiers. Commanding figures on the international scene voiced their approval of Mussolini. Had not Pius XI (1922–39) hailed him as "the man of Providence" when, in 1929, the concordat between Church and State restored (in the words of the same Pope) "God to Italy, and Italy to God"?[3] Between Him and the Duce, Fascist propaganda asserted similarities. Pronouns referring to Him (Mussolini, not God) were capitalized. Devotees groveled before their "spiritual father" and "sublime redeemer in the Roman heavens," while proclaiming their belief in his infallibility. The superman pretended to scorn these tributes, and silently encouraged them. Understandably. How could a former journalist and permanent thug resist taking seriously the spectacle of peasants kneeling before him in the fields, mothers imploring his blessing for their children, ministers running to his desk, then exiting at the double? No one laughed. "Laughter," a high priest of Fascism, Giovanni Gentile, solemnly declared, "is of the devil."[4]

Diabolically cunning, in its mixture of the sacred and the profane, was this cult of the Duce's "divinity." Accompanied by prayers and parades, ceremonies and salutes, it was staged, first and foremost, at Rome. The Rome in which Mussolini intended to realize the paradise that he promised had nothing to do with the other world. The City of God cherished by Christians seemed, to this cynic, an illusion. His urban reality amounted to an alternative and an opposition to the capital of Catholicism. And if Rome had to be rebuilt, that meant creating rubble. Construction was not the primary feature of Fascist architecture and town planning.[5] Its chief characteristic was destruction.

To the brutal eye of the dictator, trained on an ideal city of his own making, the medieval, renaissance, and baroque beauties of Rome were obstructions to the monuments of his megalomania. Think, for example, of plans that (mercifully) were never carried out, such as a new "Mussolini forum," between Monte Mario and the Tiber, dominated by a bronze colossus, eighty meters high, in the form of Hercules. Above one hand brandished in a Roman salute and another bearing a truncheon was to loom the truculent mug of the Duce.[6] Celebration of Fascism and its leader was obviously one aim of the statue and its setting, but so too was intimidation.

Intimidation was essential to this thug's mode of being. Always insecure, even at moments of success, Mussolini wanted his new Rome to outdo what remained of the city of antiquity and eclipse all that had been built by the Church. Not by chance did he order that the scale and dimensions of his forum should be grander than those of St. Peter's and the Colosseum. And if money ran out for this project, others were carried out by leveling to the ground treasures of the classical and Christian past that stood in the way of his ruthless ambition. No less than fifteen churches and several palaces were demolished in order to build his Avenue of the Empire between the Capitol and the Colosseum. There, to the delight of the Duce, military parades were conducted over the obliterated remains of what he regarded with contempt as "centuries of decadence."

The "decadence" of almost two thousand years—from the age of Augustus to the advent of Fascism—was what Mussolini wished to sweep away. Between himself and the Roman emperor whom he exalted was to yawn a chasm of emptiness. There, amid the fasces (or bundles of rods enclosing an ax) and the numbers, slowly increasing, of the new era, he found the consolation, or the illusion, of unrivaled dominance. That is one reason why the results are so pitiful—why so much Fascist architecture and urban planning, intending to impress by its grandiosity, depresses by its vacuity. Cold and anemic, it stands apart in the self-imposed isolation desired by the Duce. Or it fails, comically, to cohere with surroundings intended to link him with one of the few historical figures whose company he could bear: the Emperor Augustus.

The Piazza Augusto Imperatore provides an example of this incoherence. Here, in the center of Rome, stands a complex designed and built during the 1930s by the architect Vittorio Morpurgo, which was meant to celebrate the bond between Mussolini and his imperial model. The Emperor Augustus's return to the city was commemorated by the Roman senate with the famous Ara Pacis (the "altar of peace," built in 13–9 B.C. and reconstructed by the Fascists). Transparent glass surrounding that monument enabled spectators to gaze in wonder at its sculptures. But, as the eye traveled from the side to the center of the square, the stomach sank.

Up to the light and air of antiquity, then down to the darkness and clutter of an archaeological site. In the middle of Piazza Augusto Imperatore, reachable by subterranean stairs, the mausoleum of the emperor lurks. It lurks below street level, in jarring contrast to the position of the Ara Pacis. No harmony, no sense of proportion regulates the remains of Mussolini's model in the square planned to proclaim his affinity with Augustus.

That, however, is the least of the incongruities. The greatest and most grotesque are between the ancient and the modern monuments. On the north side of Piazza Augusto Imperatore stands a balcony topped by mosaics representing the Roman past and Roman virtues. Beneath that balcony a Latin inscription boasts the link between Mussolini the Duce and Augustus the Emperor. Here the cult of Fascism's two Romes—ancient and modern, with nothing in between—is explicit. Here, one imagines, the ruler of the revived empire intended to address, from his rostrum, cheering crowds. Then a doubt obtrudes. What crowds, and where? The space available will scarcely accommodate a rally of Boy Scouts, let alone throngs of applauding Fascists. As cramped and confined as the mind of Mussolini, it resembles less a stage for totalitarian triumphs than a hodgepodge.

Nor does the hodgepodge stop there. Despite the Duce's boast, in his Latin inscription, that he had cleared away the "antique clutter" that disfigured the area, he was forced to yield to pressure groups and spare three churches in the vicinity (San Carlo al Corso, San Rocco, and San Girolamo). The last two were attached by a traverse, while San Carlo was aligned, by Pius XI, with the Piazza Augusto Imperatore through statues of saints (Ambrose and Charles Borromeo) known for their connections not with Rome but with Milan—the city of which the Pope had been archbishop.

Not concord between Church and State is evoked by this setting, but a standoff that menaces a clash. That clash is already enacted within the muddled medley of reliefs that the Fascists set on the north side of the square, next to the balcony. There images of peace, frugality, and prosperity are aligned with weaponry and gas masks used during the Ethiopian campaign and the First World War. How do they cohere with the other side of Piazza Augusto Imperatore, where, attached to the apse of San Carlo, Latin inscriptions praise the two saints of Milan and the role of Pius XI as architect of Lateran Pacts? In such a setting, what did "Romanness" (*romanità*) mean? The "Romanness" of the Church or that of the Fascists—or both? The answer pleased neither side. Modern Duce, ancient emperor, and reigning Pope were unavoidably bound to one another. The "centuries of decadence" represented by Pius XI would not go away.

Immovable like the mountains which, earlier in his career, he had loved to climb, Pope Pius XI[7] painted a self-portrait when, on November 16, 1929, he addressed a pilgrimage of alpine guides: "A clear head, a staunch heart, courage, calm, prudence and, on occasion, ambition, proper ambition . . . combined with the noblest awareness of one's own duties and responsibilities . . . [8] As solitary and strong-willed as Mussolini, Pius XI was said to have favored, in 1932, a form of "Catholic totalitarianism."[9] What the Pope meant by that unhappy expression was nothing like what it signified to the Duce. But if his words misled, that was Pius XI's own fault, for no one who had to do with him failed to notice his authoritarian streak.

Meeting that steely gaze behind the spectacles, many trembled in fear. Unpredictable and incalculable, the Pope seldom hesitated to speak his mind. Thick-set, slow-moving, with a regal formality of manner, Pius XI attempted (not always successfully) to exercise control over his temper. Passionate but disciplined, cold and loving by turns, he was uncompromising in his demand for obedience. Subordination, not collaboration, was expected from those who worked with or (more accurately) under him.

The Pope had little use for democracy. A staunch conservative, he believed in a hierarchy with himself at its summit. To himself he referred, in the royal plural, as "We" or, in the third person, as "the father of all" and "the Vicar of Christ." Christ was visualized, by his representative on earth, as a king whose monarchy was spiritual.[10] The spiritual and supernatural realms lay beyond the reach of the state whose authority was confined to mundane matters of this earth.

In the higher sphere of morals and of faith, the Church reigned supreme. Laymen should know their place. To trespass into Christ's kingdom, as the Fascists tried to do, was "absurd in theory and monstrous in practice."

Authoritarian or democratic, the form of the state was indifferent to the Church, according to a Vatican doctrine formulated by Leo XIII (1878–1903). Pius XI followed that doctrine to the letter.[11] In 1929—the year in which he signed a concordat with Fascist Italy—he also concluded one with Prussia, then ruled by a majority of Socialists, while maintaining cordial relationships with the secularist governments of France. In this sense, it is correct to describe the Pope as an "opportunist."[12] Pius XI exploited every opportunity that presented itself in the interests of the Roman Church.

That Church's relationship with Fascist Italy was marked by an ambivalence that would also characterize its policy toward Nazi Germany. Catholics were recommended to vote for "the government of the Hon. Mussolini" in 1929 to ensure that Parliament would ratify the Lateran Pacts. Did that mean, as was asserted by an enthusiastic supporter of the Duce, Cardinal Ildefonso Schuster of Milan, that the Pope had "blessed Fascism"? The Fascists had reason to think otherwise. After Mussolini, in a speech on the Lateran Pacts delivered before the Chamber of Deputies, claimed not only that Christianity was born in Palestine and became Catholic in Rome, but also that, had it remained in its birthplace, it would have vanished without a trace,[13] Pius XI, in an address printed on the front page of the Vatican newspaper, *Osservatore Romano* (May 16, 1929), described the Duce's views as "heretical and worse than heretical."

Heresy, a mortal sin of the will and the intellect, was to be judged by Rome—not the headquarters of the Fascists but the capital of Catholicism. Different and ultimately incompatible concepts of the city were being employed, by Pope and Duce, before the Lateran Pacts were signed and, after their ratification, the gap between the two sides yawned ever more deeply. Condemning Fascist attacks on Catholic organizations and deploring Fascist attempts to monopolize the school curriculum,[14] Pius XI declared that the education of children was the "divine right" of the Church. "Nationalism," he informed an audience of missionaries on December 7, 1929, "has always been a calamity and a curse for the missions." [15] Damning "pagan worship of the state" in his encyclical *Non abbiamo bisogno (We have no need)* of 1931, without attacking the party or the regime directly, the Pope steered a course between criticism and conciliation.

The point was often lost on Mussolini. What he grasped was the patriotic zeal displayed by Italian bishops and clergy for the Ethiopian war. The alliance, proclaimed by Cardinal Schuster,[16] between "Christian civilization"—represented by Italian troops using gas against Africans—and "Catholic faith" was something the Duce was capable of understanding. Yet the general aloofness of Vatican circles bewildered him. The Pope, bent on educating native peoples in Africa and China and on taking the unprecedented step of ordaining them priests and bishops, could not countenance racist imperialism. Nonetheless Mussolini saw that the one Rome was outflanking the other. As he remarked to his brother Arnaldo, a devout Catholic: "We intended that the Church should become a pillar of the regime. We never thought that the regime would become the servant of the Church." [17]

The head of that church, in a dig at the Duce, once announced that he was prepared to negotiate with the devil, if it were a question of saving souls. Both of them were opportunists, eager to seize the moment, yet both of them yearned for immortality. Immortality of the soul, in which Pius XI believed, meant nothing to Mussolini. Craving the enduring fame of having created a new society, he counted up the diminutive figures of the Fascist era and, recognizing how short his achievements fell of his tall target, chafed against the bit of time. Pius XI, impetuous and impatient though he could be, did not suffer from the same insecurities. Divine providence, in which he placed his trust, had preserved the Church for two millennia. From the vantage point of the Vatican, where he ruled as master, the Pope regarded time with indulgence as a servant or an ally.

This fundamental difference between the authoritarian personalities of the Pope and the Duce found expression in their attitudes to Rome as a sacred city. In virtue of its "particular significance . . . , as the episcopal see of the Supreme Pontiff, for Catholicism." Rome had been recognized, in the Concordat of 1929, as a sanctuary and a place of pilgrimage. That was not enough for Pius XI. He believed that holiness, guaranteed by a long succession of apostles, saints, and martyrs, spread out over the entire urban area on which, by a vigorous campaign of religious initiatives, he aimed to impose a Catholic stamp.[18]

That did not please Mussolini. He had his own ideas about holiness. The sacredness of the city, for him, derived less from the spirit or the monuments of the Christian past than from the more recent Tomb of the Unknown Warrior, from the Altar of the Fatherland, and from the Altar to the Fascist Revolution. There they stood on the Capitol, gazing defiantly at the Vatican. Against the edifices of Catholicism were set the shrines of a political religion allegedly celebrated in the masterpiece of Italian literature. Was this not what Dante meant when—anticipating the Duce—he declared that the founder of Christianity owed everything to "that Rome, due to which Christ is Roman" (*Purgatorio* XXXII, 100–102)?

No, is the answer: Dante meant nothing of the kind. The quotation refers to Beatrice's prophecy of his entry into Paradise, the heavenly Rome, in which Christ is a citizen. The Fascists' attempt to twist the text and reduce it to their earthly slogan was not lost on that Dante-lover Pius XI. In a series of speeches, delivered throughout his reign, he dwelt on Rome, using the same quotation to different ends.

> We have a unique claim to be Roman, because it is not only with reference to Dante's Rome—the Rome of the *Divine Comedy*'s "Paradise"—but also to this earthly Rome that it can be said, with historical truth, that "Christ is Roman." And if Christ is Roman, it follows that he too is Roman whom everyone calls the Vicar of Christ . . . the Pope.[19]

Not by chance these words were addressed, on December 27, 1933, to a congress of *Asian* students. The message was not only valid for Italians. Pagan Rome, declared Pius XI, had an imperial ambition of conquest; Catholic Rome a Christian mission of peace. And if the Church saw itself as the bearer of civilization throughout the world, the universality of Catholicism was contrasted—implicitly but unmistakably—with the nationalism of the Fascists.

That universality hinged on "the father of all." No pope had a loftier, more learned, more historical sense of his office than Pius XI. He had acquired it by reading voraciously. This combative ex-librarian viewed books as weapons to be used in a "splendid . . . battle fought for truth and good." [20] That is why it was significant when he compared Rome with a book, "enormous and infinite," which comprised, among its pages, history and art, faith and religion. The city could not be annexed to Fascism because it was "the fatherland of all." [21] And, more particularly, it was *"Ours, Our* diocese, *Ours* in the highest and truest sense of the word." [22]

This sense of possession was shared. Like one of those "unique, incomparable books that belong not to a single nation but are the patrimony of mankind as a whole," Pius XI's ideal of "Romanness" emphasized and exalted what Mussolini minimized and scorned. The unity of Christendom was the Pope's principle. United during the Middle Ages, whose monuments the Duce demolished, Christian society had then been ruled by the Vicars of Christ the King. Their successor, in the second quarter of the twentieth century, was inspired by that medieval ideal.

If Mussolini's model was Augustus, Pius XI's might have been Gregory VII (1073–85)—the pope who made an emperor do penance, barefoot in the ice and snow, for three days at Canossa. Such was the glorious age to which the "father of all" looked back. Before Protestantism—which he deplored as a "corrosive force" [23]—before freemasons, liberals, socialists, communists, and other subversives of the clerical order, there had existed principles of hierarchy and discipline wrongly rejected in modern times. Against them and their abuses, Pius XI set his face.[24] Turning, in his first encyclical, to the Middle Ages, when supreme pontiffs had provided governments and peoples with leadership, he drew a pessimistic picture of modern mankind alienated from the Church, confronted by temptations, and struck down by disease.

Freedom, independence, private initiative—these were the illnesses which, in the medical language favored by Pius XI, needed to be healed from the ailing body of Christendom. Excision was the remedy that he prescribed for the faithful. Separated from the rest of society, they were to have their own schools, hospitals, banks, and newspapers—all of them directed by the Church. Catholicism consequently emerged as the state's competitor. That competition was intensified by the Pope's belief in the superiority of his ideal over "modern errors," and the stage was set for a conflict.

Rome stood at the center stage of that conflict. While Mussolini sought to provide an alternative to, or a substitute for, Catholicism, Pius XI attempted to tame Fascism and make it Catholic. As tension mounted, the Pope was prepared for violence. He referred to it, again and again, in addresses on the subject of martyrdom. The fate of the Scottish Jesuit, St. John Ogilvie (1579–1614), offered a key to understanding the history of the Church. Persecution and combat marked its entire course.[25] This sixteenth-century priest—executed by the Protestants, proclaimed a martyr on November 30, 1929, and beatified the following December 22—set an example still valid in the present. Ogilvie had died a heroic death in the cause of "Romanness" and the "papacy." [26] In the eyes of Pius XI, he had given his life for the same ideal that the Pope defended against the Fascists. Rome was not a myth or a symbol of political ideology: It was the universal standard in the battle "between State and Church, error and truth." [27]

Fighting words. Confrontation combined with diplomacy maintained Catholic institutions in Fascist Italy. In Germany, the situation was already disturbing. On April 4, 1934, less than nine months after the signing of the Concordat between Nazi Germany and the Holy See (July 20, 1933), when violations of the agreement were already flagrant, three hundred and fifty German Catholics received in audience heard the following declaration from Pius XI:

> You may be certain that the Pope will always state the truth
> ... What remains of Christianity—true Christianity—with
> out Catholicism, the Church, its doctrine, the Catholic way of
> life? Nothing or next to nothing. Or rather, after all that has
> occurred recently, one can and must say: not only a false
> Christianity but a real paganism.[28]

What did Pius XI mean by these words? The reference to the Nazis and to the menace posed by the "neo-paganism" of Alfred Rosenberg, chief ideologue of the Party, and his likes is evident.[29] The

very existence of Catholic Christianity appeared, in the spring of
1934, to be at stake. Was the Pope demanding martyrdom from the
German subjects of Hitler? Was he announcing that condemnation
which, many lament, never came? To answer these questions, let us
look behind the scenes into parts of the Vatican where few have penetrated.

Inside the Vatican

As BOTH A COURT and an administration, the Vatican between the two World Wars was shaped by the personality of its ruler. More and better than most states, it understood how to enact its authority. Personified in the Vicar of Christ, that authority was vividly conveyed to all present at the ceremony of a papal mass:

> Borne aloft in the *sedia gestatoria*, wearing the tiara, and accompanied by his entourage, the Pope enters St. Peter's. Silver trumpets resound. The choir sings *Tu es Petrus* . . . When the Pope approaches the high altar, the first of the cardinal-deacons removes the tiara from his head and he alights from the *sedia gestatoria* before praying and taking his seat on the throne . . . The hierarchy assembled in St. Peter's advances to do homage to its prince. Cardinals are permitted to kiss his ring; patriarchs, archbishops, and bishops kiss his right knee; mitred abbots and others kiss his foot . . . [1]

From the hand to the knee to the foot: A hierarchy of obeisance was marked out on the papal body. The ritual mirrored a dispensation ordained by God, that the person of the Vicar of Christ mediated between the human and the divine. As Pius XI expressed it to Cardinal Pietro Gasparri in 1929: "[the Pope] does not represent but personifies and exercises sovereignty by direct divine mandate." [2]

Many within the Vatican, both before and since 1933, believed that because the Church's authority was divinely mandated, its sovereignty was superior to that of the state.[3] They were convinced that they were working for a higher organization. Its rights and duties had been set out, as recently as 1917, in a new code of canon law. Legalism of a lofty kind was an outlook widespread among Vatican officials in the 1930s. In law, they believed, the Catholic Church enacted its sense of justice. When the landholdings of the Holy See had been "usurped" by the state in 1870 at the unification of Italy, depriving Pius IX (1846–78) of his temporal powers, he lamented that he was a "prisoner in the Vatican." By the 1930s, however, the Vatican had reemerged on the international scene as a power with which to be reckoned.

If the popes had lost territory in 1870, they had since won prestige. The interventions of Benedict XV (1914–22) on behalf of peace had been respected (if not followed); the diplomatic activities of the Holy See expanded; and concordats were established with a series of states. When, after his election in February 1922, Pius XI gave his blessing from the external loggia of St. Peter's—for the first time in more than fifty years—the significance was greater than a gesture of reconciliation to Italy. The papal benediction also indicated the Vatican's desire to make its worldwide presence felt. As one of the Pope's German friends, the Jesuit Cardinal Franz Ehrle, wrote proudly: ". . . the man on the throne of St Peter will impose himself on even the powerful in this world as a remarkable power, a figure who commands solemn reverence."[4]

Law and peace were the grand themes upon which Pius XI insisted. One of the Holy See's most distinguished representatives abroad, Eugenio Pacelli, linked them both in a series of well-publicized addresses while serving as nuncio in Munich and Berlin between 1917 and 1929. In 1926, for example, he contrasted "the primacy of law" with "the dark demon of force," and opposed "the gentle empire of legal rights" to "the brutal idea of power."[5] Catholics, according to Pacelli, were missionaries in the cause of peace and law among the peoples.[6]

Human law, in the Church's eyes, was both inferior to divine or natural law and answerable to it. The rulers of the state had responsibilities to their people that were imposed by God. He set limits to political power.[7] When those limits were overstepped, it was the duty of Catholics to speak out, reminding governments of the bounds established by divine law. As a papal diplomat in 1920s Germany, Pacelli displayed none of the timidity before the powerful for which he has been reproached. He emerged, from his speeches, as a prophet of that divine and legal order centered in Rome.

Rome, as viewed from the Vatican, held moral sway over the world. Some of its influence was exercised by the Secretariat of State, the Vatican department responsible for political and diplomatic affairs. Its officials exhibited a kind of Catholic imperialism. In 1937, one of them, Domenico Tardini, already a prominent figure in that department,[8] voiced the spirit that moved him and his colleagues in tones of triumph as ringing as any used by Pius XI: "Rome now has with the Pope a truly universal authority; an authority which, although of a spiritual quality, must necessarily be expressed through an entire organization of external government based and centered here. So it is that, at long last, Rome truly governs the world."[9] As officials of a world power that was smaller yet more impressive than any state, such representatives of the Vatican felt warranted to pronounce on the errors of modern society with the authority of judges.

Judgment, in moral and doctrinal issues, was the prerogative of the Pope. He presided over debates about National Socialism, Fascism, and Communism that were conducted in the Supreme Tribunal of the Catholic Church. Known as the Inquisition from 1542 to 1908, that tribunal had been feared and mocked. There was nothing comic, however, about the functions that this department of the Roman Curia continued to perform. Elevated above all others, as its title stated, the Supreme Congregation of the Holy Office was responsible for the purity of Catholic doctrine and morals. On its benches sat the modern inquisitors.

The competence of the Holy Office was as wide as the range of human failings. To sit there in judgment could mean anything from assessing and, if necessary, condemning political ideas that threatened to undermine the faith to disciplining clerical misdemeanors and banning books. The Holy Office's activities were conducted in strict secrecy and its membership was recruited from a broad cross-section of the Roman Curia. The members believed that this breadth was a strength. Men of different experiences and backgrounds cooperated there, and an appointment in another department of the Vatican did not exclude membership in the Holy Office.

Pacelli, for example, became a member of the Holy Office in 1930 by virtue of his office as head of the Secretariat of State. He was a product of the younger generation, which set store by diplomacy and prized legalism in the Vatican. There, on the benches of the Supreme Congregation, he shared the company of older and grayer eminences who had made their careers in a different world and a less calculable atmosphere.

The leading cardinal in the Holy Office when Pacelli joined was Rafael Merry Del Val, former secretary of state under Pius X (1903–14). Both that pope and his protégé were firm opponents of the "heresy" of "modernism" [10]—any form of activity, intellectual or political, that conflicted with the Pope's ultraconservative principles. Outside the Vatican, this led to a breach between the Church and the intelligentsia; within the Vatican, the antimodernism of Pius X and Merry Del Val led to the rise of a self-appointed spymaster, Monsignor Umberto Benigni. Benigni, while an official in the Secretariat of State, made himself infamous for the sentiments that guided his activities: "History is nothing but a continual desperate attempt to vomit. For this sort of human being, there is only one remedy: the Inquisition." [11]

The powers of the Inquisition or Holy Office were now limited to moral and religious sanctions—indicative of the Vatican's disapproval but less violent than torture and less fiery than the stake. Nonetheless there remained, among the senior members of the Holy Office who were Pacelli's colleagues, hostility to innovation and suspicion of new ideas.

Hostility to innovation and suspicion of new ideas are vividly illustrated by an episode that occurred within the Holy Office shortly before Pacelli joined its ranks. In 1928 a Catholic movement called the Friends of Israel, composed of eighteen cardinals, two hundred archbishops or bishops, and two thousand priests, petitioned the Vatican to have the expressions "perfidious Jews" and "the perfidy of the Jews" removed from the Latin liturgy for Good Friday.[12]

There was "something odious" about such terms, argued the Friends of Israel. They lent themselves to "anti-Semitic interpretation." They should be replaced by words that corresponded more closely to the reality that the Jews "were not far removed" from Catholicism. Instead of "Jewish perfidy" the expression "the Jewish people" was proposed. This well-meaning proposal was referred to the Holy Office, where it caused an uproar.

Only one reaction within the Holy Office was positive. It came from Ildefonso Schuster—then abbot of San Paolo fuori le mura at Rome and a leading expert on the liturgy—who urged in two brief but incisive notes that the prayer should be altered in the sense desired by the Friends of Israel. As it stood, it reflected the "mentality of a different age . . . which is not in keeping with the spirit of the Church today." Schuster added that such expressions as "perfidious Jews" represented a practice that was "late and superstitious." His frank words brought down on his head the wrath of the cardinal-secretary of the Holy Office.

"Completely unacceptable and senseless," fumed Merry Del Val. "These are prayers and rites of great antiquity in the liturgy of the Church . . . inspired and consecrated by centuries." According to him, individual Jews, who might convert to Christianity, were not being cursed. The curse was directed against the Jewish people as a whole, which was responsible for having "shed the blood of the saint of saints." For this "rebellion and treason" the Jews deserved to be execrated.

Merry Del Val cited various texts by St. Paul in support of his views and elaborated on them with forthrightness. "Today, after the war" the Jews were attempting "more than ever to reconstruct the kingdom of Israel in opposition to Christ and His Church." They penetrated modern society, seeking to hide their history and win the confidence of Christians while forming alliances with Masonry and practicing usury.

Merry Del Val insisted that the Church was not anti-Semitic. Yet, knowing the nature of its opponents, it should refuse to compromise with them. The liturgy was to remain unaltered, and the Friends of

Israel must be dissolved. Behind that movement—to which he himself had belonged—the cardinal-secretary of the Holy Office detected "the hand and the inspiration of the Jews."

Pius XI was impressed by this idea. He ordered Merry Del Val to ask Schuster to explain why he had voiced opinions "so grave and offensive to the Church." Schuster groveled. The Holy Office then proceeded to examine a publication of the movement's central committee—*Peace upon Israel (Pax super Israel)*—and found faults such as the assertion that Jews, like Catholics, had a priesthood and that both "were joined in the life of grace."

The Holy Office deemed that unconverted Jews were alien to Christians, and they should not be permitted to come too close. Catholics could pray for them—that was laudable—but Jews were too dissimilar to be fully embraced by the Church. Even as Pius XI was dissolving the Friends of Israel, he cited its clerical membership as proof that the Church took its condemnation of anti-Semitism seriously.

Hatred of Jews may have been forbidden, but so were concessions to them. The movement was suppressed for violating the Church's traditions in its proposals for liturgical change. With friends such as Cardinal Merry Del Val in influential positions, Israel did not lack opponents in the Vatican.

In the Vatican, during the 1930s, the rise of revolutionary movements—above all, Communism—economic depression, and political instability were registered with concern. That concern was often expressed in highly traditional terms. Several of Merry Del Val's colleagues in the Holy Office reacted and behaved as if they still lived in the Counter-Reformation. Like champions of the Catholic faith against Luther, such figures as Cardinal Donato Sbarretti saw menace and conspiracy everywhere. The Protestants, according to Sbarretti, were on the march, aided and abetted by traitors to the Roman cause. For these turncoats there was no more fitting term than the ancient label of "heretic." The threat of heresy was horrifying and, to combat it, "a vast plan of defense and offensive against heresy" [13] needed to be worked out. What Sbarretti meant by such a plan, he did not specify.

Nor is his tone of alarm justified by the results of a pastoral visitation conducted in 1932 at Rome.[14] At that time only two out of seventy-one dioceses registered activities of "Protestant propaganda" (any form of non-Catholic religious activity).

"Protestantism" was also regarded with suspicion by the Fascist police. The brutality shown toward Pentecostalists—their meetings were disrupted and their members shut up in lunatic asylums—was the product of a convergence of views between Church and State towards such "aliens." Cardinal Francesco Marchetti Selvaggiani, vicar of the Pope at Rome (who was bishop of the see) and Del Val's colleague at the Holy Office, guided the Church firmly on this issue. Marchetti's energy, combined with his ability to maintain cooperation with the regime, focused on the organization known as Catholic Action, described by Pius XI as the "apple of my eye."

The Pope referred to Catholic Action as a "Christian army" of laymen and laywomen. Led by the clergy and formally recognized in the Concordat of 1929, Catholic Action saw itself as an organization of crusaders, an instrument for Pius XI's reformation of society. That reformation entailed stamping out public signs of "immorality," such as dances, female athletics, and sexually explicit films, plays, and books. The spirit in which this organization worked and the targets it selected were defined by its ecclesiastical head, Monsignor Giuseppe Pizzardo, in these ebullient terms: "Life today demands a new flowering of the methods and the zeal of the primitive Church."[15] Pizzardo was a consultant to the Holy Office who, since 1929, was also secretary of the Congregation for Extraordinary Ecclesiastical Affairs, the first sub-department of the Secretariat of State chiefly concerned with diplomatic matters.

One of his tasks within Catholic Action was to regain the allegiance and sympathies of the working classes alienated by Communism.[16] Communism, to Pizzardo, was both the cause and the symptom of Europe's crisis. That crisis, as viewed by his colleagues in the Holy Office, could only be resolved by a new kind of evangelism. In the Vatican between the two World Wars, evangelism was much in the air.

Pius XI, the "Pope of the missions," attached prime importance to the task of conversion. He made sure that *Propaganda fide*—the powerhouse of missionary activities—was represented in the Supreme Congregation by Carlo Salotti, a modern Jeremiah given to deploring the evils of the age. Family, schools, learning, liberty: all these values, according to Salotti, were undermined by contemporary decadence.[17] As negative about his own times as any senior member of the Holy Office, Salotti typified the attitude of suspicion with which the modern world was regarded in some quarters of the Vatican.

All these modern inquisitors were Italian, which was typical of the Roman Curia between the two World Wars. "Foreigners," or non-Italians, represented a minority in the organization that governed the universal Church, which was (and remains, in certain quarters) a reason for the misgivings with which Eugenio Pacelli has been viewed. Member of a family with a tradition of service to the Holy See, noted for his privacy, dignity, and discipline, Pacelli has seemed, to many, an embodiment of qualities predestined to achieve high office in the Vatican.

The reality is more complicated. The rise of Eugenio Pacelli was neither automatic nor inevitable. It is true that ability and obedience were virtues that merited promotion. Yet his career depended upon Pius XI and, when he was appointed cardinal–secretary of state in 1930, Pacelli succeeded a man who was his opposite in many respects. Pietro Gasparri looked and, at times, behaved like a peasant, with none of Pacelli's aristocratic reserve or refinement of manner. But Gasparri's absence of polish was more than offset by a sophisticated understanding of power. It was he who was thought to be the prime mover behind the codification of canon law, the negotiator of the Lateran Pacts, the leading and most influential figure in the Roman Curia.

As such, by reputation or in fact, Gasparri represented a challenge to the supremacy of Pius XI, who removed this insider from the corridors of power and replaced him with Pacelli, a diplomat who had been absent for twelve years in Germany. Absence from court for such a long period meant weakness on return. As the Vatican's new secretary of state, Pacelli had fewer connections than older hands; and that made him more dependent than Gasparri on the will of his master. Such was Pius XI's intention.

Rumors that the Pope intended to replace Pacelli circulated more than once in the Roman Curia. Neither he nor anyone else was capable of acting as the éminence grise of the Vatican between the two World Wars. The papal court was filled with competing voices, which Pius XI sought to orchestrate but could not dominate. With the feline subtlety of courtiers or the fiery convictions of missionaries, the Pope's underlings were officials of a Rome that was both Catholic and Fascist. They gazed in these two directions with the insight, and the limits, of the distinctively Italian vision—on the horizons of which, with growing urgency from 1933, impinged the menace of Nazi Germany.

—∞∞∞—

Voices from Germany

IN 1933, when the Vatican ratified a concordat with Nazi Germany, enthusiasm was not high in Rome. Pacelli said shortly afterward that he had signed because a pistol had been pointed at his brow. There were those within the Curia who believed that he would have done better not to yield to the pressure of "professional treaty-breakers."[1] This group argued that National Socialism was incompatible with Christian beliefs and that German Catholics would feel themselves abandoned by the Vatican.[2] Others, reckoning with struggle and persecution in the future, were convinced that the attempt to reach a settlement with the Nazis would later represent a "source of moral strength." And a third group, suspecting that violations of the Concordat were inevitable, believed that its abrogation would be a powerful weapon to use against the Nazis. To make breaches of the agreement public, they argued, would be to strike a blow against Germany's international prestige. To this third group probably belonged Eugenio Pacelli,[3] who, as cardinal–secretary of state, was in vantage position to observe events in Germany. How well was he informed?

One of the chief sources of official information came from his successor as nuncio in Berlin, Cesare Orsenigo.[4] Seldom has the same office been held by two men of more different abilities. Orsenigo could not compete with Pacelli's flair, skill, and urbanity. The nuncio lacked professional training as a diplomat, having begun his career as a representative of the Holy See at the no longer tender age of forty-nine. He owed that career to Pius XI, who had known him at Milan.

To Orsenigo's objection that he had no qualifications for the job, the Pope—doubtless thinking of his own appointment in 1918, after decades spent as a librarian, to be apostolic delegate to Poland—replied that a good priest can become a good diplomat.

Pius XI was optimistic. Conscientious and cautious, always fearful of giving offense, Orsenigo was taken seriously neither by the Führer at Berlin nor by the cardinal–secretary of state at Rome. Pacelli excluded his predecessor as nuncio from all important negotiations about Germany (including the Concordat), which he concentrated in his own hands.

In the hesitant hands of Orsenigo lay the task of reporting on events in the German Reich. His attitude emerged clearly during and after the elections that brought Hitler to power. On February 16, 1933, he wrote to Pacelli that it would be "ingenuous and incoherent" to support the new Nazi government, which had been condemned by the Catholic bishops, but equally rash to oppose it openly in the name of religion because that would lead to a *Kulturkampf*.[5] (Catholics' memories were scarred by that struggle between the secular state and the Roman Church, from which they had suffered in Bismarck's Germany.) Struggle, combat, resistance: These were already, and would remain, the specters that haunted the papal nuncio at Berlin.

Orsenigo did not believe that German Catholics were capable of standing up to Hitler. One of the main reasons for this disbelief was stated in his dispatch of March 7, 1933. Of thirty-nine million voters, one-third were Catholics; and some six to seven million of them, on Orsenigo's estimation, had elected the Nazis. This "immense number of transgressors" (as he described them) gave strong reasons for doubting whether instructions, issued by the episcopate against National Socialism, would be followed by a "people made fanatical by the new ideas."[6]

Uncertainty, voiced as caution, characterized the nuncio's reports to the cardinal-secretary of state. As early as March 1933, Orsenigo was seeking grounds for compromise and conciliation with the regime. The German bishops' earlier condemnation of the Nazi movement, he claimed, had concerned only its religious—not its political—ideas. With a little goodwill, it ought to have been possible to make declarations that would avoid a clash, which Orsenigo dreaded above all else.[7]

Wishful thinking marked his attitude, with its curious mixture of realism and timidity. As early as June 18, 1933, Orsenigo was aware that the Nazi Party intended to "absorb" everything outside it. Recognizing that intolerance was the hallmark of Hitler and his followers, the nuncio nevertheless persisted in his desire to believe that religion formed an exception. "Now is the moment," he wrote to Pacelli, "to make a virtue of necessity . . . and save what can be saved."[8]

What could be saved? One of the grounds for Orsenigo's belief that advantages might be sought was a conversation held with Hitler, about which he reported on May 8, 1933, with all the "ingenuity" that he had previously decried. The Führer, as described by the papal nuncio, was convinced that neither a private life nor a state—especially the German state—could be imagined without Christianity. An alliance between them was essential, since the Church was not strong enough to defeat, by itself, liberalism, socialism, and Bolshevism.[9] (Or, by an implication that Orsenigo appeared not to realize, National Socialism.)

From hypocritical reassurance the Führer had passed to frank menace. The real problem, he stated, was posed by the Jews. Recalling with admiration what he took to be the repressive policy of the Church "up to 1500," Hitler had declared that he saw in that "race . . . a danger for state and Church." Disavowing Rosenberg, whose *Myth of the Twentieth Century*, in its neo-paganism, did not represent the policy of the Party, the Führer offered pledges of his sincerity to live in peace with Catholicism. So, without further comment, came the dispatch of Cesare Orsenigo, betraying no sign of awareness that he was being told what Hitler reckoned he wished to hear.

The nuncio appeared to hear little about the terror already being directed against the Jews by the regime.[10] The silence of his dispatches on that subject was, however, compensated by other sources of information. As early as the spring of 1933, protests against the harshness with which the Jews were being persecuted reached the Secretariat of State.[11] On April 4 of that year, Pacelli transmitted the following instruction, direct from the Pope, to Orsenigo:

> As it is a tradition of the Holy See to pursue its universal mission of peace and Christian love towards all men, whatever their social position or religion, imparting to them its charitable services, where they are needed, the Holy Father charges Your Excellency to look into whether and how it may be possible to become involved . . . [12]

At the outset of Nazi persecution, both Pius XI and his second-in-command recognized the Church's duty to intervene in order to alleviate the suffering of German Jews. Not only Jews converted to Catholicism but all people—irrespective of race, rank, or religion—in need of Christian charity. Politics did not enter into Pacelli's dispatch to Orsenigo except, implicitly, in the words "whether and how."

That was the loophole on which the nuncio seized. In a telegram, dated April 8, 1933, to Pacelli he reported that "the anti-Semitic struggle . . ." had assumed a "governmental character." [13] It followed, according to Orsenigo, that an intervention by the Holy See would be interpreted as "a protest against that government's law." That such an interpretation might be desirable and justified, on moral grounds, never appears to have entered the nuncio's head. Nervous as ever, Orsenigo was concerned less with the principle of the Church's "universal mission of peace and Christian love towards all men" than with the political consequences, for German Catholics, of the regime's disfavor. The moment, he argued characteristically, was not ripe for a protest.

From within Germany an influential member of its episcopate, Cardinal Michael von Faulhaber of Munich, took a more direct but not dissimilar line in a letter to Pacelli on April 10.[14] Why were the bishops not intervening on behalf of the Jews? the faithful were asking. The answer was blunt: Intervention was impossible because otherwise the campaign against the Jews would be directed against the Catholics as well. And besides, the Jews were capable of helping themselves . . . Not that Faulhaber was unmoved by the persecution.

What he found particularly "unjust and painful" was the suffering being inflicted on those converted from Judaism to Christianity. The bishops too were in a sorry state. Their authority was in crisis. The people did not understand their shifts of position toward the Nazis.

Neither from the German hierarchy nor from its diplomatic representative at Berlin did the Holy See, in 1933, receive support for its initiative on behalf of the Jews. The Pope and Pacelli did not insist on their own teaching that Catholics, as missionaries among the peoples, must stand up to secular rulers on matters of moral duty. Instead they adopted the course of silence. And it was that silence that was challenged, in terms which had once been their own, by a Carmelite nun of Jewish origin, who was to be murdered in Auschwitz and who is now venerated as a saint.

On April 12, 1933, Edith Stein wrote to the Pope.[15] Her letter, transmitted to Pacelli by Rafael Walzer, the arch-abbot of Beuron, was accompanied by his praise (in Latin) for her sanctity and learning and by an appeal for assistance: "in this extreme emergency . . . my only hope on earth is the Holy See." Against a background of boycotts, suicides, and virulent anti-Semitism, Edith Stein prophesied, with grim exactitude, that National Socialism would exact "many victims." Then she posed the question of responsibility—the responsibility of those who chose not to speak out. Both Jews and Catholics were waiting expectantly for the Church to raise its voice. To the head of that Church, Edith Stein directed some of the burning questions that, the following year, would be considered not by the Secretariat of State but by the Holy Office: "Is not this idolization of race and of the state's power, which is hammered into the masses daily by radio, an obvious heresy? Is not the campaign of destruction being conducted against Jewish blood a profanation of the most holy humanity of our Savior . . . ? [16]

Nowhere, among the extant documents addressed in 1933 to the central authorities of the Vatican, are the moral and religious issues raised by Nazi anti-Semitism more clearly perceived or more profoundly interpreted than in this letter written to Pius XI by a Jewish nun. The future saint shared the view then being taken by the cardinal of Munich that the campaign against the Jews might become, or already was, a campaign against the Catholics. But Edith Stein drew the opposite conclusion. She feared the worst for the standing of the Church, if its silence continued.

The cardinal–secretary of state informed the arch-abbot of Beuron on April 20, 1933, that this letter had been laid before the Pope.[17] But Pacelli, in his reply, did not refer to the Jews. He prayed for God's protection of the Church and for "the grace of courage and generosity." Neither of those qualities appears to have been granted to the Vatican's representative at Berlin. Orsenigo assured his superior that he was doing his best, while noting, on April 28, 1933, that "the social elimination of the Semitic element [sic] continues on a large scale."[18] And as the nuncio wrote, negotiations to conclude the Concordat had begun in the same month of April.

Alarm entered Orsenigo's reports only when he touched on two issues. One was fear of the "ferocious Bolshevism" to which he believed the German people would swing if disappointed by Nazi promises of economic revival.[19] The other was scorn for the Protestants. "This mastadonic mass," as the nuncio described it, was led by pastors more concerned with the government than the gospels. Politically the Protestant Church might enjoy success but, in religious terms, it was a failure.[20] "Sterile and inert,"[21] it lacked the strength to survive in the catacombs.[22] Such were the questions that occupied Nuncio Orsenigo. Concerning the Jews and the Church's mission toward them, he reported little and did less.

The Secretariat of State was informed better by spontaneous sources than by official channels about the threats posed by the Nazis. The acuteness of Edith Stein was matched by the penetration of Friedrich Muckermann.[23] This German Jesuit had fled to Holland, where he published, in the weekly *The German Way* (*Der deutsche Weg*), a series of attacks on the Nazis. They, considering him a force with which to reckon, had attempted to win him for their side. In vain. Muckermann remained unwavering in his opposition to this "kind of religion," the evil character and disastrous consequences of which he perceived with prophetic insight.

The Vatican's diplomatic service transmitted Muckermann's insights to Rome. On November 16, 1934, after meeting the Jesuit (who had come to him in disguise), an official at the Bavarian nunciature, Giovanni Panico, forwarded to Pacelli a report, composed by Mucker- mann, on the situation in Germany. "National Socialism," it declared, was identical to neo-paganism and was characterized by its hostility to the Church. What the Nazis meant by "positive Christianity" in the program of their Party was nothing more than the neo-paganism advocated in the writings of Alfred Rosenberg. "Negative Christian- ity," for them, was represented by Roman Catholicism, with its dog- mas and sacraments. Blood and race, not revelation, were the constitutive elements of this new religion.[24]

"National Socialism," according to Muckermann, styled itself "the heir of Luther's Reformation, in order to do away with every- thing that Luther had left untouched. So we are dealing with a reli- gion . . . directed by men with no religious or moral inhibitions. It functions with a revolutionary dynamic which makes its appeal, above all, to sub-human instincts." Faced with such a terrible phe- nomenon, people were asking whether the bishops had done what was necessary to protect the Church and Christianity.

Muckermann accused the German episcopate of failure—failure of courage, of unity, of modern methods. Slow to explain that Na- tional Socialism meant neo-paganism and unclear when they at- tempted to do so, the bishops had left the faithful in the lurch. "Why, the people now asks and the entire world will soon enquire, does the Church not move against the Nazis with the same energy which it found [in its attacks] on the Bolsheviks and Socialists?" Muckermann, in 1934, was calling for a condemnation, open and uncompromising. Finding no response to his appeal in Germany, this Jesuit turned to Rome to combat "the danger facing the world" that was represented by Adolf Hitler and to avert the coming "catastrophe." Such was the message, grave and urgent, being sent to Pacelli in November 1934.

Lack of knowledge about the situation in Germany during 1933–34 was not the Vatican's problem. Greater difficulties were posed by its sources' diversity of attitudes and conflict of interpretations. In the discrepancy between the facts transmitted and the conclusions drawn from them emerged a shuffling of responsibility between Rome and its representatives. An example is provided by the wavering line taken on the Nazi laws on sterilization.

Orsenigo had informed Pacelli on July 21, 1932, that Nazi misuse of "eugenics" amounted to a challenge to the teaching of the Church.[25] Careful watch was kept on Catholics who supported the measures (including Friedrich Muckermann's brother Hermann, a professor in Berlin).[26] When the law on sterilization was enacted, Pius XI instructed the nuncio to look for an "opportune remedy."[27] Orsenigo attempted to organize a campaign of protest in Catholic newspapers,[28] and the head of the Fulda bishops' conference, Cardinal Bertram of Breslau, wrote to him, on August 4, 1933, seeking instructions from Rome.[29] Sterilization, recognized Bertram, violated a principle of natural law expressed in Pius XI's encyclical on Christian marriage and contraception, *Casti connubii* (December 30, 1930). And yet, in a case so plainly at odds with orthodoxy, neither Bertram nor his colleagues were capable of action.

Believing that a protest might endanger the Concordat, this senior member of the German hierarchy sought to avoid taking responsibility: "It would be a great relief for the episcopate if the Holy See itself would decide whether it is opportune to make a stand or give an indication to the bishops who, on account of this matter's implications, cannot proceed . . ."[30] The German bishops passed to Rome a choice that they hesitated to make. Accountability to the Vatican was represented as grounds for inaction. If Pius XI and Pacelli had concentrated, in their own hands, power to negotiate the Concordat, they were now faced with the consequences in this moral indecision masked as deference.

That is why the Pope's tone was probably tart when he ordered the bishops to follow the line taken in *Casti connubii*.[31] Yet that instruction is striking for its ambiguity. It did not encourage an open campaign against the law on sterilization, nor did it rule one out. Discretion, in these circumstances, prevailed—with meager results. Behind the scenes Bishops Conrad Gröber of Freiburg and Wilhelm Berning of Osnabrück attempted, unsuccessfully, to intervene with the authorities[32]; and Orsenigo read the Catholic vice-chancellor,

Franz von Papen, a lesson on how the legislation represented "an offence against divine law." To little effect. The government replied to these confidential remonstrances with "systematic silence."[33]

In the course of this dialogue of the deaf, voices were raised in the Vatican. On April 18, 1934, Pacelli sent a letter to Sbarretti—then Merry Del Val's successor as cardinal-secretary of the Holy Office—informing him of a discussion that he had had, on February 6, with Hitler's envoy, the ministerial director Rudolf Buttmann, about sterilization. Was it possible for a Catholic to publish a book on that subject expounding the doctrine of the Church without encountering difficulties from the government? All depended on the form, was the answer that Pacelli had received. A scholarly book would have a restricted readership and might be permitted. A declaration from the pulpit, addressed to everyone, might incite to disobedience. To affirm: "According to Catholic teaching, these matters are viewed differently" was perfectly acceptable, Buttmann had explained. What the government regarded as provocative was the bishops' statement: "This is not allowed."[34]

Why, it is often asked, did Eugenio Pacelli, as cardinal–secretary of state, not act against the moral outrages being perpetrated by the Nazi regime? Here, in this document addressed by him to Cardinal Sbarretti, is evidence of action taken by him to inform the Supreme Tribunal of the Roman Church about the infringements of its liberty to teach in the Third Reich. No comment was passed on the information conveyed. The Holy Office had to draw its own conclusions. If it did so, no record remains of them, nor is there any trace of a call for condemnation—despite (or, perhaps, on account of) the fact that, in 1934, no less than seven of the cardinal-members of the Holy Office also belonged to the Congregation for Extraordinary Affairs.

Headed by Pacelli, that congregation operated with his colleagues' knowledge. How much they knew about the material that passed over his desk cannot be determined, because no record of their oral deliberations is preserved in the documents accessible in the Vatican. Yet it is legitimate to infer that, as authoritative members of the subdepartment responsible for "foreign affairs," these men were aware, at least in outline, of developments in Germany. If none of them acted, in this case as in others, that was because they had reason to feel that an impasse had already been reached. The nature of that impasse had emerged a year previously.

On March 29, 1933, Pacelli, following instructions from the Pope, had written to Sbarretti to ask whether it would be "opportune"—his word—to condemn the Communist agitators known as the "Godless." [35] This was a case in which all ecclesiastical parties to the problem of Germany played a role. Orsenigo consulted the German episcopate, a majority of which was opposed to any condemnation. To condemn would not help, argued Cardinal Bertram: The only antidote to Communist and Socialist "poison" was preaching. What he wanted was encouragement for priests and Catholic organizations, which, he claimed, were doing excellent work.

This view was shared by other members of the German hierarchy from the north to the south. In the south, at Munich, it was Cardinal Faulhaber who was most alert to the political implications of the case. If the Holy Office condemned the "Godless," the government would regard the act as praise for its policy, while the Communist Party would claim that it was carried out on orders from Rome. Neither would do. Hitler wanted to destroy the Communists, declared Faulhaber with disbelief: "With the violent methods of the police-state alone . . . the danger will not be eliminated." Nor was the Führer's goal the same as that of the Church. "The Church's aim is not the destruction of the Communists, but their edification." [36]

No action was taken by the Holy Office, in this case as in the other. But both had served to set discouraging precedents for the authorities in the Vatican. From the German bishops, Rome had come to expect counsels of caution on moral and doctrinal issues. Caution dictated by political factors weighed the scales against any form of open condemnation, although, by the autumn of 1934, there existed grounds for a more dynamic policy.

One of the most pressing concerns of Vatican policy was the education of the young. Their teachers, Rome knew, were being indoctrinated in hostility to the Church. How else were such declarations to be interpreted—made at a training course for female teachers of economics in 1934 and promptly transmitted to the Secretariat of

State—as "A Church corrupted by the drive for power has poisoned the German people. Where is this opponent? The Church in Rome." Or "We have a millennial enemy, the enemy in Rome." Or "Rome is guilty of the lost war?" [37]

The anti-Roman drive in Germany, at levels ranging from legislation to education, was apparent, to the Vatican, from multiple and convergent sources. Silence alternated with discreet protest, in the form of Pacelli's diplomatic notes, but coordination between the Secretariat of State and the Holy Office was little in evidence. More than the bureaucratic principle of separating spheres of competence is needed to explain why the work of these two powerful departments failed to find a focus in the problem of the Nazis until late 1934; and the reason is not to be found in the sympathy felt for the Führer by the man who was allegedly to become "Hitler's Pope."

Eugenio Pacelli's strengths were also his weakness. A faithful servant of his master, he is never disclosed, by the extant documents, as taking the initiative. Diligent, clever, and correct, the cardinal–secretary of state to Pius XI followed the orders of the Pope. It was the Pope who decided when information reaching one department should be taken further by the Holy Office.

When did a violation of the Concordat or an act of Nazi brutality become an issue that touched on the fundaments of the faith and morality? For much of 1933 and 1934, Pius XI avoided that question. He chose the line of negotiation that Pacelli followed in that spirit of diplomatic legalism appropriate to his role and congenial to his character. And if other characters, more fiery than his, in the Holy Office did not broach the German question, that was not only because they knew the Pope's mind but because their own were occupied by different matters. One of them was nudism.

Nudism was much in the Holy Office's thoughts during the early 1930s.[38] Days before his death on February 26, 1930, Rafael Merry Del Val had begun to fume against "one of the most detestable and pernicious aberrations of our times." The cardinal-secretary of the Holy Office did not mean National Socialism, Fascism, or Communism. He referred, with violent hostility, to naked bathing and other practices that represented, in his opinion, "an attack on Christian morality." Nudism, in the view of this modern inquisitor, amounted to a doctrine—a doctrine that was contrary to the faith. Thousands of nudists, with their "magnificently illustrated" publications, were encouraging "materialism and bestiality." They denied the shame that ought to have been felt at the naked body ever since Adam and Eve disobeyed God's commandments at the fall. About to depart for a better world, the cardinal struck his last blow in this one. The ancient doctrine of original sin prohibited the modern doctrine of nudism, which should be condemned.

Merry Del Val's death did not win the nudists respite. Quite the contrary. The Holy Office and the Secretariat of State began to work together with an efficiency that proves, beyond doubt, that collaboration was possible. Germany was one of their main targets because it was there that the movement was believed to have begun. The diplomatic service was mobilized with urgency. Even Orsenigo swung into action. No report that he composed, during the 1930s, on Nazi Germany matches the detail or the enthusiasm with which, on June 8, 1930, he wrote about nudism.

Tracing a German tradition of nudism back to the nineteenth century, he identified, in the years 1918–19, the point at which the "last leashes on shame were broken down publicly." Then both sexes went swimming and sunbathing together. This "total depravation," this "collective madness," was spread by propaganda. Some five million nudists were to be numbered in Germany, according to Orsenigo. Yet the papal nuncio consoled himself with the thought that most Catholics—warned off nudism by the bishops' conference at Fulda in 1925—had nothing to do with the movement. The few who did were "mentally imbalanced."

Reports, pouring into the Secretariat of State from all over the world, were forwarded to the Holy Office. Memoranda were particularly numerous from France, where the nuncio shared Orsenigo's zeal. The archbishop of El Salvador denounced an illustrated review that he accused of spreading nudist dirt. As material amassed and indignation mounted, the Holy Office may have become one of the leading clearinghouses of information about this "fetish of the flesh."

Such was the zeal that, after more than three years of determined labor, that pious Dominican Marco Sales submitted, in July 1933, a report arguing that the scope of the investigation should be enlarged. He wished to distinguish between nudism, seminudism, and naturalism; and he knew much about their differences, having examined numerous illustrated reviews and noted the degrees to which sexual organs were exposed. Not, of course, from prurient interest. Sales was concerned that the young, corrupted by nudism and its variations, might "no longer regard human bodies as temples of the Holy Spirit."

This was an issue which, well into 1934, occupied the combined attention of the Holy Office and the Secretariat of State. As late as December of that year, information was still streaming in, while the highest authorities of the Roman Church debated whether "a solemn papal act" condemning nudism might be opportune. They decided that it would not. Four years of effort and a mountain of labors had produced a mouse.

It was in this context, distracted by nudism and fraught with tension from Germany, that denunciations of the Nazis began to be made to the Supreme Tribunal by one of its members.

The Politics of Condemnation

THE FIRST TO CALL for a condemnation of National Socialism from the Holy Office in 1934 was Alois Hudal. The observer of the papal mass quoted at the beginning of Chapter 3 was born, the son of a shoemaker, at Graz in 1885.[1] Small in stature but lofty in ambition, Hudal was determined to make a name for himself. Pushy, combative, and no victim of false modesty, this Austrian was also conscious of being a member of a minority in the Roman Curia dominated by Italians. For Italians, the climb up the slippery pole could be facilitated by helping hands. Those stretched out to Eugenio Pacelli, a Roman who had begun his career in the Vatican, were not in easy reach of Alois Hudal, who felt this difference acutely.

At Rome, Hudal enjoyed none of Pacelli's advantages of social standing or insider knowledge. An outsider on the make in the Eternal City needed connections, but he was not a member of one of the major religious orders such as the Dominicans, the Franciscans, or the Jesuits, which had headquarters and influence there. In 1908, after studying theology at the university of Graz, Hudal became a secular priest. As professor of New Testament studies in his native town, he craved opportunities that neither pastoral nor academic work offered; and he sought to forge them for himself, by addressing Catholic organizations and by publishing.[2]

Publicity attracted Hudal, who commanded a fluent pen. During a period of service as an assistant military chaplain in the First World War, he composed a number of sermons to the soldiers, which he published in 1917.[3] Filled with emotive appeals to defend "the holy soil of our fatherland," they also warned against "national chauvinism." "Kinship of blood" had been preferred to the "community between men in religion, scholarship, and art." Now was the time to "heal this error of the human spirit, the decadence of Christian love." [4] How these statements were to be reconciled with his declaration that "loyalty to the flag is loyalty to God," [5] Hudal did not explain to the troops. But his ever more determined attempts to figure in current debates continued after the war.

In a book on the Serbian-Orthodox Church, published in 1922, he wrote that one of the consequences of that war had been to pit the Germanic and the Slavonic peoples against each another.[6] Bridges that had been torn down by violence and hatred now needed to be rebuilt. And he made it clear that no one was better qualified to undertake this task of mediation than a scholar—like himself.

Scholarship, organization, and writing on issues in the public domain served Hudal for the next step in his career. In 1923, he was appointed head of Santa Maria dell'Anima, the German national church at Rome, in the hospice of which he had lodged while studying for his doctorate. Run-down and in poor financial condition the Anima had become a focus of rivalry between the Germans and the Austrians. Nevertheless Hudal, from his position there, set his sights on higher things.

The highest—the supreme—congregation in the Roman Curia was the Holy Office. To that department was passed a memorandum which, on December 10, 1927, Hudal addressed to the Pope about the "crisis of culture" in Germany,[7] which was to become one of his main themes. That crisis was evident among candidates for the Catholic clergy whose theological training was being poisoned, according to Hudal, by an overdose of Protestant methods. The remedy was to remove them from these corrupting influences and bring them to Rome, where they could be grounded in the doctrine of the faith at such orthodox institutions as the Anima.

In 1927, the protector of the German national church at Rome was none other than the cardinal–secretary of the Holy Office, Rafael Merry Del Val. With him, this champion of Roman conservatism got on famously. Not by chance, Hudal was appointed a consultant to the department headed by Merry Del Val in 1930.[8] There he began to assert himself with an assurance that had been more difficult to muster at the Anima.

As rector of the Anima, an Austrian like Hudal was susceptible to pressure from the Germans.[9] Alert as ever to the direction in which the political wind was blowing, he began to embrace, in his sermons and other public pronouncements, the very pan-Germanic nationalism that he had earlier condemned. Opportunism, combined with desire for recognition, played a driving role. A model of curial success had been set by Pacelli, with whom Hudal collaborated in negotiations for a concordat between Austria and the Vatican.[10] Elevated to the rank of titular bishop for his services in 1933, in the presence of Nazi dignitaries and representatives of Hitler Youth, he proclaimed, at a ceremony performed before the German-speaking community at Rome, that no contrast existed between nation and Church.

In the same year, Hudal was beginning to speak a language which the Führer—who, when it suited his purposes, spoke in favor of Christianity—could understand. Even more comprehensible to Hitler would have been Hudal's invectives against the Jews. The Roman ghetto, he argued, had not been an instrument of repression. The Jews had manipulated it to create a "state within a state" and become the financial masters of the Eternal City. The "Semitic race," linked with the nefarious movements of democracy and cosmopolitanism, sought to set itself apart and dominate.[11]

These were sentiments worthy of Hudal's patron, Merry Del Val. The difference between them was that such hostility, expressed by the cardinal in a secret memorandum to the Holy Office,[12] was stated by Hudal in public. Publicity, always one of his objectives, became a mania in 1933. He was forthright about his intentions, referring, on July 18 of that year, to "the total German cause, whose servant and herald abroad I always wished to be."[13] At Christmas Hudal lamented that the Germans had few friends in the world.[14] Their natural ally was the Church. Rome represented the true "principle of leadership" (*Führerprinzip*).[15]

The eager tone and headstrong purpose of these utterances are plain. Already in 1933, Hudal was casting himself in the role of a mediator between the German nation and the Roman Church. That is why he has been described as the "brown bishop" or, hardly less negatively, as one of the "bridge-builders" between Catholicism and National Socialism. Yet neither description does justice to the complexity of his character and the duplicity of his roles.

This sympathizer with the Austrian chancellor, Engelbert Dolfuss, was capable of writing a preface to an Italian biography of him, published in 1935, without ever mentioning that his "exemplary and Christian life" [16] had ended in murder by the Nazis during their attempted coup in June of the previous year. But if Hudal had no scruples about turning a blind eye when it furthered his aims, he was also equal to the opposite. Under the cover of secrecy—unknown to the Nazis, whose favors he had been courting—he denounced them to the Holy Office a few months after Dolfuss's death.

What did a denunciation amount to, what did a call for condemnation mean, if accepted and implemented by the highest Roman authority in matters of faith and morals? That authority derived from the Pope's. As he was the head of the Holy Office, a negative judgment passed on the Nazis by the Supreme Tribunal over which he presided would almost certainly have been interpreted by them as a declaration of spiritual war. But how did Rome view its options? What procedures existed, what precedents had been set, in such cases?

The Pope might intervene directly. This Pius XI had done in 1929, when he damned works by Charles Maurras and the periodical *L'Action Française* for their extreme nationalism and their challenge to papal authority. [17] That authority, however, was exercised after consulting studies made during the reign of Pius X; and the condemnation was issued in the traditional form of a decree by the Holy Office. Such matters of moment customarily passed through the Supreme Tribunal of the Roman Church.

Passage could be simple, when the matter was, or seemed, straightforward. On May 23, 1930, for example, Father Agostino Gemelli, an eager denouncer and founder of the Catholic University of Milan, wrote to Pius XI about a work by the Dutchman T. van de Velde on the perfect marriage, which had been translated into German and was about to appear in Italian. [18] Appalled by the success of this book, which he believed encouraged sexual explicitness, Gemelli feared that it might circulate among schoolteachers, who would be able to corrupt the young. And, as he added in a further note: "The diffusion of [van de Velde's writings] was part of a program of nudism and sensualism that was invading Mediterranean countries from the nations of the North."

To the Holy Office, in 1930, nudism seemed one of the most pressing threats to Mediterranean morals.[19] Action was taken swiftly and, on March 14, 1931, a decree banning the book and translations of it was issued. That had the effect of making the work better known and of boosting its sales. Indignant at the publicity that it was drawing, on April 6, 1933, Pius XI sent his intermediary with Mussolini, the Jesuit Pietro Tacchi Venturi, to protest. If the Duce did not intervene, the Church would "be obliged to take further measures" (unspecified). Dismissing the work as "filth," Mussolini promised to have it confiscated and to silence the journalists—an edifying example of collaboration between Church and state.

Collaboration of that kind was impossible in the case of the Nazis. There the Church stood on its own, reliant on weapons of its making. One of them, by now four centuries old, was both antiquated and double-edged. Since the sixteenth century, the Index of Prohibited Books had been intended to warn Catholics of publications detrimental to the faith and to morality, which they were forbidden to read on pain of religious sanctions.[20] In the preface to the new edition of the Index, published in 1930, Cardinal Merry Del Val expressed the spirit in which it had been drawn up:

> The Holy Church, over centuries, endures great and terrible persecutions . . . but today hell is waging a battle against it that is even more terrible . . . No danger is more serious than [bad publications] which threaten the integrity of the faith and morals . . . The Holy Church, which God has appointed the infallible teacher and unerring guide of the faithful . . . has the duty and consequently the sacrosanct right to prevent error and corruption . . . contaminating the flock of Jesus Christ.[21]

Anxious to immunize Catholics against the "infection" of "bad books," the officials of the Supreme Tribunal of the Roman Church continued to cling to their faith in the effectiveness of bans. Not that the Vatican, during the 1930s, was insensitive to the mass communications of the modern age. In 1931, Pius XI installed a radio station in Vatican City and was the first pope to use it for pastoral purposes. The Vatican newspaper, *Osservatore Romano,* was also employed to comment, in a semiofficial manner, on current events.

In 1933–34, those comments on Germany were reserved to the point of reticence. The persecution of the Jews, the establishment of concentration camps, the law on sterilization—these issues provoked little more than a muted response.[22] No stand was taken against Hitler, who the *Osservatore Romano* continued to insist had only good intentions, in contrast to those of "radical" Nazis. In that contrast (based on his own assurances)—between a well-disposed, conservative Führer and the extremist or "left-wing" opponents of the Church—Rome still wished to believe. It was an illusion that explains why, when action was first taken within the Holy Office, it was not against Hitler's *Mein Kampf* but against *The Myth of the Twentieth Century* (1930) by Alfred Rosenberg.

Rosenberg's book is a document of intense hostility to Christianity and in particular to Catholicism. But it is not the work of an author with theological training. Rosenberg had studied architecture at Riga and Moscow.[23] Like Adolf Hitler, that amateur architect and dilettante of ideas,[24] Alfred Rosenberg acquainted himself, through wide and confused reading, with the subjects about which he wrote. There lies one of the fundamental differences between the leading Nazis and those who read them at Rome—a difference that can be reconstructed, although the censures of *The Myth of the Twentieth Century* made by members of the Holy Office, including Hudal, have not survived in the dossier that originally contained them.[25]

An abyss of culture and education yawned between the author of this book and his Roman censors. They were not only members of a church that Rosenberg attacked but also intellectuals or professors— a category that both he and Hitler despised. "Entrust the world for a few centuries to a German professor," the Führer mused on February 17, 1942, "and you'll have a mankind of cretins." [26] Rosenberg's similar contempt for those who possessed that scholarly competence which he lacked only boosted his confidence in his own intuitions. It was at that level—of crass speculation or brutal polemic—that his works were interpreted at Rome. No one there made the mistake of looking for an argument in *The Myth of the Twentieth Century* because none existed in Rosenberg's rantings.

"A fanatical and violent book, disseminating hatred," wrote the *Osservatore Romano* (drawing on an article published in the Jesuit periodical *Civiltà Cattolica*) on February 7, 1934—the day when the Holy Office issued its decree banning *The Myth of the Twentieth Century*. "Anti-educational, anti-Christian, and anti-human," the condemned work proclaimed the death of Christianity and the birth of a new man from its blasphemous myth of blood. In his denial of Catholic doctrines and his "racist mania," Rosenberg committed such enormities as asserting that Jesus Christ was of Nordic origin and that St. Paul had promoted the interests of the Jews.

It was not difficult to see that *The Myth of the Twentieth Century* advocated a neo-paganism that the Church was bound to reject. But Rome was slower to understand that, in Rosenberg, it was dealing with an apostle of a political religion. With a mystical mumbo jumbo that demanded the assent of dogma, he elevated the doctrines of people and race above not only individuals but also the state itself.[27] All that was heresy, which Rome identified and condemned. But, in 1934, the authorities did not see—or did not wish to perceive—that it was a heresy to which the Führer also adhered.

At the beginning of 1934, many in the Vatican were reluctant to acknowledge that Hitler, as the messiah of this political religion, placed his faith in its articles. Although they estimated that no less than 75,000 copies of *The Myth of the Twentieth Century* had been sold since it first appeared in 1930—obviously with the backing of the Nazis—Rome still insisted on the "private" character of the publication. Why the central authorities of the Church attached such importance to this point was stated plainly by the *Osservatore Romano*. Rosenberg's ideas were not those of the Party; Hitler had declared that he wished to found the Third Reich on a Christian basis; and

Vice-Chancellor Papen maintained that the Führer thought differently from his followers. In that distinction emerged a tactic. By banning *The Myth of the Twentieth Century* in February 1934, the intention was not to launch an assault on National Socialism as a whole. Rome was attempting to divide its unacceptable wing from the one with which it then seemed that Catholics could live.

Catholics could not live with the idea of a national church, separated from and opposed to Rome. Rosenberg was not the only Nazi to propose such a heresy.[28] In 1933, a leading member of the "Movement for German Belief," Ernst Bergmann, professor of philosophy at Leipzig, also published a book that the consultants of the Holy Office examined and condemned in January of the following year.[29]

Hudal played a role in that condemnation, and his censure of Bergmann has survived. The prime objection that he leveled against the work was its assumption that the Germanic race, set apart from others, required a "national" church "as the symbol and expression of its race." Catholicism was alien to the "Nordic race," Bergmann argued. "Infected by the spirit of Semitism," the Bible had promoted a false image of Christ. He was a "pantheist" of "Indo-Germanic" origins.

This was the information received from Germany that the Holy Office examined most closely at the beginning of 1934. No attempt was made, then or later, to compare the errors identified in Bergmann's writing with those that had been denounced by Edith Stein and others. Neither Stein's letter nor Muckermann's memorandum was made available to the Holy Office; and, in the absence of coordination between departments in the Vatican, if anyone possessed an overview of the German situation, it was Pacelli or the Pope.

The notion that they harbored sympathies for National Socialism because they continued to negotiate with its leaders must be rejected. At the level of diplomatic relations, they continued to hope, with more than a touch of wishful thinking. But at the level of ideas and belief, both of them approved the condemnation of Bergmann's work because the arguments for putting it on the Index of Prohibited Books were irrefutable. How else could they have reacted to the claim that Christianity, born in a state of Mediterranean corruption, was incapable of improving the German race? Or that Christian doctrines—from original sin to redemption through Jesus Christ—had impeded the progress and undermined the morals of the Germans? The vision of Catholicism conjured up by Bergmann before the horrified eyes of the Roman authorities was a caricature of their faith.

He described that faith as a form of ancient paganism, as an "alien element" in the Germanic state, as the Italian national religion, and as a cult of Mithras revived, concluding: "We cannot be good Germans, if we remain Roman Catholic." And Bergmann, as summarized by Hudal, went further: "Christianity and true national feeling are incompatible. We must refuse the cross of Christ and despise this religion alien to Germanic genius." But it was not merely the fanaticism that disturbed Hudal. A committed nationalist, he was also shocked by "this disgrace to the Germanic race" that Bergmann's book represented.

There lay one of the paradoxes that, within two years, would erupt into contradiction. While damning Bergmann's excesses, Hudal shared one of his criteria. This titular bishop, whose motto was "for the Church and the Nation," believed that the first power should moderate and guide the second. For Hudal, there existed not only a wrong but also a right form of nationalism. Here Bergmann erred rather in degree than in kind.

The errors of extreme nationalism were dangerous because they were liable to corrupt the young. Bergmann, Hudal argued, was representative of a horde of similar propagandists who threatened German youth. The Movement for German Belief, which, according to him, counted more than 100,000 members, was attempting to organize an alternative church based on its racist ideas, with support from the Nazi Party. A hint of mistrust toward the government, understated but plain, was made in Hudal's observation that it was a "bit strange" that the police, known for its surveillance of the press, allowed such offenses to the Holy See to be published. But that hint was not followed to its logical consequence, which led to Hitler.

In the Führer's entourage, not in his person, Hudal identified the menace with a mixture of directness and circumspection typical of Rome at that time. He was able to quote from a speech that the leader of Hitler Youth, Baldur von Schirach, delivered in November 1933, in which he rejected Christ in favor of the nation. This was the kind of source that was not normally available to the Holy Office. There, at the beginning of 1934, it carried weight when Hudal concluded: "If Catholic young people are forced to enroll in the Hitler-Youth of Schirach—an adherent of "German religion"—and educated for a decade in these dangerous and, from the nationalist standpoint, fascinating ideas, the Catholic churches in Germany will be empty."

Condemnation of Bergmann, Hudal argued, would also be in the interests of those Protestants who had retained their faith. Spurred on by the Catholics' example, they might even return to the Roman fold. Reaffirming its authority, he was inspired not by ecumenism but by the kind of imperialism displayed by other Vatican officials between the two World Wars. The consequence was that Bergmann's book joined Rosenberg's on the Index in two decrees of the Holy Office published in the *Osservatore Romano* on February 14, 1934.

At the beginning of 1934, no one in the Roman Curia had taken a stronger yet more selective position against National Socialism than Alois Hudal. His standing was enhanced by his command of German, his native language, and by his knowledge of recent publications. Neither Pius XI nor Pacelli—although both gifted linguists, fluent in German—possessed, at firsthand, Hudal's acquaintance with so many of the Nazis' writings. The Pope and the cardinal–secretary of state received diplomatic dispatches, private communications, reports, newspaper clippings, memoranda, and appeals. This was enough to inform them about the character of National Socialism, but it had not been sufficient to acquaint them with the details of Nazi ideology. The examination of Rosenberg's and Bergmann's works served as a lesson that, although incomplete, alerted them to aspects of the problem hitherto neglected. And the banning of these books moved the confrontation on to a different and more public plane.

A polemic followed between Rosenberg and his Catholic critics.[30] On February 7, 1934, in a conversation with Cardinal Karl Joseph Schulte, the archbishop of Cologne, Hitler declared that he identified with Rosenberg as the "maker of party-dogma," not as the author of the banned book[31]—a distinction without a difference, since Rosenberg was to be made responsible, on February 24, for overseeing the "world-view" of the Nazi party. Acclaim in Germany followed condemnation by Rome. The message was obvious, and Hitler rubbed salt into the wound by asserting that it was the Catholic Church that made *The Myth of the Twentieth Century* popular by its ban.

Hostility and mistrust mounted on both sides in the course of 1934. During the summer of that year, Hudal traveled in Germany and Austria. Returning to Rome in the autumn, he was received in audience by Pius XI.[32] Asked for his impressions of the situation, Hudal commented on the difficulties with the Concordat. The Pope was moved to indignation: "What? We did not demand the Concordat. It was forced upon Us!" Hudal then pointed out the contradictions in the Church's attitude to the Nazis in different countries. In Germany, a National Socialist could be absolved at confession, but not in Holland. The same party, with which the Vatican had seen fit to sign a treaty in 1933, was being attacked from the pulpits in neighboring Austria. This, according to Hudal, was producing confusion among Catholics. The Church needed a new strategy.

The architect of that new strategy, in Hudal's view, ought to be himself. His ambition and assurance in his own gifts are nowhere more manifest than in his admiring and envious references to Giovanni Gentile, the high priest and philosopher of Fascism.[33] Hudal aspired to play a similar role on the international stage, ranging from the Vatican to Germany: as a thinker and a mediator, less committed but more influential than Gentile, because he fancied himself acceptable to both sides.

His role, as Hudal explained it to Pius XI, involved separating the good from the bad in National Socialism. The bad, already condemned in the cases of Rosenberg and Bergmann, was represented by the "left wing" of the party. The "conservatives"—headed, he believed, by Hitler—should be redirected toward Rome. An "injection" of Christianity into the National Socialist movement would strengthen it in its "providential mission against the incursion of nihilism from the East."[34] Hudal's strategy was to make the Nazis Catholic and use them against the Communists; and he intended to reach this goal by writing a book on the "intellectual foundations" of the movement. "There you make the first mistake," objected Pius XI: "There is no intellect in this movement. It is a massive materialism." Despite the papal warning that he was tilting against a windmill, Hudal continued on his headstrong way.

A double strategy had emerged, in Hudal's mind, by the autumn of 1934. On the one hand, the Church should condemn the Nazis' errors. On the other, it should Christianize their movement and achieve a reconciliation. Obsessed by his plans for the future, Hudal did not grasp how far removed from reality those objectives were. Revealingly, he lamented that, in Germany, there was no figure like Tacchi Venturi, the Jesuit who smoothed out differences between Pius XI and Mussolini behind the scenes. That was another part that Hudal would have loved dearly to play, and his sympathy for certain Nazi positions may have seemed to qualify him. But even as he prepared his book on the intellectual foundations of National Socialism, he returned to the negative part of his strategy. Before his work appeared, the ground should be cleared by the Holy Office

The condemnation of Rosenberg's *The Myth of the Twentieth Century* was, according to Hudal, only "the first step." It was insufficient in the face of a movement "all the more dangerous for being accompanied and supported by the other two false doctrines of nationalism and the totalitarian state." [35] On October 7, 1934 he wrote a letter of denunciation to the cardinal-secretary of the Holy Office, Donato Sbarretti. A member of that organization for several years, Hudal knew that he was addressing a hard-liner who had called for a campaign against heresy.[36] In just such terms he launched the next attack on those aspects of Nazi ideology that needed to be excised before Christianity could be "injected" into its wounds.

During his vacation in Germany and Austria, Hudal explained, he had studied National Socialist ideas of race and blood. Taught everywhere throughout the Reich, they permeated intellectual life and were being used to indoctrinate the young. A radio broadcast to Hitler Youth that Hudal had heard made the following assertions:

(1) Race, which derives from the blood, is decisive in the formation of the culture of each nation; culture originates in race.

(2) The laws of race are as invariable as those of nature. Different races cannot be united.

(3) Scientific research has proved that belief in supranational cultures and religions is out of date.

(4) The doctrine of race is capable of creating, for the Germanic peoples, a new culture and a new religion.

At the conclusion of this broadcast, a chorus of Hitler Youth sang "Holy, holy, holy is blood."

The danger posed by such propaganda was urgent especially for the young, Hudal declared. The "Arian-Nordic" religiosity cultivated by the Nazis did not recognize the concepts of original sin or redemption. Exclusively concerned with life on this earth, they denied the conflict between body and soul and set no value on a morality of asceticism. Their aim was to preserve, through healthy families selected by eugenics, the heritage of the Germanic race. While Christianity sought to flee the world, "Nordic religion" attempted to dominate and enjoy it. The conclusion to be drawn was clear: "It is false to pretend that National Socialism is merely a political party like Fascism, for example, or that it has nothing to do with religion or that, founded on a "positive Christianity," it has protected religion in Germany against the danger of Bolshevism."[37] Only those unacquainted with Nazi writings could claim that such views were confined to radicals who had no influence on the education of party members. Exponents of these errors, like Alfred Rosenberg, were important figures in public life. They were imposing their sinister stamp on the schools and youth organizations.

In the autumn of 1934, Hudal's tone of apparent anger mounted. Nazi ideas of blood and race undermined the foundations of the Christian religion. They were all the more dangerous in an age of extreme nationalism that, in itself, amounted to a heresy. Totalitarianism was equally heretical because it contradicted Christian thinking about the State. For Christianity in general and Catholicism in particular, these heresies "over the next years" were going to present "a very serious danger."

Hudal identified that danger in the Nazi belief that Christianity was "an Oriental and Semitic product," alien to the "Nordic race," which should therefore replace it with "a new and revived paganism." That paganism amounted to a form of "nationalist mysticism," with its own cult of saints and martyrs and a deification of blood and race.

Condemnation of Nazi publications on these subjects, declared Hudal, would not be enough. The Church needed a rigorous examination of "the three modern heresies" of nationalism, race, and blood with a view to publishing a papal encyclical or a document as momentous as the Syllabus of Errors—with which Pius IX had damned the false doctrines of the modern age in 1864.

Even these dramatic measures, warned Hudal, would not be sufficient. He proposed further that the Holy See instruct the bishops, "in the countries particularly threatened by these heresies," to mobilize Catholic Action in each diocese and begin "a unified struggle . . . with every means at disposal." That struggle, as he envisaged it, was to be conducted on the plane of ideas. No account was taken of the Nazis' brutal use of force. In 1934, from the benches of the Supreme Tribunal and the universal perspective of Rome, National Socialism seemed a provincial aberration, capable of being healed of its infections by a salutary dose of Catholic dogma.

Or so it appeared to Hudal, in the flush of his fervor. Fervid but calculating, he knew that he ran no great risk because there was next to no chance that the Nazis would learn of his initiative. It had been taken behind the scenes, in the most secret department of the Roman Curia. Indiscretion could mean excommunication—which was tantamount to a capital sentence for a member of the Holy Office. His colleagues would maintain confidentiality and he, having established his credit with them as an opponent of National Socialism, could then emerge as a reconciler with the other side once they had completed their work. The game was double, and the stakes were high. Only one other person was in a position to decide whether the risk was worth taking.

Although Pius XI was of the opinion that the matter was delicate, when it was presented to him at a congregation (or meeting) of the Holy Office on October 25, 1934, he gave permission to proceed. A decision was taken that reveals much about how policy was formulated within the Vatican. As the case of the Nazis was one that required careful study, the Pope announced that he would speak with the general of the Jesuits.

The Jesuits and the Racists

THE NAZIS ADMIRED, and detested, the Jesuits. According to Heinrich
Himmler, chief of the SS, this "most important and politically most
active of the orders" stood at the summit of the Catholic Church.[1]
The SS even spied on the Jesuits—less to discover evidence of subver-
sive activities than to learn the tricks of what they took to be their
trade.[2] As the "storm-troops of the Vatican" with many-sided connections, superb training of its members, and brilliant tactics of operation, the order presented a model of what a secret service should be.
The Jesuits were able to defend the Church against its opponents and
to attack its enemies.[3] Little did the SS know how accurate its assessment was.

The Pope too held his "secret service" in the highest regard.[4] After
three centuries of opposition, it was Pius XI who had made the Jesuit
Robert Bellarmine a saint and *doctor* of the Church. Papal favor for
the discipline, dedication, and learning of the order had been marked
throughout his reign. The Jesuits, for example, had been put in
charge of Vatican Radio, with which Rome aimed to reach a worldwide audience; and to their general, the energetic and autocratic Pole
Wlodomir Ledóchowski,[5] was delegated the task of selecting those
who were to examine, from the standpoint of Catholic doctrine, Nazi
ideas on race and blood.

Ledóchowski's choice did not fall on Friedrich Muckermann,
then (or soon to be) in Rome,[6] perhaps because his position was too ex-

posed. Muckermann was already known as a leading figure in the struggle against the Nazis[7]; he published, in *The German Way (Der deutsche Weg)* of December 23, 1934, a call for condemnation of them; and at an audience with Pacelli, in which he vigorously expressed his views, he received short shrift. Too forthright, too controversial, and too much in the public eye, Muckermann (already contested within the order) was passed over by its general for another figure whom both of them knew and respected.[8]

Franz Hürth taught at the Jesuit seminary at Valkenburg in Holland. A prominent theologian, he was regarded as an expert on moral questions whose advice was widely sought. Why it was sought, in this case, by Ledóchowski is clear. Hürth had taken a stand against the sterilization of the mentally ill during a debate on that issue in Germany during the late 1920s,[9] which raised profound questions of Catholic morality and its relationship to the politics of the State. Was that State justified in legislating to sterilize those incapable of producing healthy offspring in order to safeguard the "hygiene of the race"?

There were Catholic theologians who argued that such measures were legitimate in the interests of the common good. One of them was Joseph Mayer, who was prepared to countenance abortion if the life of the mother was threatened by the birth of a child. Mayer, in his publications on the subject, reasoned from the standpoint of emergency. Should one life put another in danger, the state was obliged to save that of the mother.

To Hürth, this position was abhorrent. For him, the chief issue was the prohibition to kill, founded on the Bible and on natural law. All life was sacred, and the state possessed no right to destroy it. But the problem went deeper. One of the implications of Mayer's reasoning was that the individual was subordinated to the well-being of the community. That opened the doors to euthanasia—to the legalized murder of the mentally ill and of others, which, Hürth argued, the Church must oppose.

Years previous to the Nazis' seizure of power, long before the attempt to erect a totalitarian state, Franz Hürth had condemned in no uncertain terms some of the key elements in what was to become the ideology of National Socialism. That his stand was known in Rome is certain because, in 1928, he was asked to write a censure of Mayer's book on "the legal sterilization of the mentally ill" for the Holy Office.[10]

Referring to the Holy Office's decree of May 22, 1895, which prohibited the sterilization of women, Hürth argued that even "inferior beings" had a natural right to marriage and offspring. This was the position taken by Leo XIII in his encyclical *Rerum novarum* (May 15, 1891), from which Hürth argued that the policy of the state could not take precedence over the interests of its citizens. Laws aimed at sterilization or at preventing sexual intercourse in favor of "racial hygiene" were "erroneous, mistaken, dangerous, and absolutely prohibited." Citing Pius XI's statement, made in the consistory of December 20, 1926,[11] that the idea of the state as an end to itself was unacceptable and must be condemned, Hürth delivered a judgment that commanded unanimous assent within the Holy Office.

Hudal added his voice to the chorus. Typically, he spoke in political tones. Unless Catholics made their position clear, he argued in 1931, the abuses liable to be committed by the state would be incalculable. Why should "lives unworthy of being lived"—a sinister formula that the Nazis would appropriate—not be suppressed in what the state took to be its own interests? There was no reason to suppose that the horrors would stop there. "State sterilization" might be extended to other categories of people.

The issue, however, lingered, for the sentence passed on Mayer was lenient. At the suggestion of Pacelli, he was given the option of retracting and of rewriting his book in the light of Pius XI's encyclical *Casti connubii.* Should he fail to do so, a decree of condemnation would be issued by the Holy Office and his work would be put on the Index. Characteristic of Pacelli's proposal was its diplomatic conciliation. As doubts persisted, the German bishops had to commission yet another memorandum from Hürth at their annual conference at Fulda in 1933.[12] But, as early as 1928, he had raised the fundamental issues that were to occupy the Holy Office during the 1930s: not only sterilization and its legitimacy but the natural rights of the individual as opposed to the overweening power of the state.

• • •

To this moral theologian in distant Valkenburg was passed Ledóchowski's order from Rome. Hürth was to examine National Socialist
ideas on racism, nationalism, and the totalitarian state with a view to
condemning them. A proposal made by a consultant led to a command by the Pope and an assignment by the Jesuit general: Such was
the process by which the Catholic Church, in 1934, moved into action.
Each step of that action was taken in strict secrecy—not only because
the proceedings of the Holy Office were *sub secreto pontificio,* the
highest grade of papal security, or out of concern that the Nazis might
learn of the moves being made against them, but also because the operation was improvised and its outcome uncertain. If Hudal had a
strategy (only part of which he divulged), the Vatican did not. Franz
Hürth was given the task of providing the basis on which a potential
strategy might be worked out.

Hürth, understandably, sought assistance in this daunting task.
His colleague at Valkenburg, Johannes Baptista Rabeneck,[13] collaborated with him, bringing to the task encyclopedic knowledge and a
lively interest in current events. The results of their labors were two
reports and some forty-five pages of notes. One report—described as
longer but less clear than the other—was hardly considered; the
other, more succinct and to the point, was examined by the Holy Office when Ledóchowski presented it on March 17, 1935.[14]

To appreciate the form and the intention of these documents, it is
helpful to know how the Holy Office worked. For almost four hundred years, the Supreme Tribunal of the Roman Church had operated according to fixed procedures, which derived from the methods
of debate and analysis employed in the medieval schools. In the Middle Ages, it had been customary to select a statement or a "proposition" that summed up a belief, an attitude, or a theory that was then
examined in terms of its coherence and its orthodoxy, before judgment was passed on it.

That was the setting in which Hürth's and Rabeneck's work was
considered: a cross between a courtroom and a forum for debate. They
presented the case for the prosecution; they brought the Nazis before

the dock. More than a decade before the trials at Nuremberg, they called for a condemnation of National Socialism from the highest doctrinal and moral authority of the Church.

The reports were written in Latin—the language of the universal Church used for papal encyclicals and inquisitorial decrees. A censure of a book like Mayer's on sterilization might be, and was, submitted in German by Hürth in 1928 because, for such routine matters, a summary or translation into Italian would suffice. But this matter was not routine, and the work had to be intelligible to all the modern inquisitors—which meant turning the Teutonic turgidity of *Mein Kampf* into the clarity of the learned language.

Mein Kampf (in an unspecified edition) was the main source for the Jesuits' analysis of Nazi views on racism, supplemented by some of Hitler's speeches and by the writings of his followers, and this may have been one of the motives why the documents were transported to America in 1940. Had Adolf Hitler—admirer of the "logical training" provided by an education in Latin grammar, which he did not have—been able to read the list of propositions to be condemned, he would have had good reasons for concluding that they were directed primarily at himself. All of which marked a change. Before 1935 many members of the Roman Curia (including Hudal) had been inclined to take Hitler at his word. Now the Führer's word was being exposed as heretical.

The doctrine of "purity of blood," the preservation of which Hitler declared to be a "most holy duty," was the first point that the Jesuits singled out. Yet the religious language of *Mein Kampf* and of the Führer's speeches[15] was neither translated nor commented on in the analysis that opened the list presented to the Holy Office. Hürth and Rabeneck attempted to introduce rationality, factual and objective, into a mode of expression that was mystical, muddled, and subjective. They conveyed the stark core of Hitler's ideas, but not the exalted tone with which he proclaimed his racist faith.

Faith, to the Jesuits at this first stage of their work, meant something quite different from the Führer's violence. Their culture and their analytical cast of mind prevented them from taking seriously

Hitler's appeal to the basest instincts. How base those instincts were, they did not fail to see. The idea that differences in blood distinguished one race from another, separating the "lowest" from the "highest" by more distance than the "lowest" man was set apart from the "highest ape,"[16] was contrary to the Church's teaching on the unity and dignity of human nature, the brotherhood of mankind, and Christian spirituality.[17] The Jesuits then linked that heresy to Hitler's belief in the superiority of the "Arian race."

The first proposition, chosen with care, was fundamental to Nazi ideology and it was certain to shock the arbiters of orthodoxy in Rome. No reconciliation was possible between the chief article of racist faith and the doctrines of Catholicism; and the propositions that followed were intended to bolster the effect created by the beginning. Blood was the basis of everything that was praiseworthy in human history, the foundation of a racial character unchanging and incapable of development or improvement: Such were the assertions, unargued and unproved, with which Hitler stated his dogmas in *Mein Kampf.*

The Führer was anything but a systematic thinker. But Hitler, in the hands of the Jesuits, almost became one as they took passages from the entire confused text of *Mein Kampf* and lent them an order which, in the original, they lacked. In doing so, Hürth and Rabeneck did not falsify anything that Hitler had written or said. By reading him with the eyes of rationalists, they presented a digest, clear and comprehensible, of Nazi racism. Yet they communicated little of the hysterical fervor with which Hitler thrust his ideas on his readers or hearers.

Transported onto the plane of the eternal verities, *Mein Kampf,* as analyzed by Hürth and Rabeneck, acquires the timeless quality of heresy: "Mixtures of different bloods can only produce inferior stock"; "Those of the best blood must be preserved and propagated so that, in the struggle between the superior and the inferior, the stronger will triumph and the weaker perish." The Jesuits rightly referred these propositions to Hitler's belief in the laws of nature. What is not transmitted, in the austerity of their presentation, is the fanaticism with which the Führer wrote his racist gospel.

Racial mixture was, for him, "the original sin of this world."[18]

Among the races, it was the Arian that "beyond doubt . . . occupied pride of place." So Hürth and Rabeneck interpreted *Mein Kampf.* Yet they do not note how, in the glowing terms of a true devotee, Hitler attributes Arian predominance to divine will or describes the Germans as "the image of the Lord" and the Jews as the agents or offspring of the devil.[19] Demonizing the Jews, the Führer heroized himself as a savior and redeemer of Arian blood. A Christlike figure in the Germanic people's struggle between "good" and "evil," the Hitler of *Mein Kampf* spoke in apocalyptic tones.

Those tones were most strident on questions of race, the implications of which were hardly conveyed by the Jesuits. To read their work is to obtain the impression that National Socialism was nothing more than a "massive materialism," as Pius XI had stated to Hudal. Mandated to extract what was essential in the writings of Hitler, they neglected a mode of expression, fundamental to his message, that they may have attributed to ignorance. Ignorance (or worse) would have been ascribed to them by this despiser of German professors, had he known of their analysis. Hitler used, or perverted, the Christian language of faith because he was constructing nothing less than a political religion. Yet the threats posed by a political religion were something that members of the Holy Office—who lived in Fascist Rome, with its cult of the Duce and its secular rituals—were wellplaced to understand.

Few, if anyone, understood, in 1934–35, the terrible "logic" of demonizing the Jews that led from *Mein Kampf* to Auschwitz. In that pseudo-religious sphere, where Hitler trespassed most directly on their own territory, the Jesuits were least disposed to take him seriously. The radicalism of *Mein Kampf* was silently dismissed as if it were the outpouring of a crank. Although Hürth and Rabeneck underestimated the reasons for alarm in this central aspect of Nazi ideology, they showed their strength on more familiar grounds. The "defense of good qualities founded in blood," they noted, led inevitably to the assumption that "inferior beings" should be prevented from procreating and therefore to "legalized" sterilization. So it was that Hürth, in 1934, found confirmation of what he had conjectured in 1928.

Blood and the defense of its purity also lay behind Nazi views on education. Hürth and Rabeneck regarded with suspicion the emphasis placed by National Socialism on sports and physical training. When absolute priority was given to the body, the mind and the soul were endangered. That danger was indicated in terms both vague and sinister. Education, according to the Nazis, was to be aimed at developing an "instinct" for the "common good."

The Jesuits grasped that the subordination of the individual to the state and, through it, to the race was an idea with sinister implications. But it is less clear that they understood the term "instinct" simply because their thought was rational. An expression such as "instinct of blood" is hardly translatable into rational terms, nor was it easy to render, in the concrete clarity of Latin, the froth of Nazi gibberish. Unable to explain its appeal, rooted in an anti-intellectualism that was alien to them, the Jesuits concentrated on its effects.

Hürth and Rabeneck extracted from a speech made by the National Socialist minister of justice at Leipzig, on September 30, 1933, the proposition that law should be decided upon and enacted according to the "instinct of blood." What he and other sources meant by this mumbo jumbo was, argued the Jesuits, a political doctrine of leadership. The true, the sole interpreter of the "instinct of blood" was a führer selected, by nature, because he was stronger than others.

Little more than the law of the jungle was the basis of Nazi legal and political thought, and that had direct consequences for the faith. Everything in the Christian religion at odds with this doctrine—humility, gentleness, tolerance, repression of the desire for revenge— was to be abolished. Only "active virtues," such as courage and zeal, might be admitted. The Jesuits doubted the Nazis' belief in a personal God and suspected that many of them wanted to do away with Christianity. Their suspicion was not simply based on the "neopaganism" of Rosenberg and others; the analysis went deeper. Down in the depths of the cult of blood, there was no room for the sacred or the transcendent. In the negation of all that the Jesuits held holy, the Nazis showed their true character. For them, the only relationships that mattered were ones of dominance and subordination, power and force.

The tyranny of this bleak vision, asserting its sway over every aspect of daily life, was plain in the sphere of economics, where "blood" took precedence over all other rights. The "common good" overruled the well-being of individuals, who might be denied their own property. Insignificant in themselves, they counted only as members of the state—with one language, one territory, and one mode of thought or feeling. That, according to *Mein Kampf* as interpreted by Hürth and Rabeneck, was what Hitler meant by the economic interests of the race.

The race was the content, the state, the vessel that lent it form. The "common good" of the race was the purpose and the goal, the state no more than a means to an end. And if, through struggle between the fittest, nature determined that one leader should dominate the unified and disciplined race, its health and prosperity were to be his prime concerns. That is why the Führer should prevent "racial contamination" through sexual contact with "the worst examples of a different blood." Even the sacrament of marriage presented no obstacle to his unlimited powers. He might intervene to "remove the desire to produce offspring." And offspring, when produced, were to be educated in public schools. No private schools were to be allowed, unless they followed the dictates of the state to the letter.

The power of the totalitarian state was absolute and unlimited. Opposition was prohibited and "unnatural" because individuals had no right to existence except as members of the race. The race, founded on blood, represented the first and the last principle of political life: "What individuals possess belongs to the race, and what the race possesses belongs to individuals."

It followed that the realm of the conscience, private and inviolable, no longer existed. The citizen's duty was not to think, but to obey. And if Hürth and Rabeneck refrained from stating that Hitler came close to substituting his idols for God, that was their implied conclusion.

• • •

In fourteen points, or propositions, the Jesuits summed up the chief errors of National Socialism from the standpoint of Catholic orthodoxy. Their list was independent, based on their own work and unaffected by political criteria. Nonetheless it touched directly on politics—in the fullest and widest sense of the word—and it amounted to the most comprehensive account yet presented to the Vatican of the threats posed by National Socialism to the Church in particular and to Christianity in general. Neither the dispatches by Orsenigo nor even the memoranda from other informants writing to Rome offered a picture so many-sided or so menacing. Yet the Jesuits made no comment on actions. They were concerned with ideas.

Dismissing the biological basis of Nazi racism out of hand, they noted that scientists derided such theories—without, however, registering that Hitler's claims for racism were made less on biological than on "religious" grounds. The animus of the scholar against the charlatan came to the fore in the verve with which Hürth and Rabeneck attacked the Nazis' "arbitrary interpretations" and preference for assertions over facts. But the fundamental point on which the Jesuits rejected Nazi racism was its denial of the unity of mankind.

"Essentially the same nature is present in all mankind, according to the principles of the faith," they declared. Irrespective of race or circumstance, everyone was entitled to the rights and privileges derived from that common nature. To emphasize the differences between races, rather than their points in common, was to deny all peoples' subjection to divine providence and to negate God's desire for their salvation and eternal happiness. Christ, who died for all, had founded the Church. Its mission excluded no one. "By one Spirit we are baptized into one body, whether we be Jews or Gentiles" quoted Hürth and Rabeneck from I Corinthians 12.

If the Jesuits did not address the "Jewish question" directly, it was because their first concern was with the biblical doctrine of mankind's unity. For racism, as Hürth and Rabeneck viewed it, threatened not only the Jews but also the Germans. The Nazis exalted those characteristics that men and women shared not with one another but with brute beasts. And the bestiality of the doctrines of race and blood was doubly dangerous because they were forced on German youth by an education that urged them to follow "the law of the flesh that is opposed to the law of the spirit." Self-control, sexual abstinence, and discipline were the values that the Jesuits affirmed against Nazi amorality. They were also the values the absence of which senior members of the Holy Office had been deploring in contemporary society. In Hitler and his adherents, as described by Hürth and Rabeneck, the judges of the Supreme Tribunal were invited to detect the horns of the devil.

The consequences of the doctrine of the purity of blood seemed diabolical to the Jesuits. This led to the "grave error" of prohibiting marriages between Arians and those of "inferior race." Worse still was the practice of sterilization and, most abominable of all, the "murder of unborn children" suspected of some physical defect. "All this offends against natural and divine law, as explained . . . by the Supreme Pontiffs."

A society based on Nazi ideology, it seemed to Hürth and Rabeneck, could only be a travesty of Christian ideals. "The state is not founded on blind instincts of blood, but on human nature, which is rational; and its goal is the common good of its citizens, whatever their blood may be." Law—natural law, derived from God—provided the supreme authority, not a Führer with unlimited powers acquired by violence. The "totalitarian state" ruled by such a figure was an absurdity, they stated, quoting Pius XI. Individual rights, particularly those of the family and the upbringing of offspring, were prior to the state and superior to it.

From an attack on the Nazi ideal of society, the Jesuits passed to a catalog of the rights that were being denied to individuals: to life, protection of the body, the use of one's faculties, personal liberty, worship of God, marriage . . . "Citizens do not exist for the sake of the state; rather it is the state that exists for the benefit of citizens." Totalitarianism repudiated, in doctrine and in detail, the Holy Office was offered a vision of Christian society diametrically opposed to Hitler's.

• • •

These results were achieved, at its first attempt, by what the Nazis saw as an organization of spies. Yet Hürth and Rabeneck had no access to secret sources. Nor would they have acquired them if they had been members of the Holy Office at Rome. The Secretariat of State made very little of the information that it was receiving available to other departments. They were consulted only when the Pope decided that their advice was needed; and if that occurred in 1934, it was not on Pacelli's initiative but on Hudal's. He had posed a problem and offered a lead. But he had not reckoned with the consequences of his move.

Hürth and Rabeneck had gone far beyond Hudal's criticisms of the Nazis. His attack had been aimed at compromise. Correct the "extremists" by pointing out the errors of their ways, he believed, and the result would be an equilibrium in which the Church could prosper. That belief was encouraged by the hypocrisy of Hitler, who never ceased to be a nominal Catholic and who always denied that National Socialism wished to be, or become, a "mystical cult." [20] If there were those at Rome, such as Hudal, and in Germany, such as a number of the Catholic bishops, who wished to give credit to such declarations, the Jesuits Hürth and Rabeneck did not make that mistake. They treated the Nazi doctrines of race and blood as the inseparable articles of a new heresy.

Hürth and Rabeneck saw that they were dealing with a movement that was not simply political. "Politics," as conceived by Hitler and his followers, encompassed every aspect of human life. Life, for the Nazis, was not sacred but instrumental to their racist aims of dominance, which might be achieved by "legal" murder. Yet murder and persecution were not the only consequences of these doctrines, as the Jesuits interpreted them. Hürth and Rabeneck considered that life itself was robbed of its meaning and transcendence by the totalitarian state. They drew no distinction between the state and the Party—and rightly so, because the Nazis were doing all in their power to obscure that difference. It followed from their clear and uncompromising analysis that a strategy of accommodation had to be ruled out on moral and religious grounds.

• • •

Such was the counsel given to the Holy Office by two external advisers of standing. Their views were examined on March 21, 1935, at a congregation over which Pius XI presided. Only his opinion is recorded. He was in favor of proceeding against the Nazis. What he wanted, in order to do so, was a "synthesis . . . of the erroneous principles that form the basis of . . . National Socialism, racism, and the totalitarian state." When it was drawn up, the Holy Office would consider those principles in detail.

This was a move to prepare for action at the highest level. No opposition, on grounds of political expediency or for other motives, was voiced. The Church, in the first quarter of 1935, had already taken the first steps in the direction of a condemnation that presaged a conflict. Neither disagreements nor comments by Pacelli are recorded. Yet the attitude, by 1935, of the future Pius XII toward the Nazis can be gauged.

Appeasement and Opportunism

WEAKNESS TOWARD THE NAZIS and authoritarianism in the Vatican
are charges made against "Hitler's Pope" when he was cardinal–secretary of state.[1] Between 1933 and 1939, Eugenio Pacelli is said to
have followed a policy of appeasement. "Tragic weakness" is alleged
to have determined his tactics; and his protests—threatened, then
withdrawn—amounted to nothing more than "diplomatic play."[2]
Diplomatic correspondence needs to be assessed in the language in
which it was written. When communicating with the government of
Nazi Germany, the Holy See wrote in German.[3]

In German, Pacelli stated positions that had been agreed between
him and the Pope. If other collaborators played a role, it was advisory
and minor. The diplomatic notes sent by the Holy See to the government of the Third Reich were confidential, although it is probable
that they were composed with a view to future publication as a
"white book" intended to demonstrate the Vatican's efforts to maintain the Concordat in the spirit with which it had been signed. Since
then, experience had been discouraging. Negotiations between Rome
and Berlin were stalled in the spring of 1934. Irritated at the German
failure, for months, to respond to his protests, Pacelli forwarded, via
Hitler's ambassador, Diego von Bergen, a memorandum dated May
14, 1934.

To the excuses offered by that government for crass and multiple
violations of the treaty by forces allegedly beyond its control, Pacelli
replied that these were all the less credible, coming from an authoritarian regime.[4] This has been taken to be an example of Pacelli up-

braiding Hitler for "failing to be sufficiently dictatorial" or making "a gesture of heavy irony." [5] In the measured tones of diplomatic language Pacelli was actually stating his disbelief in the lie that the Concordat was being broken by extremists whom their rulers could not restrain.

Less restrained and more passionate was his defense of German Catholics—an integral part of the whole German people, entitled to equal rights. Prepared to be loyal and make sacrifices, they refused to support those who, under the cover provided by politics, pursued aims that were antireligious. Members of the Roman Church would give the state its due, but their first loyalty was to Scripture's command: "One must obey God more than men." [6]

Informing Hitler clearly that the Vatican believed that the Party was behind Nazi attacks on Catholicism, Pacelli refused to accept their spurious distinction between politics and religion. Party politics, he stated flatly, had no influence on the judgment of the Holy See, whose mission was the salvation of immortal souls. [7] If the cardinal was speaking a language which, to the Führer, had little meaning, he was employing terms that recall his declarations, as nuncio in Germany, about Catholics' moral mission. [8] The moral and religious mission of the bishops had led them to condemn National Socialism before it had come to power and, after its accession, the faithful had been bitterly disappointed, noted Pacelli. [9] He presented a long list of the offenses reported to his department that illustrated "the unparalleled trampling of the conscience by the state's representatives." [10] Against such representatives, not the state itself, the Church defended its members. Nazis must be resisted in their attempt to attribute to their movement "cultural and religious" functions that were irreconcilable with the Christian faith. [11]

The Christian faith, Pacelli pointed out to the government of National Socialist Germany, aimed to encompass "the total religious person." [12] Any attempt to limit religious education led, inevitably, to "a crack in the moral foundations of a citizen's sense of duty to the state." "Totality" did not mean "totalitarianism" in the sense in which that word was used in the Third Reich. "Totality" signified a supernatural realm, into which the state's attempt to intrude had been described, by Pius XI, as "absurd" and "monstrous." [13]

False in theory and suicidal in practice, Pacelli argued, the claims of the state in the sphere of education were to be rejected. Without religion, no people could achieve well-being. Human norms were unthinkable unless anchored in the divine. The divinization of the race or of the nation was nothing more than "self-imposed limitation and narrowness." To exalt Fascism as a substitute religion was to follow the path of error; and it was Rome's duty to prevent the young from making such mistakes.[14] That lay in the interests of both Church and state.

Six months before Hürth and Rabeneck had received, from the Jesuit general, the order to examine Nazi doctrines of racism, nationalism, and the totalitarian state, Cardinal Eugenio Pacelli had stated forcefully the Church's position on these issues to the German government. Whole passages of his memorandum employ terms similar to those used in the Jesuits' work. All three expressed the same concerns, such as (in Pacelli's words):

> The Church, as guardian of the faith that is Christ's bequest, cannot stand by without resistance when to young people, the sustainers of future generations, is preached the false and deceptive message of a new materialism of race instead of the joyous news of Christ's teaching, and state institutions are misused to this purpose.

Anticipating the moral and religious position that was to be taken by those who presented the case against National Socialism to the Supreme Tribunal of the Roman Church, Pacelli argued in defense of Catholicism's public role. Argument never ceased to be his weapon against opponents who, by his own standards, were clad in an impenetrable armor plate of irrationality. His aim was not only to protect but also to persuade, and there lay its flaw. For persuasion implied, on the part of the government to which his memorandum was addressed, an openness, an honesty, and a susceptibility to reason which, already in May 1934, were absent. If the cardinal–secretary of state had doubts on that score, they should have been dispelled by the events of the following weeks.

On June 30, 1934, on the "Night of the Long Knives," Ernst Röhm and other SA leaders were arrested and shot without trial. It was scarcely possible for Rome to consider this an "internal affair" of the German Reich because Erich Klausener, the popular leader of Catholic Action in the diocese of Berlin, was also murdered, together with a number of prominent Catholic laymen. Pacelli was informed, in detail, about the acts of terror.[15] He received not only dispatches from Orsenigo but also a copy of a letter (dated July 21, 1934) from Klausener's widow in which the Nazi claim that her husband had committed suicide with his own pistol was flatly denied. (The government accused Klausener of high treason for being implicated in a plot with France.) Contrary to Catholic practice, the corpse had been cremated on the instructions of the secret police.

The Nazis had replied to Pacelli's memorandum of the previous May. He remained silent. The German bishops issued a pastoral letter that did not satisfy the faithful. Protests became loud, and unflattering contrasts were drawn between the episcopate and St. Ambrose, who had compelled the Emperor Theodosius to do penance for his brutality.[16]

That type of outspokenness was lacking among the ecclesiastical authorities both at Rome and in the Third Reich. Pacelli, the master of diplomatic protests, was no more an Ambrose than were the German bishops. He stated his mind and declared his convictions, when called for, in terms of the Concordat. In circumstances not foreseen by that treaty, he held back. Events later in the year would reveal whether Pacelli suffered from excess of prudence or lack of courage.

Silent on some issues and eloquent on others, the secretary of state, by the end of 1935, had learned much about the nature of Hitler's government, and none of it was positive. Throughout that year, Pacelli was informed, by Orsenigo and others, of an organized campaign against the Church.[17] Insults directed at Cardinal Faulhaber, repression of youth organizations, and the arrests of monks accused of teaching the orthodox doctrine on sterilization were noted. Yet none of these actions prompted the Holy See to respond with rigor. The reason for its hesitation is disclosed in a letter of December 18, 1935, that Pacelli sent to Cardinal Schulte of Cologne on the subject of sterilization:

> It would be difficult for the Holy See to take a step, as suggested, on the issue of the Church making a stand on sterilization by that preaching from the pulpit customary in Germany. Should the government of the Reich decide against this, the situation of the bishops would only become more difficult. The form of the announcement can, unity assumed, be left to the conscientious estimation of the Reverend Episcopate . . . Should the . . . bishops believe that an act of courtesy toward the government would make their situation easier, they may, immediately before reading [their announcement] . . . , give notice of it to the authorities responsible, with an indication that the reading occurs in conformity to the Concordat . . . [18]

By the Concordat, which the Nazis were systematically breaking, Pacelli judged each and every case. To the government, whose supporters had attacked a cardinal of the Roman Church, he envisaged an act of diplomatic "courtesy" before the German bishops spoke out. Rome itself would hold its tongue, for fear of making matters worse. That they were bad, he knew from a report (undated, but probably from late 1935) in which it was declared that:

> . . . the Catholic Church, in the last months, has gradually lost prestige. Its tactic of non-resistance is considered a sign of weakness . . . The government neither slows down the struggle nor compromises. The *détente* of the moment serves only to send the masses to sleep and separate them more easily, imperceptibly, and gradually from the Church's forms of organization.[19]

Even Orsenigo shared this sense of alarm. On December 20, 1935, he wrote to Pacelli requesting a "brief and eloquent reference," by the Pope, to the "sorrows caused to his heart" by events in Germany.[20] This would comfort Catholics as the "repression of religious freedom" continued.

The same nuncio had reported, on January 23 of that year, that Hitler's gratitude for the bishops' support in obtaining a favorable vote in the referendum on the Saarland would ward off "anti-Christian attacks"[21] and, on May 16, had relayed his "good hopes" that an intervention by Papen would avoid a "religious struggle."[22] Months later those illusions were dispelled. And Pacelli, in December 1935, was not willing to take a stand on the issue of sterilization, which, a few years previously, had been debated and decided by the Supreme Congregation of the Holy Office, of which he was a member. He was less an appeaser, in the sense which that term has acquired by hindsight, than an opportunist, as the Vatican used that expression during the 1930s.

Moral and doctrinal considerations were not lacking in his strategy. The cardinal-secretary of state was as alert to recent decisions of the Holy Office as he was convinced by the traditional teachings of the Church. Nor did he hesitate to state them to the Nazis, as his memorandum of May 1934 shows. But as a diplomat—the first diplomat, in rank—of the Holy See, he had to judge the moment. "Opportune" and "inopportune" are terms that recur throughout Pacelli's state papers. He was answerable to a great opportunist—Pius XI—who had signed a treaty with the Fascists in 1929, when the time seemed ripe. Developments in Italy since that date had not always been happy, yet the Church had secured several of its objectives. In Germany the aim was similar and, from August 19, 1934, Pacelli was dealing with a Führer who had united the offices of head of state and head of government on the basis of a plebiscite that had offered him 89.9 percent support.

The cardinal had to calculate the opportuneness of the moment. But as he calculated, the moment passed—and the official voice of Rome remained silent.

•   •   •

In that silence, one of the figures on the Roman scene raised his own voice. Alois Hudal suffered from none of Eugenio Pacelli's inhibitions or scruples. Nor was the titular bishop of Ela satisfied with his status. He, the self-styled mediator, needed to speak out. In tones of urgency Hudal published, in 1935, a pamphlet on the German people and the Christian West.[23]

The tone of urgency stemmed from his belief that he was living at a historical turning point, when "an old world was collapsing." The unity of the West was threatened and, with it, the intellectual leadership of Europe. But "the West," as Hudal wished to interpret that term, was not a geographical or political concept, but a cultural one. For him, each culture was influenced by national and racial factors. Yet Hudal, who (unknown to the Nazis) had so recently called for the condemnation of their nationalism and racism, hastened to add that he was not in favor of the idea of any land's superiority or hegemony. What he wanted was harmony between "the Germanic and Romanic geniuses."

For that harmony, he had a model. It was provided by Italy. There the "two personalities of world-historical importance, Pope Pius XI and the brilliant Duce," had repressed extremists and furthered cooperation between state and Church. That was the ideal that Hudal was holding up to Germany—of a leader, in league with the papacy, who repudiated the cult of the nation, of race, and of blood.

The addressee of this pamphlet, unmentioned by name, was Adolf Hitler—the same Hitler a condemnation of whose ideas had been prepared, in a memorandum written for the Holy Office at Hudal's prompting, and submitted in March 1935. As Hudal's pamphlet was not approved by the archbishopric of Vienna for publication until July 29 of that year, it is more than probable that, while writing it, he was aware of the line then being pursued by the Roman authorities. That, however, did not inhibit him from striking out on his own. What the Jesuits had identified as the essence of Hitler's thought, Hudal continued to ascribe to Nazi "extremists."

The illusion of "Hitler the moderate" was, in defiance of the evidence, still alive in Rome in 1935. Its chief proponent was Hudal, who persisted in his attempt to separate the Führer from his followers. The compromises that his ambition dictated were far removed from the tough line that the rector of the Anima had advocated previously. The "idea of race" seemed now valuable to him, provided that it did not obtrude into the sphere of culture or become a substitute for religion.[24] It was all a question of degree. Nation or race, elevated to a "worldview" *(Weltanschauung)*, was incompatible with Christianity. In milder and measured forms, however, both might be accepted. So it was that the self-appointed mediator formed his policy of "appeasement."

Adapting Nazi language, Hudal claimed that what was now needed was "an intellectual Führer" whose name was Christ. As absolutely as any totalitarian ruler, he should hold sway over "the whole of cultural life." There, in the realm where National Socialism was weakest, Hudal saw the Church's chance. It provided unity and vision, which served the state's purposes. And the attractiveness of Rome, at this time of cultural crisis, was proved by the return of Protestants to the true Church.[25]

Rome offered the stoutest defense against that "cultural Bolshevism which was alien to German blood." Using terms reminiscent of Hitler's, Hudal cited *Mein Kampf* on the Führer's duty to preserve, inviolable, the religious institutions of his people.[26] And this declaration, blatantly belied by Nazi practice in 1935, was derived from the book on which the Jesuits based many of their arguments for a condemnation of National Socialism by the Holy Office.

Inside the Holy Office, Hudal had advocated the strategy of attack. Outside those secret confines, he was using the same strategy to "negotiate" from a position of strength. Condemnation could be avoided if the other side was ready for compromise. In milder forms, Nazi doctrine might be tolerated.[27] Tolerance and compromise with the Catholic Church were in the interests of the state. Nothing was to be hoped for from Protestantism, now a spent force. And as Hudal warmed to his theme, his voice became charged with imperialistic tones.

The Church, like a lighthouse, loomed over the present's "field of ruins." "Millions, in the darkness of [these] times, waited for her word of leadership." A longing for power, not simply intellectual or spiritual, is evident in the role that its author envisaged for Rome: "as

more than a legal authority, more than a religious organization . . ." [28]
Guardian of culture, continuity, and tradition, the Church of Hudal's
fantasy could become an equal partner of National Socialism, closer
to which its former critic was now moving.

One step followed another, at a swift pace. In the same year (1935) in
which his pamphlet appeared, Hudal published a book on the Vatican
and the modern states.[29] Both works had much in common—the
"leadership-role" of the Church, its cultural preeminence, and
(above all) its rights, founded in natural law. With the same monoto-
nous confidence in his own judgment, Hudal repeated the theory of
the "left-wing extremists" and "conservatives" to be found in every
dictatorship.[30] Rome, he declared, wanted an "adaptation" between
such conservative forces and "modern circumstances." [31]

"Adaptation" was achieved in Hudal's use of Hitler's terms. The
German people lacked space to live[32]; expansion was necessary; and
Bolshevism represented the main enemy. Then these ideas were
linked to one another in a *fortissimo* that must have sounded musical
to Nazi ears:

> . . . the religious and moral dregs of Jewry which today, from
> Moscow, keep the Christian peoples of Europe in a state of
> permanent unrest in order to prepare the way for the world-
> dominance of a race which has given the world precious cul-
> tural goods and outstanding personalities but which, as soon
> as its religious roots are upturned, is impelled to supplant
> every other culture . . . [33]

Equating the Jews with the "Bolsheviks" and linking them in a plot
for "world-dominion," Hudal sought to form a common front.

Those who have sought an "appeaser" in the Vatican before the
Second World War have looked in the wrong place. "Adaptation,"
meaning "appeasement" followed by alliance, was the strategy beginning to form in the mind not of the cardinal–secretary of state but
of this titular bishop of the Church.

• • •

One of its princes, Eugenio Pacelli, spoke at Lourdes in the same year on a number of the same issues. On April 28, 1935, he deplored:

> . . . the present reality . . . in which minds, guided by teachers of error, drink at poisoned springs . . . It matters little that they flock, in masses, round the flag of social revolution, that they are inspired by a false conception of the world and life, that they are possessed by the superstition of race and blood. Their philosophy . . . rests on principles fundamentally opposed to those of the Christian faith and the Church will never, at any price, have dealings with them.[34]

Pacelli denied that "the Church of the catacombs, the Church of the martyrs and intrepid, heroic bishops" was a thing of the past. He affirmed that it was a "living reality," equal to facing the "infernal dragon," the "demon's rage," the "power of darkness."

Less than six months later, on September 14, 1935—the day before the "Nuremberg Laws," denying the Jews German citizenship and forbidding marriage and sexual relations between them and non-Jews, were promulgated—an archbishop who was not notably "intrepid and heroic" wrote to Pacelli from Berlin.[35] Nuncio Orsenigo knew what was about to be enacted. He remarked that it was difficult to find a single non-Jewish German who dared to disapprove of the measures. The "campaign was boundless," denunciations and persecution rife. In a moment of rare insight, Orsenigo concluded:

> I do not know whether Russian Bolshevism is the exclusive work of the Jews but here the way has been found to make this believed and to take measures in consequence against Jewry. If, as it seems, the Nazi government will have a long life, the Jews are destined to disappear from this nation.

Pacelli, prince of "the Church of the catacombs and the martyrs," neither acted on that information nor did he forward it to the Holy Office, which, at that time, was examining the issue of racism. He continued to alternate between relative forthrightness and absolute silence. Meanwhile, Hudal's overtures of "appeasement" began to clash with Rome's other strategies.

Three Strategies

THROUGHOUT 1934–35, the Secretariat of State, the Holy Office, and Alois Hudal pursued different approaches to the Third Reich. Inconsistent with one another, each of their strategies sheds light on tensions within the Vatican.

The first strategy was adopted by the cardinal–secretary of state, who attached prime importance to the terms of the Concordat. Pacelli was neither unaware of the outrages of the Nazis nor sympathetic to their movement, yet he saw no alternative to negotiation, punctuated by protests made in the form of diplomatic notes. Those notes seldom exceeded the bounds defined by the treaty. In the exceptional cases, such as his memorandum of May 1934, in which he went further, the cardinal–secretary of state explained, clearly and cogently, the Church's motives. The result, for him, was a martyrdom of patience. Pacelli's communications did not always receive answers. When they did, the replies from the government of the Third Reich were often late, seldom sincere, and never on the same level of argument. The approach that he maintained, and wished to foster on the other side, was that of a correct partner to the treaty. Correctness, legal and diplomatic, was not only fundamental to Eugenio Pacelli's understanding of his institutional role but also a key to his character.

Within these limits, the cardinal–secretary of state was capable of speaking out. But the limits were circumscribed by Pius XI. During the nine years of Pacelli's "apprenticeship" to become that pope's successor, there is no sign, among the official documents in the Vatican, that he ever overstepped them. To ask about his "personal role" is to put the question in misleading terms. Distinctive of Pacelli was his selflessness in the execution of his duties and his subordination to the will of his master.

These are the attributes of a dedicated servant. They are not obviously the qualities of a hero. Nor do the state papers and public addresses of Eugenio Pacelli reveal original ideas. If he thought for himself, he was careful to remove any trace; and behind the public facade of this intensely private person no one was invited to penetrate. Reserve and scrupulousness affected his conduct of affairs. Pacelli was aware that the Church needed champions of its cause. He said as much while nuncio in Germany, and repeated it more forcefully in his speech at Lourdes in 1935.[1] Yet he was not inclined to strike out on his own account, nor to force the hand of what must at times have seemed a hesitant episcopate in Germany. That is why his alleged authoritarianism has been overstated.

Personally timid, Pacelli was in favor of strong government of the Church from its center. But as cardinal–secretary of state, he was too prudent to issue orders that would, or could, not be followed. An instruction to the German bishops might lead to difficulties both with the government and with the Catholic faithful, of whose support for Hitler he was convinced. The consequence was not a firm chain of command between Rome and Germany but a never-ending series of consultations marked by doubts and uncertainty on both sides.

Their back-and-forth exchanges failed to produce a firm line of resistance.[2] Confronted with cases, such as the Nuremberg racial laws of 1935, which were—narrowly interpreted—outside the sphere of church-state relations as defined by the Concordat, Pacelli did not return to the policy of intervention on the Jews' behalf, which, on Pius XI's orders, he had recommended to Orsenigo two years earlier.[3] Perhaps pessimistic about achieving any useful result, the cardinal hung back. And where Pacelli hesitated, Hudal leapt in.

Alois Hudal's position, in the mid-1930s, was not comparable to that of Eugenio Pacelli. Direct access to the Pope and control over the Vatican's diplomatic service, combined with other distinctions, made the cardinal–secretary of state a central figure at Rome. More marginal in the establishment and lower in rank, the rector of the Anima could not compete. Yet that, in a sense, is what Hudal attempted to do. Secret or public, all of his activities were aimed at securing influence—both with the Germans and with the Roman authorities.

Hudal's position, in his own wishful thinking, was pivotal. As head of the German national church in the holy city, he might become the privileged interpreter of the Reich to a Roman Curia dominated by Italians. For the Germans, he could perform a similar service, steering Rome in the direction of what he took to be the nation's interest. To achieve both aims, he had the advantage of a double role—hidden, in the Holy Office, where he could play the part of the Nazis' critic, and open, when he published for a general audience in the Reich. Driven by ambition to seize the chances offered by what he regarded as a historical opportunity, Hudal was a man in a hurry. In his haste, he forgot that the Vatican worked with the timetable of eternity.

By the time that Pius XI ordered the Jesuits' work to be synthesized into propositions that formed the foundation of National Socialism, racism, and the totalitarian state, Hürth had transferred to Rome as a professor at the Gregorian university and been appointed a consultant to the Holy Office. He was joined by a new collaborator, Louis Chagnon, a Canadian sociologist and expert on natural law.[4] They labored to produce a long list of the damnable beliefs held by the Nazis by May 1, 1935. What neither Hürth nor Chagnon nor anyone else then knew was that, two years later, the revisions and expansions of that list would still not be complete.

The Vatican's sense of time was ably defined by Pacelli when he referred, in a note to the German government of January 29, 1936, to the "tasks assigned by its supranatural mission and the experience gained in two thousand years of activity."[5] That was the spirit, unhurried and serene, in which Hürth's and Chagnon's list was examined by his colleagues in the Holy Office, to the chagrin of Hudal's impatience. They were accustomed to proceeding at a more stately pace.

The success or failure of the day was a matter of indifference to the Vatican, as Pius XI would put it; and its officials had difficulties in approaching recent problems from a traditional standpoint. One of those difficulties lay in the language used by Hürth and Chagnon. When their list was presented to the Holy Office by the general of the Jesuits, Ledóchowski remarked that it had been at times impossible to find a word suitable to translate the concepts analyzed. "Totalitarianism," for example, had no equivalent in Latin. So it was that, at Rome during the mid-1930s, modern inquisitors pondered over how to render, into the ancient tongue of Latin civilization, the new slogans of barbarism.

Hürth and Rabeneck had summed up the heresies of National Socialism in fourteen propositions in the first part of their report to the Holy Office. Twelve counter-propositions were listed in its second part. By May 1, 1935, Hürth and Chagnon had produced a list of no less than forty-seven items that deserved to be condemned (Appendix I).[6] That list differed from the first not only in its length but also in organization and emphasis.

Nationalism, not racism, was now the prime issue. What Hudal regarded, in its "more moderate" forms, as a virtue, the Jesuits were calling on the Holy Office to damn. Their call paid closer attention to the nature of the threat than before. In particular, they now recognized that they were dealing with a political religion that deified the state (1).* As state-worship amounted to a form of neo-paganism, it entered into direct competition with Christianity (2).

From these two heresies followed a series of lesser evils—the "extreme nationalism (3) that declared the state a law unto itself and (4) the consequent contempt for private or international law. Here and elsewhere throughout their list, the Jesuits did not hesitate to move from religious questions to political and legal issues. While the grounds on which they did so are not spelled out, the context is indicated in two diplomatic notes that Pacelli sent to the German government."

On January 31, 1934, he declared: "it is far from being the

---

* Numbers within parentheses refer to numbered clauses in Appendix I of this book.

Catholic Church's intention to refuse [to acknowledge] a form of state or a re-organization or a new organization of a state. [The Church] lives in correct and good relations with states that have the most different forms of government and the most diverse internal structures. It has concluded Concordats with monarchies and republics, with democratic and authoritarian states."[7] And on January 29, 1936, he added in another note: "[The Church] judges each form of the state according to its value and success in achieving the true well-being of the people, which can never be reached by alienation or struggle with revealed Christian truth . . ."[8]

These two statements by Pacelli repeat, in concise form, a Catholic doctrine of neutrality formulated by Leo XIII.[9] Between the first and the second of these statements, however, an extension of that doctrine had been proposed within the Vatican. A state that took account of nothing but itself, in disregard of natural, private, or international law, was irreconcilable with Christianity and, on the recommendation of Hürth and Chagnon, should be condemned. This was one of the chief issues raised by National Socialism, as it was appraised for the Holy Office in the spring of 1935. Probably like Pacelli and certainly unlike Hudal, the Jesuits drew a line at neutrality not only when it was at odds with "revealed Christian truth" but also when the legal basis of peaceful coexistence between states was undermined.

The desire to expand, in quest of *Lebensraum*, was condemned by Hürth and Chagnon four years before the Second World War broke out (6). Militarism and aggression, in the interests of power and glory, were linked by them with that "national fanaticism" which they found in *Mein Kampf* (7, 8). These Jesuits were hardly prophets who had seen through Hitler's war aims,[10] but they understood the drives that lay behind them. A warning was issued at Rome in 1935; and it was not that the "appeaser" Hudal failed to hear it but that he chose to remain deaf.

Racism, previously the core of the Nazi creed, was now relegated to second place. The overriding concern remained the Church's teaching on the unity of mankind (9 ff). Although the Jesuits retained, among the propositions to be condemned, that the "lowest of races" differs more from the "highest" than it does from brute beasts (9), they did not spell out the implications of Hitler's bestial idea, which was directed against the Jews.

Why were Hürth and Chagnon silent on this point? Was it because:

> ... the anti-Semitism of the Nazis was a problem for the Church in the 1930s not because of its negative portrayal of the Jews, much of which was shared by the Church itself; the problem stemmed, on the contrary, from the danger that the Nazis would exploit an appeal that had previously been identified with the Church to attract Catholics to a non-Christian cause. In denouncing Nazism, Church leaders were eager to show people that they did not have to join the Nazis to be against the Jews ... ? [11]

The "Church leaders" in the Holy Office of 1935 had reason to recall the dissolution of the Friends of Israel a few years earlier.[12] Then anti-Semitism had been condemned, but hostility to the Jews had been shown by Merry Del Val. His protégé, Hudal, who had followed the same course, would travel even further in that direction in 1936.[13] Yet Pacelli had deplored racism in his memorandum to the German government of May 1934,[14] and Orsenigo's grim prophecy that the Jews were "destined to disappear" from Germany was still to be made when the Jesuits submitted their list. The near-absence of direct reference to the "Jewish problem," in the Jesuits' document, does not prove their sympathy for anti-Semitism.

Hürth and Chagnon now saw that they were dealing with a "religion" of racism (12 ff) that altered or eliminated the fundamentals of Catholic faith (16). That was the standard by which the Jesuits measured the heresies of National Socialism and which, in 1935, prevented them and others from perceiving anti-Semitism as an issue to itself. Of all the forty-seven points that figure on their list, only one (19) explicitly mentions the Jews, and then it deals with the prohibition of "mixed marriages" between them and Arians. When the "Jewish problem" touched directly on Catholic life, it was dealt with explicitly. Otherwise it was subsumed under the doctrine of mankind's unity. Not until 1936 was anti-Semitism mentioned specifically,[15] as the product of a slow process of reflection by the Holy Office. But, in condemning Nazi racism as a whole, the Jesuits made no exceptions.

This was the second attempt, within two years, to formulate a critique of National Socialism, and more work remained to be done. Generalizations about the "Church leaders in the 1930s" can be insensitive to how their positions developed with time. If it took time to interpret the errors of Hitler and his followers, that was because their beliefs appeared, to the Jesuits, improvised and transient. What struck Hürth and Chagnon, in the doctrines that they recommended for condemnation, was their lack of stability. The Nazis not only denied the universal validity of one religion; their faith "of blood and race" dictated a diversity that rose to coherence only in its opposition to Christianity (12, 13). Yet even faith in racism did not require active assent (15). "Passive participation" in racist rituals might serve to foster belief. Christianity could be "adapted" or "altered," so long as its absolute value was denied (16).

Denial and negation remained, for the Jesuits, central features of the Nazi creed. Realizing, however, that it could not only be based on negatives, they went further than the first analysis to consider the "instinct of race." That term, in its vagueness, had eluded the analysis of Hürth and Rabeneck. Now (17), as a supreme principle above all others, it is invested with the qualities of infallibility. Nowhere is the likeness, or the menace, to Catholicism more explicit than in this point. Seeking to make sense of the irrationality of racism, the Jesuits attributed to "instinct" what orthodoxy assigned to the Pope.

The issues posed by procreation and "racial hygiene" were simpler. Sterilization and abortion (20) had been dealt with recently by the Holy Office, and the Church's doctrines on extramarital sex and clerical celibacy were so clear-cut that the Nazi errors listed at 21 to 23 were beyond discussion. Their effect was cumulative. When supplemented by National Socialist doctrine on education (24–26), they amounted to a blueprint for destruction of Christian society. Hürth and Chagnon understood that the society or state that was to be erected on its ruins was not only to be racist, violent, and tyrannical (27–32) but also totalitarian.

Totalitarianism was, for the Nazis, a doctrine as "infallible" as the "instinct of race" (33). As the Jesuits saw it, this meant more than absolute state power (35); it also implied that everything was prohibited that had not been explicitly allowed (36). The imperious rhetoric of the Nazis may have suggested this conclusion, but it is difficult to find a law or a document making the claim in so many words. Nor did Hürth and Chagnon produce any evidence. Here their hostility to Hitler appears to have imagined a totalitarianism more total than even the Führer envisaged.

The elimination of the Church's freedom was the inevitable consequence of such an interpretation of the state's power, they noted (37–39), with no reference to the Concordat. Violations of its provisions were by now so patent and flagrant that it was unnecessary to emphasize them; and the Jesuits were concerned, in the first place, with principles rather than practice. One of those principles now found, at 41, a fresh and significant emphasis.

The Church as defender of universal human rights against the encroachment of the state was an idea present in the first version. But the notion that the totalitarians denied that the popes might champion those rights for mankind, individually and collectively, now acquires a polemical tone. Challenging the authority of the Supreme Pontiffs in the sphere where it was not restricted to Catholics, the Nazis, as portrayed by Hürth and Chagnon, were the enemies of all. It is at this point in their analysis that its general implications emerge most forcefully. Beginning with three heresies menacing the Church in Germany, the Jesuits ended with concerns that were not exclusively Catholic.

The doctrine of human rights and the duty of its defense by the papacy was familiar to Pius XI and Pacelli. Two years before, acting on similar principles, the cardinal–secretary of state had transmitted to Orsenigo the Pope's instruction to concern himself with the plight of the Jews.[16] If that line had not been pursued in 1933, it reemerged with broader force in 1935. And it pointed to a third strategy incompatible with the alternation between protests and silence adopted by the Secretariat of State or with the "appeasement" initiated by Hudal. This third strategy urged condemnation of National Socialism in the interests of a mankind whose defender, according to divine and natural law, was the Pope.

> Human rights are in danger. No one dares to speak out against those dictators who treat people as though they were slaves. Faced with the concentration camps, the murders, the violations of freedom, no one declares God's word: "That is not allowed!" Were the Church to speak out, were it to fulfill its high calling, the entire world would echo it with enthusiasm . . . ! [17]

So Friedrich Muckermann had written in *The German Way (Der deutsche Weg)* on December 23, 1934. Although Hürth's and Chagnon's list was not a reply to his call, the correspondence between their positions is unmistakable. The appeal of the one Jesuit and the propositions of the other two found focus on the same issue. Both in the glare of publicity and in the secrecy of the Holy Office these members of the same order were taking the strongest stand on human rights in evidence at Rome during 1934 and 1935.[18]

More reserved were the positions expressed in the *Osservatore Romano*. That newspaper reported little about anti-Semitism in Germany during 1935, concentrating instead on "problems with the Concordat" in its article of July 15/16 of that year.[19] This reflected the line taken by Pacelli. If the secretary of state knew of Muckermann's call, no evidence of that knowledge is available; but it is certain that, from May 1935, he was aware of the forty-seven grounds for condemnation submitted to the Holy Office by Hürth and Chagnon. They were presented to the cardinals in printed copies.

From within the Vatican, Pacelli was placed in a delicate position. Based on criteria similar to (if more extensive than) those expressed in his memorandum to the German government of 1934, the Jesuits' draft recommended a strategy of confrontation as strong as Pacelli's rhetoric of resistance, but tougher than his practice. The practice of dealing with the National Socialists, in the Secretariat of State, was, and had to be, influenced by consideration of *Realpolitik*. The Holy

Office was concerned not with the details of current policy but with the principles for which Catholicism did, or should, stand. As Pacelli meditated on his stand, he had to take into account the concrete circumstances described in such reports as that dated February 6, 1935, from Warsaw, which stated:

> Very seldom indeed does one meet people [in Germany] who reject the regime on grounds of principle, and I have encountered nobody who would be ready to engage in active opposition ... The daily poison of mendacity and monotonous optimism . . . has an effect like that of opium on people's spirits, even on those who think that they have seen through to reality and believe nothing that is served up, day by day, from Goebbels's kitchen of lies. No one exposed to this poison on a daily basis can, in the long term, avoid its paralyzing effect on the spirit.[20]

What was the antidote to that "poison"? Pacelli had to judge whether the cure might not be more dangerous than the malady. And that was not easy to do, as the same report noted:

> The work of the Catholic Church is bearing unmistakable fruits. But the danger is already more and more evident that the impulses given by the resistance to the Nazi's ideological experiments are not leadiing to an active opposition in the religious sphere but end in a Christianity of the catacombs— i.e.: that one gives up [all hope of] having an effect outside the confines of the Church.[21]

This depressing picture was made more somber by the perception of lack of unity among the German bishops and by a sense of "stagnation."[22] Was the Vatican now to break through these clouds with a lightning bolt of anathema? Or, while the condemnation was being prepared in the Holy Office, would it be content with a rumble of thunder from Rome?

• • •

Rumblings of papal discontent had been audible since Easter 1934. At that time Pius XI had written to the leader of a Catholic youth organization threatened by Nazi measures, assuring him that the Pope identified with its cause. A year later he declared, to German pilgrims in Rome, that attempts were being made to destroy Christian and Catholic life in their country by a "barbaric paganism." And in 1935 the Pope's protests were swelled by a *basso*, unobtrusive but not insignificant, because it derived from a figure of note in both the Holy Office and the Secretariat of State.

Now remembered as a leading conservative at the Second Vatican Council,[23] Alfredo Ottaviani, in 1935, was both a consultant to the Holy Office and, as *sostituto* (or undersecretary of state), one of Pacelli's closest collaborators. In that year he published a textbook of canon law[24] that attacked doctrines embraced by the Nazis and the Fascists. Citing the works of Mussolini, Hitler, and Rosenberg, Ottaviani condemned, for example, the idea that the state possessed all rights which it might deny to individuals.[25] Totalitarianism's claims to dominate were unfounded; the secular authorities were incompetent in spiritual matters.[26] These were issues with which, at the time Ottaviani's book appeared, the Holy Office was dealing; and his denunciation of the "recent German error by Hitler" that the function and aim of the state lay in preserving the "purity of blood" might have been taken from the first or second versions of the Jesuits' reports.

If this was not a planned leak, it resembled one. In 1936, Ottaviani was transferred to the Holy Office as its *assessor*—the highest full-time official, after the cardinals, who had a weekly audience (on Thursdays) with the Pope. The right man in the right place, he reissued his book in an abbreviated edition that was noticed in Germany.[27] Formally a "private" publication, the work was nonetheless printed by the Vatican; and it would have been wholly inconsistent with Ottaviani's prudence had he acted without authorization. A signal was being sent that bore the mark of Pacelli's subtlety. Too subtle for some, it nonetheless offered a glimpse into what, at Rome, was being planned behind the official facade.

———⚬⚬⚬———

The Grand Design

MONTHS PASSED AND LENGTHENED into almost a year. On July 16, 1935, the Nazis founded a ministry for ecclesiastical affairs, led by Hanns Kerrl. His ill-defined brief was mocked in his nickname of "minister of heavenly and earthly organization," and his powerlessness was exposed, a week after his appointment, by Hermann Göring's edict forbidding Catholic youth organizations to engage in any activity that was not of an exclusively religious nature. Repression continued, with attacks on groups of Catholic workers and fruitless appeals by German bishops to the terms of the Concordat. Trials against the clergy on drummed-up charges of immorality and currency-smuggling took place; and measures were introduced to eliminate confessional schools. Kerrl was not always informed about these actions that affected his ministry, and his policy of ignoring Catholic protests heightened tension.

Meanwhile, three consultants had been asked by the Holy Office to comment on Hürth's and Chagnon's reports. Not until April 4, 1936, did they do so. The Vatican's majestic sense of time was not the only reason for this pace. A consultancy in the Holy Office was, for members of the Roman establishment, a part-time job.

Each consultant was to state his own position, which was then compared with those of the others. The orthodox view, on the issues posed by National Socialism, was reached by discussion—first between the consultants and then, on the basis of their recommendations, by the cardinals of the Holy Office. Its head, the Pope, would take the final decision. In theory, Pius XI's freedom to act was not limited by this process. But, in practice, the Vicar of Christ was influenced by consultation. Consultation, within the papal monarchy, was a means of achieving consensus. The Pope might be an autocratic ruler, but he was not absolute. More than a totalitarian dictator, he relied on his experts.

Expertise, in the Vatican, was not reckoned in purely academic terms. Consultants might be theologians or canon lawyers, but they also represented the interests of the Vatican's bureaucracy and the Church's institutions. A principle of balance influenced their recruitment. Jesuits had undertaken the first and second stages of the work on National Socialism, and it was no accident that its assessment was entrusted to the master-general of the Dominicans.[1]

Head of a religious order that had provided the Holy Office with members for centuries, Martin-Stanislaus Gillet enjoyed the reputation of being an intellectual. That says much about the torpor of ecclesiastical circles at Rome. Wide-ranging but not deep in his knowledge, Gillet was an addict of simple ideas. In November 1932, for example, he gave a speech about the Church and international relations.[2] In it emerged his governing notion: the family. Just as the family provided the model for protection of human dignity, so nations and societies were children that the Vatican guided with maternal authority. No one, after Christ Himself, had done more in this cause than Pius XI, Gillet was to assert a few years later.[3]

All of which might have made the master-general of the Dominicans receptive to the Jesuits' defense of human rights and condemnation of racism. Not a bit of it. Gillet's sole interests were in the Nazis' "deification of the state" and "absorption of the individual." He argued that they had led to a confusion between the personal and the social conscience. In the moral chaos that followed, a new pagan religion had emerged.

At that point in his report, Gillet performed a mental somersault. Leaping from the solid ground of Hürth's and Chagnon's document, he soared through the hot air of his own speculation. In that lofty sphere, unhampered by facts, every distinction drawn by the Jesuits became blurred. Nationalism, Communism, totalitarianism, racism: The terms did not matter, because they all amounted to the same. A "new idol," recognizable to everyone by its common features, had emerged. Its name was "social modernism."

"Modernism" was also the name that senior members of the Holy Office applied to their old enemy. Combated by Pius X,[4] it was now reviving in new forms, according to Gillet. The struggle against National Socialism was nothing more or less than a continuation of the battles of the past. On this ill-defined basis the master-general of the Dominicans favored a condemnation of the "various errors of the modern age," which he attempted to reduce to a common denominator.

A more realistic but equally selective line was taken by Ernesto Ruffini, secretary of the Congregation for the Seminars and Universities and a consultant to the Congregation for Extraordinary Ecclesiastical Affairs. He emphasized those aspects of the problem that were most "political." "Ultra-nationalism," as Ruffini called it, was "the heresy of our times." All peoples and even some priests were "infected" by it. That was the main reason why he held it "absolutely opportune, not to say necessary," that the Holy See speak out. Not, however, in the form proposed by the Jesuits. Their work was too detailed, yet insufficiently precise.

Both Ruffini and Gillet identified precision with simplification. One term, they recommended, should be employed to get to the core of the problem. That the problem posed by National Socialism was complex and many-sided could only be ignored by paring away layers of Hürth's and Chagnon's analysis. Racism, for example, was not mentioned by Ruffini or Gillet. Although they detected, in the state's claim to be the supreme source of law and the final arbiter of morality, a usurpation of the Church's rights, they wished to return to "fundamentals" rather than maintaining fullness. A difficulty had emerged that was addressed most interestingly by the third member of this trio of consultants.

Domenico Tardini was a man of many parts.[5] In 1936 he had succeeded Ottaviani as *sostituto* or undersecretary of state. Closer than Ruffini to Pacelli (of whom he was to paint a portrait[6]), Tardini had links with several departments, including the Papal Commission for Russia. Commanding an overview of Vatican policy, he was capable of approaching the problem in "geopolitical" terms.

Less than a month previously, on March 19, 1936, Pius XI had condemned "atheistic Communism" in his encyclical *Dilectissima nobis.* Tardini had that document in mind when he commented on the Jesuits' list. The world, he declared, was divided into two camps: nationalist and Communist. To damn the first might seem to favor the second. The Church should not "remain silent before two opposing and most pernicious errors," Tardini argued. What was needed was a double attack, aimed at eliminating them both. So it was that there emerged, in April 1936, a line of Vatican policy that Tardini was to restate in May 1943: "Two dangers threaten European and Christian culture: Nazism and Communism. Both are materialistic, antireligious, totalitarian, tyrannical, cruel and militaristic . . ." [7]

The similarities between the dangers posed by the right and the left were recognized early; and that perception became sharper in the light of persecutions of Catholics in Mexico and Spain. Tardini, however, counseled caution. At all costs, the impression of making a "political gesture" was to be avoided. Not politics but pastoral concerns should be seen to be the aim of the condemnation.

As these issues emerged into the limelight, racism was relegated to the wings. Too complex, it did not fit into the simple schema developing in the Holy Office's thought. Like Gillet, Tardini believed that nationalism and Communism could be linked easily because they had common features, such as the all-powerfullness of the state and the denial of individual liberty. There lay the opportunity that Tardini recommended that Rome should seize: "The extremes meet in this case and we could strike at them both, demonstrating once again that the Church follows a golden middle path in which consist truth and virtue." [8]

That "middle path" had to be shorter than the one followed by Hürth and Chagnon. Their work, according to Tardini, listed errors so elementary that they did not need to be pointed out. It was a mistake not to express the heresies in the terms originally used by the Nazis. Rephrasing them, the Jesuits had employed an academic language that the general public would not understand. Nor was it helpful to include, in the same proposition, both the falsehoods they asserted and the truths they denied. Some were so obvious that they would provoke, in the faithful, "a spontaneous feeling of revulsion."

While the Jesuits had attempted to be comprehensive, Tardini aimed to be selective. Selectiveness became sarcasm when he demolished Hürth's and Chagnon's claim (Appendix I, 36) that everything was prohibited by the totalitarian state that had not been allowed explicitly: "That a stupidity of this kind could have been written may be understandable, but that there is a single Nazi in the world who follows this principle in conscience is an absurdity! That is why it is useless to include such a proposition." [9]

Hardly less tough on the Jesuits than on the Nazis, Tardini was not opposed to the intention that lay behind their list. Modified, he argued that it should serve for a decree by the Holy Office condemning specific propositions that expressed the "grave errors" of the age that the Pope was also to discuss in an encyclical treating the doctrine of the Church. The papal contribution to the "double document," Tardini recommended, should be positive. The decree by the Supreme Tribunal was intended to be negative. It was of no moment which came first.

During these deliberations, Hudal's strategy was transformed. He had wished to "correct," by condemnation, the "left-wing extremists" among the National Socialists in order to form an alliance between the "conservatives" and the Church against the Communists. Now the Communists and the Nazis were being placed at the same level of menace, and both of them were to be attacked together in a solemn act by the Church. Influence on Roman policy was slipping from Hudal's grasp in the spring of 1936.

On April 20 it was decided to submit Hürth's and Chagnon's work to "a further examination"; on the twenty-ninth a commission was formed to investigate Communism. The pace accelerated. Seven meetings were held during May and June. Yet frequency did not result in progress. Struggling with the cardinals' instruction that its work was to be neither too general nor too specific, the commission became sidetracked by Gillet's insistence on reducing all "modern heresies" to "social modernism." [10] Wrapped in the blanket of that vague term, the Jesuits' draft condemnations lost their original clarity, as the commission acknowledged when submitting the shorter of two lists into which it had attempted to condense the problem:

> If the propositions which we have drawn up are understood to refer to political society, they do not reveal the doctrines or the intention with which they are advanced in Germany today. The Nazis [= *Nationalsocialistae*] do not claim that the state is the final end and supreme law, but consider it a particularly effective and necessary means of promoting the good of the race and the people.[11]

There lay one of the principal difficulties faced by the Holy Office in its work. It wished to restrict itself to doctrine, but it was continually forced, by the nature of Nazi and Communist ideology, to enter the sphere of politics. Rome refused to be demoted to the status of a church confined within the walls of the sacristy in which Hitler and his followers aimed to imprison it. Its mission embraced society, conduct, and morals in a wider sense—which meant that, while all the consultants were in favor of a condemnation, each of them feared that it would be interpreted as political.

That raises the question of whether the Vatican's choice of experts indicated political motivation. Were figures chosen who were known, within the establishment, for their sympathies with National Socialism or their antipathy to Communism? The exclusion of potential candidates points to the opposite. Obviously "political priests" were not consulted by the Holy Office.

Hudal, as one of its members, was informed of the results of the work, but he was not invited to contribute. Nor was Friedrich Muckermann, despite his extensive knowledge of Communism. Now a professor of Russian literature at the Oriental Institute sponsored by the papacy,[12] he was passed over. The task was given to Joseph Ledit, another Jesuit, who edited *Letters from Rome (Lettres de Rome)*.

Letters from Rome was a publication, founded at the wish of Wlodomir Ledóchowski, intended to document the character of Communism that the Jesuit general regarded with alarm. Muckermann wrote for that publication and his essays would be cited with respect by Ledit.[13] Yet the respect of a colleague did not offset the reservations of a superior who excluded Muckermann both in 1934 and in 1936. Although one occasion may have been an accident, two, given his qualifications, amounted to policy.

All those chosen to conduct the operation—from Ledit, Hürth, and Chagnon to Ottaviani and Ruffini—were discreet figures at Rome. Only one of them (Ottaviani) had ventured into print on the issues being examined, and then it had been in a textbook written in Latin. Far from the glare of publicity, in which Muckermann and Hudal thrived, Rome continued to plan its offensive in a secrecy that guaranteed, if not objectivity, then lack of patent bias.

Bias against the Communists and sympathy for the Nazis is a charge leveled against the Vatican before and during the Second World War. The open sympathizer with Hitler in the Roman Curia has already been identified as the "appeaser" Hudal. That the Communists had none is hardly surprising in the light of the long and troubled history of their relations with Pius XI.

The problem of Communism had exercised that Pope since the beginning of his reign. Negotiations with the Soviet state, initiated in 1922, had brought nothing but disappointments. Relations were broken off in 1929.[14] The next year Pius XI sponsored a "crusade of prayer" against the "Russian persecutors of religion." The Soviet government's newspaper *Izvestia* responded on February 18, 1930: "The Pope assumes the role of leader in the struggle against the Soviet Union assigned to him by world-capitalism." Intrigues and rumors of Soviet spies in the Vatican[15] poisoned the atmosphere further until, in 1933, the Pope voiced admiration for Hitler's "decisive and undaunted measures against Communism" (as it was described to the German ambassador by the Secretariat of State).[16] Three years later, that admiration had evaporated, and the Nazis had joined the "Bolsheviks" on the Vatican's list of enemies of the faith.

As that list expanded, the commission was charged with finding points in common between Nazism and Communism. Ledit identified them as an antireligious perversion: "Just as the Christian religion elevates the whole man, so Communism perverts him entirely." [17] The idea, often expressed by Pius XI and Pacelli, of Catholicism's ability to encompass and ennoble the "totality" of man was caricatured in Communist totalitarianism. Hürth and Chagnon had presented the degrading effects of Nazi racism in similar terms, analyzing it chiefly on the plane of ideas.

Ledit was concerned not only with theory but also with practice. Between them there yawned an "abyss," which he illustrated by citing sources that ranged from Marx, Lenin, and Stalin to Soviet textbooks (translated into French). And Ledit went further. He was capable of quoting an article that had appeared in the newspaper *Pravda* as recently as April 13, 1936, giving statistics of the weight and height of workers in the area of Moscow between 1922 and 1923. A closer contact with Soviet realities, or their distortions by propaganda, lent Ledit's work its force.

Materialism—the term that Pius XI used to define National Socialism—was, for Ledit, the first and distinguishing principle of Communism. From material production as the foundation of human society to history as the account of class struggle: Each of the classic Communist doctrines, as interpreted by Ledit, stemmed from the same idea. Its consequence had been unwelcome innovations in the social sphere. Among the novelties that he deplored were the measures that had led to women being "emancipated from the bond of indissoluble marriage, from the care of children, and from housework" and allowed to take part in economic activities and political life with the same rights as men. If the education of the young in Communist collectives appeared abominable to Ledit, no better was the notion that the state might grant women "full control over their own bodies, even during marriage," allowing them to choose between procreation and abortion. Such were the "heresies" that shocked this consultant to the Holy Office.

In the Holy Office, during the 1930s, a majority of the modern inquisitors were conservative Italians. But they were not blind to the failings, from a Catholic standpoint, of Fascism. The praise that Hudal lavished on the "brilliant Duce" [18] was untypical of his colleagues, as one of them now demonstrated when asked to analyze totalitarianism.

Angelo Perugini, whose chief occupation was writing Latin letters for the Secretariat of State, had clear ideas about the nebulous concept of totalitarianism, which he identified with Fascism.[19] His principal (though not his only) source were the nine volumes, of the *Writings and Speeches* of Benito Mussolini, published in Milan between 1934 and 1935. The Duce was unaware that, in 1936, he was being censured at the heart of Fascist Rome.[20]

Mussolini's religious policy was the chief target of Perugini's attack. A book on that subject had been published by Mario Missiroli, a journalist whom the Holy Office held in contempt. "Superficial, full of contradictions, pathetic" was the judgment on Missiroli's *Date a Cesare (Render unto Caesar)* when, on January 30, 1930, it had been indexed.[21] Special hostility was reserved for Missiroli's quotations from Mussolini's speeches that Pius XI had described as containing "obvious heresies." Deploring the follower, Perugini intended to proscribe the Duce himself.

Not every Fascist qualified for condemnation. Only "the most representative" of their speeches and writings were selected. Giovanni Gentile, for example, was left out on the grounds that his ideas were so "personal" that they had made no contribution worth noting. So much for the sometime high priest of Fascism whom Hudal had regarded with envy. So much too for Mussolini, whose every word, anticlerical and anti-Catholic, was recalled to memory.

Memories in the Holy Office were long. Many of Mussolini's declarations had been made before the Fascists came to power. Had he, in an article published as long ago as January 1, 1920, declared that he had "torn up revealed truths, spat on all the dogmas," disbelieved in the saints, and poured scorn on the "two Vaticans . . . of Rome and Moscow"? One of those Vaticans, in 1936, had neither forgotten nor forgiven. And if it was understandable that the Duce's claim, in his address to the Chamber of Deputies of May 14, 1929,[22] that Christianity would have remained "one of many sects" had it not come to Rome from Palestine, continued to smart, his exaltation of the Eternal City in a speech delivered at Udine in September 1922 might have been passed over as the bombast that it was.

Not by Perugini. After exposing the anti-Catholicism of the Fascists, he launched an assault on their objectives without flinching from politics. The state's claim to a monopoly of power, in disregard of the Church's rights, the government's design to dominate education, the exaltation of violence and militarism, the lust for a Mediterranean empire—every one of these positions, cited from the Duce, formed a list of charges almost as long and certainly as precise as that brought by the Jesuits against the Führer. Even aims of conquest particular to Fascist Italy were considered, by Perugini, typical of the aggressiveness of totalitarianism as a whole. Such was, in Mussolini's words, the nature of the "faith" in which he believed—a political religion, with its own "fallen and heroes," which the Holy Office was invited to damn.

A grand design had emerged, within the Vatican, by the summer of 1936. Grand in the sense that the Holy Office was preparing to condemn National Socialism, Communism, and Fascist totalitarianism all at once. On July 12, 1936, a draft was printed, consisting of three parts.[23] The first part set out principles of Christian doctrine on mankind both as individuals and as members of society. The second part set out "true doctrine" about race, nation, and proletariat. The third part was concerned with the "errors of racism, hypernationalism, Communism, and totalitarianism." [24]

As the operation, once so slow, gathered momentum, Tardini's call for selectiveness had not been forgotten but rejected. Fullness was now needed, the commission argued. Anticipating the objection that many of its points had been made in the past by the popes and could be assumed to be familiar to Catholics, it replied: "The opposite is the case. For the uncertainty and errors which can be observed today even among Catholics regard precisely these fundamental truths which are either not understood or forgotten." [25] These sentences might have been written in response to the criticism, often voiced in Germany during and before 1936, that the Church was failing to enlighten its members on fundamental matters of Christian principle. The problem was acknowledged in the capital of Catholicism.

That this grand design had implications for the Church's relations with secular states, the consultants were aware. As they weighed the arguments for and against publishing the third part of their draft on racism, "hypernationalism," Communism, and totalitarianism, they added a caveat that recalled the criterion of opportunism: "If we omit this [third] part, it appears easier to avoid the difficulties with governments which are perhaps to be feared when the decree is published." [26]

"Difficulties with governments" were the responsibility of the Secretariat of State. Pacelli did not make this observation, although his collaborators, Ruffini and Tardini, were members of the commission that produced it. Neither of them had illusions about the regimes against which the draft was directed. In July 1936, its consequences were predictable, and Rome was faced with a difficult choice. The option of remaining silent having been ruled out by the Holy Office's consultants, the cardinals and the Pope were presented with the choice between a comprehensive and a selective condemnation of the "errors of the age."

Much therefore depended on how the Church viewed itself. What role did the Vatican believe it should play in the modern world? Was Rome solely concerned with Catholics, their rights and their privileges, as is sometimes alleged? Was no attention paid to others of different religion or race? Each of these questions was addressed by the commission in terms as uncompromising as any used by the totalitarians: "The Church is not only a perfect society but also a universal and total one in the sense that it encompasses the whole man and his every considered action in so far as they bear on an ultimate purpose and are bound by laws of faith or morality . . ." [27]

Morality, as defined by these consultants, excluded that "savage despotism" that it deemed "contrary to the common good." State tyranny was incompatible with the rights of the individual. Between individuals, as between nations, reason should be the arbiter. The use of force was unlawful, and the commission deplored war as an "enormous and horrendous evil from which the peoples are to be protected."

The "peoples"—not merely the Catholics—were the Church's

concern. The Jesuits' insistence on human rights had made its mark on the discussion, including that of racism. As a simple biological theory, the commission now declared, racism was not "cause for a crisis." The causes for the crisis were instead moral: "The differences between races are not to be exaggerated to such a point that the unity of mankind, which revelation affirms, is abolished. And it should never be forgotten to maintain *the law of justice and love toward all races, by no means excluding the Semitic race . . .* " [emphasis added][28]

Here, for the first time among the documents of the Holy Office, the problem of anti-Semitism is mentioned explicitly. Implicit in Hürth's and Chagnon's earlier analysis, this declaration does not represent a change of policy. But it demonstrates that, already in 1936, the Vatican understood that Nazi treatment of the Jews violated "the law of justice and love toward all races" that the Supreme Tribunal of the Roman Church regarded as a binding principle.

Referring to that principle in his Christmas message of 1942, when the "Final Solution" was taking its course, Eugenio Pacelli—then Pius XII—declared that mankind should make a solemn vow to reestablish a just society. The Pope stated further: "Mankind owes that vow to the hundreds of thousands of persons who, without any fault on their part, sometimes only because of their nationality or race, have been consigned to death or to a slow decline." [29]

A specific reference to the Jews is striking by its absence. Yet a precedent existed for condemning anti-Semitism in a similar context among documents made available to Pacelli by the Holy Office almost six years before he delivered his Christmas message. Those documents did not only affirm that "the law of justice and love" applied equally to the Jews. The commission also condemned, as un-Christian, the notion of a "master-race." No race, by itself, was capable of achieving perfection, it was declared. There had been only one perfect man, and his name was Christ.

Speculation about "what Pacelli might have said" on the "Jewish question" is no longer needed. In 1942 he returned to a question addressed, and answered, by the Holy Office in 1936, when he was not yet pope. It is therefore not only the silence of Pius XII that requires explanation but also that of Pius XI. For the statement about the "law of justice and love toward all races, by no means excluding the Semitic race" was intended for an encyclical by Pius XII's predecessor, which, in the form recommended by the commission that prepared it, never appeared. Why not became clear in the course of the following months, and their implications would extend far into the future. Before the Second World War and the horrors of the Holocaust, the Vatican was confronted by its experts with a moral issue that is still debated. And that issue was decided, in the first place, not by Eugenio Pacelli but by Achille Ratti, Pius XI.

To Pius XI was presented a document which, firm but not vehement, condemned the errors of National Socialism and Fascism (identified with totalitarianism) as though they were equivalent "errors of the age." Equivalent in kind but not in degree was the other major heresy damned without reservation: ". . . the entire teaching of Communism about human society is incompatible with the true Christ; they say that Communism and Christianity are at odds and irreconcilable: no one can be, at one and the same time, an upright Catholic and a sincere Communist . . ."[30]

If there is no mistaking the criticisms, forthright and far-reaching, of Hitler's and Mussolini's ideas in the work of the Holy Office, there is no denying its uncompromising hostility to Stalin's. All three enemies of Catholicism, as presented by the draft decree, were equally reprehensible, but one of them was more equal than the others. Ledit was ordered to continue with his work.

By October 13, 1936, the investigation was far enough advanced for twenty-five propositions to be laid before the cardinals of the Holy Office (Appendix II). Little more than half the number presented in the Jesuits' previous version (Appendix I), they were nonetheless numerous and forceful enough to present ample grounds for alarm on Hudal's part. If National Socialism was not mentioned by name, it was easy to identify on the basis of the quotation from Hitler (Appendix II, 1) or the reference (ibid. 6) to the elimination of Catholic periodicals, schools, and associations as a feature of the "racist-state." Worse still, in Hudal's eyes, must have seemed the position of racism and "hypernationalism" as practiced by the Nazis—at the head of the list, followed by Communism. The archenemy of the Church and

Outbursts and Intrigues

OUTBURSTS WERE NOT CUSTOMARY at the Vatican. Measured nuances of disapproval were generally preferred to howls of protest by Pius XI and Pacelli. Diplomats registered their tone with attention. Orsenigo, on December 20, 1935, transmitted his thanks to the Pope for the "paternal concern" he had recently expressed, in an address to the cardinals, about the situation of Catholics in Germany.[1] Nonetheless there were few signs of improvement. "The repression of religious freedom continues," lamented the nuncio, "with painful sporadic incidents motivated by political accusations which are almost always unfounded." Orsenigo was aware of charges, made by Goering and others, that Catholics were meddling in politics and that the religious orders were violating currency laws or corrupting the young. The nuncio did not know, when he wrote that dispatch, that Pius XI had been pondering a condemnation of the Nazis for more than a year.

Boiling with rage, the Pope met the German ambassador, Diego von Bergen, at the New Year's reception for diplomats of 1936. Defying all convention, Pius XI dressed Bergen down on the subject of "persecutions" and other outrages to which Catholics in Germany were exposed. The Church would not vanish, declared its head, but "the others." Bergen, in his report to the foreign ministry in Berlin, claimed that the Pope had spoken of Bismarck.[2] Pius XI, in his own version of the incident, said that the allusion was to Napoleon.[3] Which enemy of Catholicism was meant was of less moment than the indignation: "Friends do not behave in this manner," was the papal

understatement; "we are truly filled with pain and profoundly dissatisfied." [4]

Grounds for dissatisfaction had been provided by Orsenigo. On
Christmas Day 1935, he had sent Pacelli a list of imprisoned Catholic
priests and laymen from all over Germany.[5] The Pope, replied the
Secretariat of State on January 8, 1936, had received the information
"with deep grief." [6] A month later, on February 8, Hitler tele-
grammed Pius XI to congratulate him on the anniversary of his coro-
nation. The Pope replied with a telegram, sent to the Ministry of
Foreign Affairs, which stated: "Apart from sincere thanks for the con-
gratulations, the general situation regrettably requires [Us] to refer to
the profound worries caused by the state's attitude to the Catholic
Church and recent news about measures taken by the police against
priests and Catholic youth organizations." [7] Constantin von Neurath,
the foreign minister, expressed "pained surprise" on receiving this
communication. He doubted whether he could present it to Hitler.[8]
Neurath complained that normal diplomatic channels had not been
respected and denied, as "absolutely mistaken," the Pope's assertion
that the National Socialist state was hostile to the Church.[9]

Pacelli's reply to the information sent to him by Orsenigo is revealing.[10] Exceptional circumstances, he stated, called for exceptional
measures. The cardinal–secretary of state recalled the Holy See's
many diplomatic notes of protests and concluded that, in Germany,
there existed: ". . . an attitude of indubitable hostility towards the
Church on the part of persons who had official roles and in view of
continual press-attacks on the Catholic religion, priests, bishops, and
the Pope himself . . ."

Yet Pacelli, with typical correctness, was concerned not only with
the substance but also with the form of Pius XI's telegram. If the
form was unusual, that was due to Hitler's unusual position as head of
state and government and as Führer. This was the aspect that appealed to Orsenigo. On April 23 he explained to Neurath that "the
Holy See had to be careful that its acts, in public, do not draw mistaken interpretations." [11] In the exchange of diplomatic niceties what
had been meant as a papal protest became a question of style. Cling-
ing to the Concordat, Rome's representative at Berlin chose, as usual,
the path of discretion.

• • •

The path of discretion led to no clear goal. Contradictory signals reached the Vatican from Germany. At a meeting between Kerrl and Catholic bishops, on January 28, 1936, the Party offered—or pretended to offer—to stop attacks on the Church on condition that the clergy cease to "reject the National Socialism and its aims." Kerrl hoped to come to "a friendly agreement" within a matter of months.[12]

Kerrl's negotiations with the head of the Fulda bishops' conference, Cardinal Bertram, were known in Rome.[13] The government promised concessions but would not permit dual membership in the Hitler Youth and Church organizations. It had nothing against religious education, Kerrl claimed, provided that Catholics understood that

> . . . it is a self-evident necessity for every good German citizen that the state, without distinguishing between the confessions, educates all young Germans to a clear and positive acknowledgement of National Socialism, just as it is self-evident that the National Socialist state can only employ those young people who sincerely and without reserve accept the National-Socialist view of the world.[14]

Bertram understood the threat. The interpretation of it that he sent to Pacelli, on April 21, 1936, was bound to unsettle the secretary of state:

> If my view is correct, the ministry intends to behave dictatorially . . . and not to reply to our submissions or to do so briefly and evasively, while making use of every means in the state's power to incorporate all members of Catholic organizations into those of the Nazis, and branding as ruinous of popular unity and therefore unacceptable membership of both. The indirect objective is to treat the Concordat and its implementation as no longer of current concern . . . [15]

Bertram touched here on one of the points to which the Jesuits had drawn Rome's attention: the education of youth and the corrupting effect of the ideology being taught in Nazi organizations. Pacelli, in this report, was faced with a double quandary: how to avoid Nazi influence on young Catholics without exposing them to discrimination and unemployment? And how to negotiate with a partner, or adversary, who was attempting to undermine the very basis of the agreement?

The Concordat, as Bertram described it, was regarded by the Nazis as "superseded," but Pacelli, the architect of that treaty, behaved as if he had little else on which to build. No false hopes, no illusions were held out to him by the chairman of the Fulda bishops' conference. Bertram stated plainly that the ministry depended entirely on the Party. That party, in the cardinal's estimation, was conducting a campaign against the Church harsher than any in the Soviet Union:

> In leading positions of the National Socialist Party the spirit of Bolshevism as hatred against Christianity, and especially against the Catholic Church, is so acute that I have repeatedly remonstrated with the government that the publications and illustrations of the official journals of Nazi organizations are worse and more disgusting than they have been in Russia. The spirit of the leadership is similar to the sounds of official organs.[16]

The "Bolshevism" of the Nazis was, in April 1936, a new idea in Rome; but it was one which would soon be confirmed, independently of Bertram, by the consultants to the Holy Office. Their comparisons between different forms of totalitarianism, in Germany, Russia, and Italy, lent substance to what the cardinal meant as an image of horror.

Horrified at what he described as a new *Kulturkampf*, Bertram foresaw a return to the repression that German Catholics had suffered under Bismarck. Their hard-won gains, as a minority in a dominantly Protestant land, since the First World War were being eliminated by a "struggle to destroy Catholics' attempt to live according to their beliefs." [17] Would abrogation of the Concordat be the solution? Bertram did not believe so, nor did he think that the Holy See would be in favor of a move that was unlikely to produce positive results. There remained only the Führer. The cardinal doubted that Hitler was informed about "the whole naked truth." Orsenigo should intervene with him, was Bertram's counsel of despair.[18]

Pacelli, replying to Bertram on April 30, 1936,[19] shifted responsibility. Yes, Orsenigo should attempt to see the Führer, but the bishops should also take action. Would it not be better if the three German cardinals, together with the papal nuncio, requested an audience with Hitler? Pacelli no longer believed in the value of written declarations. He described Nazi tactics as an "undignified double game" (*dieses unwürdige Doppelspiel*).

Who was behind that "double game"? All indications, including those of the Holy Office, pointed to the "head of state and government." Yet the Vatican was still reluctant to act on the belief that the blame lay with Hitler. And Rome's desire to lend credit to his goodwill was reinforced by the attitudes of the German bishops. On March 22, 1936—a week before the "Reichstag election" that brought Hitler 99 percent support—Clemens August von Galen, the bishop of Münster, attempted to distinguish between the policy of the Führer and that of the Party. In a sermon delivered in the cathedral of Münster and forwarded by Orsenigo to Pacelli on April 15, 1936,[20] Galen deplored the "insults and suspicions" directed at Christianity and the Catholic Church by members of the Nazi Party. Quoting Hitler's condemnation, in *Mein Kampf,* of those who stirred up religious strife, Galen repeated the question "Does the Führer know?" and answered it with the disarming sentence "I can hardly believe it" (*Ich kann es kaum glauben*).

Both the German Catholics and Rome faced a crucial problem. Unmistakable evidence pointed to a "double game," but the assurances of the Führer (even those that dated from a distant past) were the only hope of the Church authorities. If they adhered to it with a determination belied by events, Orsenigo did much to encourage wishful thinking. Despite instructions from Rome in April 1936, he avoided seeing Hitler, who, he claimed, was busy with foreign affairs. Then, on May 9, the nuncio wrote to the cardinal–secretary of state in one of his recurrent moods of unfounded buoyancy:

Hopes grow of a relative pacification among the clergy and the people: the bishops continue in their work of defending Catholic principles and freedom in keeping with the new political orientation, accepting all that is not prejudicial to faith and morals, and clearly admonishing the people when faith and morals are in danger of being impaired, even if the danger is linked with state institutions. Certainly we are very far from the National Socialists' coming to their senses, yet in general events display faint signs of greater respect for religion . . . [21]

Clutching at straws, such as the recent silence of Rosenberg on the subject of Christianity, Orsenigo alternated between relative optimism and the bleak pessimism of his dispatch less than two weeks later. On May 21[22] he reported to Pacelli that a newspaper, the *Berliner Tagblatt*, had announced that both Catholics and Protestants would be "separated from all cultural and educational contact with society." Passive resistance, thought Orsenigo, was impossible in the "forest" of state organizations. The authorities denied that their objective was persecution but, added the nuncio in a dispatch of June 6,[23] trials for immorality were proceeding against the clergy and "the prestige of the Catholic Church is compromised."

Such was the information, disparate and depressing, reaching Pacelli during the first half of 1936. The hesitancy of Vatican policy needs to be seen in its light. A chiaroscuro of black, white, and gray, it was as inconsistent as the shifting attitudes of Rome's sources. Where lay the truth about the Nazis' intentions? In the German bishops' wish to believe that Hitler was ignorant of his followers' outrages? Or in the drafts being prepared for the Holy Office's condemnation of National Socialism? In them it was argued that both Führer and Party were, and had to be, by the nature of their ideology, committed to a conflict with Christianity. But if Pacelli accepted that argument, he was not authorized to follow its consequences. Sworn to secrecy about his work in the Supreme Tribunal, the cardinal—secretary of state was in no position to inform the episcopate that its faith in the Führer's good intentions was misplaced.

On doctrinal and moral questions Rome had clear motives for taking a stand. Politics was the vexing issue. What did that term mean? How to draw the line between a legitimate intervention in favor of German Catholics and meddling in the internal affairs of the Third Reich? The Nazis were blurring that line deliberately and without scruple. Pacelli was not duped. He meditated and consulted with the Pope, whose thoughts he transmitted to Orsenigo on July 3, 1936.

Catholic publications were being suppressed on the grounds that their aims were "political," the cardinal noted. On that controversial word he made the following observation:

> If one thinks of the meaning attributed by the present government to the concept of "politics," a completely arbitrary and unacceptable limitation on such periodicals' sphere of action is the result. Since the government does not hesitate to enact laws contrary to divine law and commit acts which violate the rights of the Church and offend its dignity . . . it follows that any possibility of legitimate defense is denied to ecclesiastical periodicals.[24]

These sentences resemble a draft of the Holy Office's condemnation (Appendix II, 6). Like the consultants to the Holy Office and unlike Orsenigo, Pacelli saw and stated, in a dispatch to the nuncio of July 20, that the government's promises were "deceptive" and its assurances "mendacious."[25] Yet he persisted in his martyrdom of patience as if, in the shifting sands of this "double game," the Concordat was the only rock on which the Church might stand. That another foundation, firmer but less diplomatic, had been provided by the Holy Office, no one receiving Pacelli's official communications would have guessed. A prisoner of the legal logic constructed by himself and perverted by the Nazis, he stuck to a policy that suggested to the other side that he had no alternative.

As Pacelli continued to protest to the Nazis, in whose word he did not believe, about trials for "immorality" trumped up against the clergy, the suppression of Catholic teachers-training colleges, and the reduction of state subsidies to the Church,[26] another figure in the Vatican, uninhibited by the cardinal's scruples, intervened.

At Rome, the course of "correcting" National Socialism that Hudal had tried to steer was beyond his control, while in Germany one of his attempts to mediate had backfired. An article that he published, in May 1935, in an Austrian periodical had been confiscated by the Nazis for what was taken to be an attack on their worldview.[27] Hudal hastened to make amends. He had been misunderstood, on his own estimation, and anonymously he set about putting matters right in the newspaper *Reichspost* during the summer of 1936.[28]

The Church, Hudal declared, should come to terms with the "conservatives" among the National Socialists, in whom he still believed. Current difficulties were due to the inflexibility of the German bishops. In their refusal to compromise, he detected the source of conflict with the government. This view was expressed, in the summer of 1936, by the same consultant to the Holy Office who, in the autumn of 1934, had urged it to ". . . order the bishops that Catholic Action in each diocese should begin a unified struggle against [the Nazis] . . . with all means appropriate and possible." [29] Cardinal Faulhaber was to describe the anonymous article as "a stab in the back of the bishops." [30] Had he known more about its background of duplicity, he might have found harsher words.

Controversy surrounded the article from the moment of its publication, and Hudal emerged from anonymity on August 5, 1936, to reveal his authorship[31] and attack his critics. "Those who attempted to play the Austrians off against the Germans, with the ample support of the Jewish press," as he originally described them,[32] had now become "the emigrants" who failed to see that National Socialism was going to last. The Church had to face this fact of life.

Naturally, the Nazis were delighted. Rosenberg, whose *Myth of the Twentieth Century* had been put on the Index of Prohibited Books by Hudal and others, showered him with praise. In the Party's newspaper, *Völkischer Beobachter*,[33] he was congratulated for standing up to the "Jews" who had attempted to sabotage the entente of July 11,

1936, between Austria and Germany and for resisting "those Catholic circles . . . which are becoming Moscow's vanguard."

With support like this, the rector of the German national church might be thought to have had no need of enemies. Yet that was not how Hudal saw the situation, nor did others. One of them was Hitler's special envoy at Vienna, the former vice-chancellor, von Papen. Papen, the very type of "conservative" to whom Hudal addressed his message, received it with enthusiasm.[34]

The memorandum was composed by a spirit akin to that of Hudal. About him, Papen wrote to Hitler on July 28, 1936: "We must keep this man ready to fight for us."[35] Bergen would later say much the same.[36] This, for Hudal, was a turning point. At last he was winning the contacts and the recognition he craved. And as he prepared, with Papen's backing, a book on National Socialism and the Church, his patron at Vienna intervened with the Führer to allow it to be published in Germany, so that it could not be said at Rome that "we beat every discussion to death with police-truncheons."[37]

The chiefs of the Nazi thought-police, Alfred Rosenberg and Josef Goebbels, were opposed. Rosenberg wanted the title changed; Goebbels was flatly against publication. The controversy was settled by Hitler, to whom first the proofs and then a copy of the book—with a dedication to the "Dietrich of German greatness and hope"[38]— were sent by Hudal. He, who less than two years earlier had set out to condemn the Nazis, was now currying the favor of the Führer, without Rome's permission or knowledge.

The Court Theologian of the Party

ALOIS HUDAL CLAIMED TO HAVE WRITTEN *The Foundations of National Socialism* with his "heart's blood." That he had a heart, in addition to a head filled with calculations of opportunism, may have surprised his colleagues at the Holy Office. If they read his work, they had grounds for feeling with Cardinal Faulhaber that they too had been stabbed in the back.

Dedicated to "the inner peace of our German people," *The Foundations of National Socialism* was published in November 1936.[1] Lacking the imprimatur of the ecclesiastical authorities, it appeared at the time when the condemnation instigated by Hudal had reached an advanced state of preparation. This timing was not accidental, nor was it by chance that he gave to his preface the dramatic date of July 11, 1936. On that "day of the entente between Germany and Austria," hopes had risen of a Reich that he now wished to reconcile with the Church.[2]

Hudal knew that reconciliation would become impossible if the Holy Office issued its decree linking National Socialism and Communism as twin "errors of the age." The very first point on the list of propositions to be condemned (Appendix II, 1) was not intended to be accompanied by the name of its author, but the "Dietrich of German greatness and hope" would hardly fail to understand that it was a quotation from one of his speeches. Another, abrogating the Concordat, would have been fatal to Hudal's ambitions.

He hoped for a resolution of the conflict between Party and Church from the Führer. According to Hudal, the German bishops were exacerbating tensions. That some of them pinned the same vain hopes on Hitler, he either did not know or did not wish to acknowledge. As Hudal presented himself, he stood alone, heroically striving to avoid a clash of "worldviews." That clash was not inevitable, if only this "great movement, faithful to its origins, would build up a purely political program, aimed at Germany's greatness, while leaving the religious domain of its members untouched in its holiness."[3]

No one at Rome had stated more forcibly how implausible such a rapprochement was than Hudal himself, in two declarations to the Holy Office: "It is false to pretend that National Socialism is merely a political party like Fascism, for example, or that it has nothing do to with religion or that, founded on a 'positive Christianity,' it has protected religion in Germany against the danger of Bolshevism."[4] And: "If Catholic young people are forced to enroll in the Hitler-Youth of Schirach—an adherent of 'German religion'—and educated for a decade in these dangerous and, from the nationalist standpoint, fascinating ideas, the Catholic churches in Germany will be empty."[5]

Unabashed by self-contradiction, Hudal, in his own book, quoted repeatedly from *Mein Kampf.* From the work that had served as his colleagues' major source for the heresies of National Socialism was extracted evidence that the Führer and his followers, who had "provided the German people with such good and valuable stimuli," might accept a separation of the "purely political" from the "ideological" spheres.[6] Toward Hitler, whose intentions he had provided grounds for mistrusting in secret, Hudal was now performing an act of faith in public.

This "conversion" had two aims: one open, the other covert. Hudal expressed his admiration for the achievements of the Nazis, who, according to him, had raised the Germans' consciousness of their historical destiny and their bonds with their own race while attempting to solve the "Jewish question." The people should be grateful that this "intellectual movement" *(Geistesbewegung)* had undermined "the ideology of human rights" and destroyed belief in formal structures of law and democracy.[7] Hudal's paean of praise deliberately included several of the items on the list of propositions that the Holy Office had been urged to damn (Appendix I, 3, 4, 35, 36, 40, 41, 44, and Appendix II, 7, 9, 23).

If he intended to show the Nazis the way to a compromise with Rome, he hoped to demonstrate to his colleagues in the Vatican that a condemnation was not needed. This was an attempt more radical than any of the efforts of those feebleminded opportunists who, in Germany and elsewhere, sought to "build bridges" between the Party and the Church.[8] Opportunistic Hudal was, but not feeble-minded. It took ingenuity, combined with a misplaced faith in his own abilities, to employ the categories of condemnation in order to argue that harmony was possible.

Hudal knew that he had no authority for his self-appointed role. He declared that it was beyond the purpose of his work "to judge National Socialism [in the light of] Catholic teaching's crystalline clarity"[9]—which was just what the Holy Office was doing while he wrote. No, no: He was addressing the same issues from a different perspective. His declared aim was to liberate "the national movement" from ideological errors so that, in league with Fascism, it might form a "solid bastion against the flood-waves of the Asiatic cultural Bolshevism which today pose an equal threat to all states and peoples."[10] No reader of that sentence outside the Holy Office would have guessed that Rome was then preparing to condemn National Socialism, Fascism, and Communism together. No reader inside the Holy Office was intended to think it possible later.

The subtitle of Hudal's book was "A study in the history of ideas." The ideas of National Socialism, not its history, had been studied by the Jesuits, who had nothing good to say about them. The Pope even denied "intellect" to the Nazis. Pius XI saw in their movement a "massive materialism."[11] Hudal ignored these judgments. In providing National Socialism with an intellectual pedigree, he sought to give it what it lacked in the eyes of his superior and colleagues: a measure of respectability.

That respectability was bought at a high price. Reading *Mein Kampf* with the eyes of a sympathizer, Hudal saw what he wished rather than what its author had written. At the turn of the century, in his native Austria, attacks on the Catholic Church had been combined with anti-Semitism by the vulgar and violent leader of the "Away from Rome" movement, Georg Schönerer. Noting that the Nazis were most strongly supported in those areas most affected by Away from Rome, Hudal denied that Hitler wished to follow in its footsteps.[12] Schönerer had indeed been criticized in *Mein Kampf*—but less for his aims than for his methods. Dwelling on the lack of national loyalty among the Catholic clergy, Hitler had concluded that a political leader should not tamper with the religious doctrines and institutions of his people.[13] That assurance, first published on July 18, 1925, had been superseded by grimmer realities eleven years later. Yet such was the Führer in whom Hudal chose to believe, by separating Hitler from one of his models.

Lack of loyalty to the cause was not a flaw of this member of the Catholic clergy who praised, in *The Foundations of National Socialism*, every writer—from the poet Stefan George to Hitler's mentor Dietrich Eckart—who might be enlisted in the ranks of "champions of the avant-garde." These were the thinkers behind a movement that was not only national but social. What then did National Socialism mean in such a context? Hudal's answer was flabbergasting, as he claimed to detect substantial agreement between the policies of the Nazis and the social doctrines of recent popes![14]

Yet just when Hudal seemed to sever all contact with reality, he drew back. Even he had to recognize limits. One of them was represented by his bête noire, Alfred Rosenberg.[15] Hudal proceeded to claim that the chief ideologue of the Party had misinterpreted its program. Its Article 24 accepted "positive Christianity," and Hitler had assured that nothing was to be altered.[16] It followed that all would have been well between Rome and Berlin, had it not been for Rosenberg and his likes.[17] Confident of understanding the Führer's purpose, Hudal believed that he was putting its false interpreters to rout.

The true interpreter, as presented by *The Foundations of National Socialism*, was its author. Hudal had no doubts that he had solved the riddle of the Nazi sphinx. Writing his book, he played the part of corrector, removing "misunderstandings." Racism was a case in point.[18]

Knowing that this was one of the main issues on which the Holy Office was preparing to take a stand, he advanced fresh motives to render it unnecessary.

The Church, he claimed, was concerned solely with the supernatural realm. Although that claim was not strictly true in the categorical manner in which he put it—since Pius XI was concerned to erect an ideal Christian society on earth—what followed, in *The Foundations of National Socialism*, dealt with one of the doctrines emphasized by the Jesuits. In God's eyes, all races and people were equal. How to square that doctrine with Nazi anti-Semitism?

By arguing that below the supernatural realm, in this world, racism could be considered a response to an emergency, which Rome would understand. Had the Church not confined the Jews to the ghetto in the sixteenth century, for religious motives? Religious, not "biological," discrimination was acceptable; and so long as racism in this form was not "radicalized," explained Hudal, there was no reason for "contrasts" or "difficulties." Many and compelling reasons had been listed by his colleagues (Appendix I, 9–31, and Appendix II, 2–8), but that did not inhibit the "appeaser." Racism, as a scientific theory, had produced results that were valuable, he now asserted. As a total explanation of mankind, he claimed that it was deficient because it neglected the spiritual personality.[19]

If the spiritual personality, for the Nazis, was an object of contempt or indifference, how could they remain indifferent to Hudal's overtures, which offered just what they wanted: that the Church should confine itself to the "nonpolitical" sphere? Yet politics, in Germany, before and after the Nuremberg Laws of 1935, included the "Jewish question"; and anti-Semitism was an issue with which the Holy Office had begun to grapple.[20] Had its position become public, there would have been little room left for the "compromise" at which Hudal aimed. As if to forestall that eventuality, he took the long view.

The "problem," he claimed, dated from the French Revolution.[21] Emigration from the East, favored by the liberal doctrine of equality between peoples and races, had led to a Jewish monopoly in finance, the arts, and the professions. This catena of clichés served to explain the need for "emergency legislation" in order to protect the German people from being overrun. No serious objection to such measures could be made by Christians. For if the Jews, judged by "racial-biological" criteria, had been deprived of their rights, they had only themselves to blame for persisting in the "soulless materialism" for which they were notorious.

Just as those who have wished to find an appeaser in the Vatican have mistaken his identity, so the search for an anti-Semite has proceeded in the wrong direction. The name of both was not Eugenio Pacelli but Alois Hudal. His concern, in *The Foundations of National Socialism*, was not to defend the Christian doctrine of the equality of races in the eyes of God so much as to prevent Nazi anti-Semitism from turning into hostility against the Catholic Church. The Church as defender of a persecuted minority, on principles of charity and love, held no appeal for this opportunist, who did not hesitate to conjure up the bogey of "Bolshevism": "We, as Christians and Catholics, have not the slightest motive for defending that Jewry which, after the [First] World War, seized the leadership of the masses of workers and misused it abundantly for selfish purposes." [22]

This sentence was written by an author who conceded that the Nuremberg Laws were "hard" and by a consultant to the Holy Office who knew the motives for "defending Jewry" that had been presented by his colleagues. Because their position was still being discussed and had not yet been laid down, Hudal felt free to gloss over the major issues treated by them and to recommend a form of accommodation. That accommodation had to avoid such "exaggerations" as national churches, organization of religion according to "blood" or biological criteria, or a gospel purged of "Jewish elements." [23] They could not be accepted because they gave rise to an opposition, on racial grounds, between Germany and Rome.

Hudal wished to avoid the nation being set apart and against the Church. Pseudohistorical arguments were marshaled in the cause of their alliance. Had not "Germanic-Frankish" components been introduced into the Roman liturgy more than a thousand years ago? [24] Was not one of the greatest Catholic theologians, St. Thomas

Aquinas, both a German and a Roman at once?[25] Mixtures and syntheses, not "racial purity," had been normal throughout history. History blurred in Hudal's pan-Germanic vision.

His confidence ebbing at the Church's ability to withstand the conflict that the Holy Office's plans inaugurated, Hudal groped for every will-o'-the-wisp. If sterilization and castration were ruled out by Catholic doctrine, Rome could have no objections to "positive eugenics" inspired by "Christian-national thought."[26] He favored care of offspring and "racial hygiene," which he reclaimed for the Church as matters of pastoral concern.

Young people should be educated for marriage in keeping with "the biological and moral laws of nature." Those "laws," as Hudal interpreted them, led him to make counterproposals. If "mixed marriages" could be forbidden on grounds of "racial hygiene," why not extramarital sex?[27] As if he were bargaining with the Nazis, Hudal silently renounced points listed in the Holy Office's draft condemnation (Appendix I, 19–21). Attempting to convert the racists, he was willing to concede them their own form of "hygiene." Such were the terms, indistinguishable from a sellout, on which he attempted to reach a compromise called "Catholic National Socialism."

That grotesque expression—a contradiction in terms for Hudal's colleagues—sums up the core of his book. The Vatican lurks in its background. In its foreground stands the "Dietrich of German greatness and hope." Designed to show Hitler that, in Rome, he had friends and allies who could be useful if conditions of compromise were met, *The Foundations of National Socialism* went far toward providing a Catholic substitute for *The Myth of the Twentieth Century.* Small wonder, then, that Rosenberg condemned Hudal's work as a "complete surrender of the sphere of [Nazi] ideology to the Church."[28] The Party's chief ideologue felt himself threatened by a potential rival, and that feeling was justified.

The Foundations of National Socialism offered a different basis for many of the same ideas modified in the light of Catholic doctrine: "National thinking and Catholic sentiments are anything but irreconcilable contrasts."[29] Legal guarantees of rights were not required. If the Nazis had abolished Roman law, that could be accepted in good conscience, providing that a concentration on the affairs of this world did not exclude those of the next.[30] As if aware that such waffling was meaningless, except as a signal of capitulation, Hudal spelt out what he considered the main dangers: "radicalization and revival of liberal ideas."[31] The radical Hitler, who played the role of the moderate when it suited his purposes, may have read that declaration with a wry grin. He was unlikely to succumb to the temptations of liberalism.

After conjuring up the specter of a nonexistent threat, Hudal passed to what he saw as a real achievement in the later part of his book. The qualifications and reservations expressed earlier are to be read in its light. The Nazis had conducted a "heroic and successful struggle" against Bolshevism and "the disgrace of the peace treaties"[32] [of Versailles, which ended the First World War on humiliating terms for Germany]. "The Germanic character" had been left unaltered by the Church and Christianity.[33] If National Socialism was not an invention by radicals but a natural development of that Germanic character[34]; if, as the Führer stated, he wanted to establish nothing more than a "political-sociological system,"[35] then it followed that the movement, when reconciled with Rome, represented a "national idea which is not only necessary but also holy"[36]: "No one in the Catholic camp denies the positive, great, and lasting [qualities] of this movement which touches on new problems and raises questions which Christianity must address, in order to find a modern synthesis of Germanness and belief."[37]

Several in the Catholic camp—among them Hudal's colleagues in the Holy Office—had denied the "positive, great, and lasting" qualities of National Socialism by the time his book was published. The "movement" that he described as "holy" had been damned by them as heretical. Because that judgment was secret, he could avoid dealing openly with its religious grounds. Yet by attempting to reduce the "problem" to its political and social aspects,[38] Hudal chose to ignore, or to gloss over, its many other features that members of the Supreme Tribunal judged incompatible with Christianity. Only as a dogma or a new "worldview" (*Weltanschauung*) was National

Socialism unacceptable. In that case, which he had done all in his power to avert, the Church had to say *Non possumus* ("We cannot"). The fan of the Führer refrained from adding *Sed volumus* ("But we wish to").

On November 4, 1936—the month in which *The Foundations of National Socialism* was published—Cardinal Michael von Faulhaber was received for three hours by Adolf Hitler at Obersalzberg. Faulhaber was impressed. A monarchist, he observed that the Führer was "more in possession of the diplomatic and social forms than a born sovereign." [39] The cardinal had no doubt that Hitler believed in God and recognized Christianity as the architect of Western culture; less clear was his understanding of the Catholic Church. [40] Hitler's agility in argument, during their exchange as reported by Faulhaber, was remarkable. He made several of the points to be found in *The Foundations of National Socialism*, the proofs of which he had read: Christianity, throughout its millennial history, had been inextricably bound up with Germany [41]; peace between the Party and the Church would mean the end of the Movement for German Belief and other sources of strife [42]; the people could not live without faith in God, because "godlessness" was "emptiness." [43]

Well-primed in Hudal's rhetoric, Hitler dwelt on two of his central theses. The struggle against Communism demanded an alliance between the Nazis and the Catholics. [44] But the Church had to give up its "struggle against the racial laws; otherwise the clergy would be regarded as state-enemies." It was not that the Nazis were attacking the Catholics, but rather the reverse. [45] The "intransigence" of the German hierarchy was the real problem, as Hudal had argued that summer in the *Reichspost.* [46]

Faulhaber, to judge by his own account, was outflanked in this battle of the wits. To the Führer's hypocrisy, the cardinal replied sincerely that Pius XI, in 1933, had praised Hitler as the first statesman to recognize the danger of Bolshevism while advertising his own qualifications as an opponent of the Communists. [47] Denying that the Church was "uncompromising," Faulhaber emphasized Catholics' loyalty: "As supreme head of the German Reich you are, for us, the authority willed by God, the legal superior, to whom we owe reverence and obedience." [48]

Whenever the cardinal mentioned a grievance, the Führer brushed it aside, returning time and again to the theme of the racial laws that were at the front of his mind. Catholic objections to *The Myth of the Twentieth Century* were trivial. The Church's prohibitions had made it popular. Hitler doubted that there were ten thousand people in Germany who understood Rosenberg's book.[49] There was no doubt, however, that the Führer had grasped how *The Foundations of National Socialism* could serve his purpose.

For Hitler, as for Hudal, the main issue, in November 1936, was harmony between Catholicism and National Socialism in the battle against their mutual enemy of Communism. The Führer hinted at concessions, but ruled out "horse trading." Generally opposed to compromises, he claimed that he was now in favor of a "last attempt." Then came the masterstroke: the episcopate should make its suggestions "before Bishop Hudal is appointed the court-theologian of the Party." [50]

Intimidation masqueraded as conciliation, all the more effectively for being spiced with arguments derived from a Roman source. The Führer believed that he could use the bishop to divide the Catholic camp. With the liar's insight into duplicity, Hitler saw that Hudal could serve his ends—which were less to create the office of court theologian to the Nazis than to sow discord at Rome. There Pacelli was faced with a new variant on the familiar "double game."

Always ingratiating with the powerful on both sides, Hudal sent a copy of his book to Cardinal Faulhaber, a former vice-rector of the Anima. A covering letter explained, implausibly, that he had not intended to undertake a "special action" *(Sonderaktion)* on his own initiative.[51] Privately, Faulhaber deplored *The Foundations of National Socialism*: "We must struggle daily with the hard reality: the clergy thrown out of the schools, the young whipped up against the Church, the pagan movement. Now a bishop who is an outsider announces from the clouds: 'National Socialism is God's grace.' " [52]

At Rome, the diplomatic verdict delivered by Pacelli was "inopportune." [53] That understatement was judicious because, as cardinal-protector of the Anima, Pacelli was answerable to the Pope for Hudal. Pius XI, who cannot have failed to understand that he and the Holy Office were addressed between the lines of *The Foundations of National Socialism,* had exploded in indignation. He wished to put the work on the Index.[54] And that would have meant nothing less than having the book banned by the Supreme Tribunal, of which its author was a member.

A scandal was brewing. Pacelli foresaw its baleful effects. With characteristic subtlety, he pleaded for a lighter sentence.[55] An announcement appeared in the *Osservatore Romano,* on November 13, 1936, that the work had been published without the prior permission of the Holy See; the Vatican's newspaper tactfully omitted to mention the writer's name. A disavowal had been issued. Rome dissociated itself from Hudal while refraining from making his book a best-seller by the publicity of a ban.

The tact was lost on the author, concerned only with the harm done to his pride and to his career. After this setback, promotion within the hierarchy was difficult to envisage. Twice considered by Pius XI for the cardinalate, the "court theologian of the Party" was now forced to recognize, in Pacelli's distance, that he had reduced his chances of a red hat.

A similar distance was maintained in a letter written by Pacelli to Faulhaber three days later.[56] Replying to the cardinal of Munich's report on his visit to Hitler, with its reference to Hudal, the secretary of state declared that "the Holy See is far from sharing [the position taken in] certain publications by His Excellency the titular bishop of Ela." A reference to the announcement in the *Osservatore Romano* completed the concise explanation. Neither the author nor the title of his book needed to be specified. Pacelli's reticence marked Hudal's fall from grace.

Rejected at Rome, he turned to Vienna, where he received, in February 1937, the ecclesiastical imprimatur from Cardinal Theodor Innitzer (later infamous for his compromises with Hitler).[57] In Austria, the book went through five editions in the course of a year; in Germany, only two thousand copies were distributed by the Party to its members. That modest result did not satisfy Hudal, who had hoped that *The Foundations of National Socialism* would make his name. The opposite occurred. In German bookshops, the work was, as he expressed it, "indirectly prohibited,"[58] after being banned in Czechoslovakia. Full and direct prohibition followed the Anschluss, or annexation, of Austria to Nazi Germany in the summer of 1938. Aiming to position himself as a mediator, Hudal had succeeded in antagonizing both the National Socialists and the Catholic authorities.

If it was his fate to be disowned by both sides, that was because Hudal, like Hitler, was incapable of accepting criticism or cautioning. In October 1936 he had received a warning from the Secretariat of State.[59] He chose to ignore it and went his own way. His own way, as he saw it, led him into conflict not only with "the emigrants, the democrats, and the Jews," but also with that "hater of Christianity, Rosenberg, who was the misfortune of the movement."[60] That last was the only perceptive observation that Hudal made. *The Foundations of National Socialism* was an attempt to do for Christianity what *The Myth of the Twentieth Century* had done for neo-paganism, but in Rome the effort was not appreciated.

The Vatican intervened to prevent an Italian translation of Hudal's book.[61] It was feared that Papen had a hand in its publication, and that fear was well-founded. While Hudal, who attributed his lack of success in clerical circles to a conspiracy by the Austrian and German hierarchies,[62] was given to overestimating the strength of his position, his duplicity did have an effect, at a delicate moment, on Rome.

When, on November 16, 1936, Pacelli assured Faulhaber that the "titular bishop of Ela's" position was far from that of the Holy See, he did not specify what that position was. The German hierarchy knew nothing about the strategy of condemnation elaborated in the Holy Office. As the time approached when that condemnation might have been discussed with the leaders of the Church in the Third Reich, Hitler's menace limited the Vatican's room to maneuver. For how was the secretary of state to admit to Faulhaber and his colleagues who, in August 1936, had called for the Pope to intervene, that preparations had already been made by the organization to which "the court theologian of the Party" belonged? While the cardinal calculated that it was better to play the affair down, events were beginning to accelerate beyond Rome's control.

———∞∞∞———

The Communists and the Cardinals

ON NOVEMBER 18, 1936, five days after the announcement in the *Osservatore Romano* disavowing Hudal's book, the cardinals of the Holy Office met to consider what should be done about the condemnation that he had tried to prevent. Although Pacelli was present, no comment by him is recorded. The cardinal-vicar of Rome, Francesco Marchetti-Selvaggiani, spoke loudly in favor of silence. Hudal later claimed that this was because Marchetti-Selvaggiani feared that an attack on National Socialism would have an adverse effect on the Church in Fascist Italy.[1] If that was what the cardinal thought or remarked privately, it was not what he stated at the meeting. His words, as reported in the minutes of the Congregation of the Holy Office, were: "*Silendum* [we should be silent]. Or, if one wants to do something, let it be in the form of a letter by the Pope, the father of all, addressed to the workers, in order to warn and enlighten them." The rest of the cardinals voted for a "brief instruction to warn the faithful against such erroneous theories and especially against the errors of Communism." Communism was only one of the "erroneous theories" on the agenda. The others, racism and totalitarianism, were omitted. A shift in strategy was taking place.

The decision deferred *sine die* (with no limit of time), the Pope pronounced on November 19, 1936. Pius XI wanted a document on the errors and methods of Communism, countering them with "a clear synthesis of the doctrines of the Church." His aim was "to invite the bishops, the clergy, and Catholic Action to make them public in higher education and popular teaching and to propagate social works that have bearing on them." For his part, he declared, "he would do something." In the meantime, the Holy Office was to prepare a decree and to condemn "the relevant propositions."

Two months earlier, on September 19, 1936, the Jesuit Enrico Rosa had published, in *Civiltà Cattolica*, an article entitled "The 'International' of Barbarism in Its Struggle Against Civilization."[2] Outraged at the brutalities of the Republicans, aided by the Russians, in the Spanish Civil War, he deplored the fact that hundreds of the clergy had been murdered; religious buildings had been burned; nuns raped; priests mutilated. Rosa's denunciation of these crimes surpassed anything that *Civiltà Cattolica* had previously published against the Nazis. "Horrendous tragedies . . . of blood, massacres, collective madness show that a satanic storm has broken on the peoples, heralding death and the profound decadence of nations." Intervention was necessary.

Fascist Italy intervened on the side of Franco and the Nationalists.[3] The Spanish Civil War brought Mussolini and Hitler closer. In October 1936 the Führer met with the Duce's son-in-law and foreign minister, Galeazzo Ciano, and the "Rome-Berlin axis" was announced.[4] Less than a formal alliance, this "axis" amounted to little more than an understanding to coordinate policies. Yet it appeared to many Italian Catholics a guarantee of security against the threat of "atheistic Bolshevism." It was not guessed that, at the end of the following year, the Italian government would sign an anti-Comintern pact with Germany and begin a program of semi-Nazification at home. Nor could it be known that, on November 19, 1936, Giuseppe Bottai, the Italian minister of education, recorded in his diary the following declaration on the "racial problem" by Mussolini: "It is necessary to face it, introduce it into Fascist literature and doctrine."[5] On that very day, in the Vatican, Pius XI had chosen to turn his attention to Communism and away from Nazi racism.

Communism, the last of the "errors of the age" to be examined by the Holy Office, moved to the head of the list in November 1936. The reasons for this change of priority were political. Nothing of moment had been added to the doctrinal and moral grounds for condemnation assembled previously. On the contrary, they remained slimmer and slighter than the evidence amassed, since 1934, by the Jesuits against National Socialism. But now the Nazis were allied with the Fascists to oppose the most brutal enemy of the Church. At its Roman center, in the Supreme Tribunal, Pacelli did not take the lead in pursuing the anti-Communist line. He concurred in the near-unanimous position of the other cardinals.

Politics came first and doctrine second in establishing the Church's order of priorities. The equation, at the same level of heresy, that had emerged, earlier in the same year, of Communism, National Socialism, and totalitarianism (in its Fascist variant) was shelved. Shelving that strategy, which Hudal had resisted, enabled him to save a measure of face. He, the fierce anti-Communist, had produced a book that had been disavowed but not condemned. Now condemnation of the Nazis and the Fascists was no longer opportune. Time and circumstances seemed to be on his side and, if he had failed in one offensive, there would be opportunities for others.

The opportunities available to Rome, in late 1936, appeared more limited than earlier in that year. Since July, Pacelli had received, from Germany, appeals for an encyclical. One of them, dated the fifteenth of that month, deplored "an unstoppable sinking into the abyss" and begged for "a word of . . . redemptive truth."[6] "Where else should that word come from, if not the Holy Church? . . . Never is it more likely to be effective than today." Representative of similar petitions being sent to the Secretariat of State, this one differed from the others by the words with which it began. "Most burning anxiety" was the opening phrase—a precedent, or a model, for the title of Pius XI's famous encyclical, *With Burning Anxiety (Mit brennender Sorge)*, of March 1937.[7]

If the position of the Church in Germany was alarming, the situation in Spain fuelled the fires of anti-Bolshevism. Their heat sustained the Nazi Party, reported Orsenigo on October 17, 1936.[8] Deploring the "cultural poverty" of a recent speech by Minister

Kerrl, the nuncio described the National Socialists' tactics as aimed at evoking faith in Hitler as a savior. "Capable of moving mountains," that faith had brought order in the chaos that followed the First World War. The population viewed the Führer as a bulwark against Communist insurrection. In the following months, as Orsenigo observed and lamented the Nazis' struggle against Christianity and their attempts to monopolize the education of the young,[9] he became pessimistic about the point of even negotiating on the basis of the Concordat, which he defined, with uncustomary elegance, as "an ironical invitation to study medicine, in order to cure a dead man." [10]

The Bavarian bishops, informed of Faulhaber's discussion with Hitler, resolved, on November 25–26, 1936, to condemn Bolshevism and reaffirm their "loyal and positive attitude to the present form of the state and the Führer." [11] In that resolution, which it was intended to carry out with the rest of the episcopate, was revealed the ambivalence of the Church's leadership in Hitler's Germany. Sincerely anti-Communist and anxious to be perceived as loyal citizens, they responded to the Führer's overtures for an agreement by playing into his hands.

That was not their purpose. They wished to take a stand vehemently against "Bolshevism" and more discreetly yet firmly against the persecution of Catholics. That the emphasis was to be placed on the first position became clear in correspondence between Bertram and Faulhaber. To the cardinal of Munich the cardinal of Breslau expressed his belief that the "hostile press" had played down the Church's anti-Communism.[12]

No one in Germany would have doubted the fervor of the Catholic episcopate on that issue, had it been possible to read the bishops' pastoral letter issued on Christmas Eve 1936.[13] Violently hostile, it compared Christianity and Communism to fire and water, emphasizing the long history of Catholic condemnations of "Moscow's armies" and the "red flag." More briefly and circumspectly, the pastoral letter referred to Catholics' rights as guaranteed by the Concordat. The measured and diplomatic tones with which the situation in Germany was described stood in flagrant contrast to the alarm expressed at "Bolshevism." Yet even that was too much. The Nazi authorities had the pastoral letter suppressed. And Bertram, on December 29, 1936, was exercised by the question of whether the German cardinals should send Hitler a congratulatory telegram for the New Year.[14]

The poverty of the tactics of accommodation practiced by the German bishops was evident by the end of 1936. Was this not the moment for Rome to seize the initiative? Pacelli was hardly in a position to demand a resolute stand because, despite his skepticism about the government's assurances, he had encouraged the episcopate "to take advantage of every real opportunity to smooth the path to a responsible agreement."[15] In the meantime, the three German cardinals (Bertram, Faulhaber, and Schulte) and two bishops (Galen of Münster and Preysing of Berlin) were summoned to Rome, where most of them (with the exception of Schulte) were accommodated in the Anima as guests of Alois Hudal. The "stabber in the back" of the hierarchy, as Cardinal Faulhaber had described him, was now its host.

A fly on the wall of the Anima in mid-January 1937 might have detected an atmosphere thick with tension. Fresh from an audience with Hitler at which he had been browbeaten with arguments employed in *The Foundations of National Socialism*, Faulhaber arrived in Rome, where he enjoyed the dubious privilege of hospitality from its author. And the other members of the hierarchy, publicly accused of intransigence by Hudal, prepared to face the Pope and the secretary of state at a point when their own endeavors at accommodation had been proved bankrupt. The tension might have been cut with a knife, and there was an ample selection of backs into which it might then have been stabbed.

In these awkward circumstances, a series of meetings took place. They are well documented, and some of the documents are previously unknown. Based on notes made by Pacelli's hand, there exist, in the Secret Archives of the Vatican, typewritten transcriptions of audiences held between the Roman and the German hierarchies, with corrections or additions in the neat italic script of the secretary of state. And because Pacelli took pains to record what was said, it will be possible to reconstruct in detail one of the most significant meetings between the Catholic bishops of Nazi Germany and the head of their Church.

They met on January 17, 1937. Two days before that audience, Bertram and Faulhaber were received by Pacelli. Either he made no notes on that conversation or they have not survived. Our source is Faulhaber, whose papers have been edited admirably.[16] That the otherwise discreet cardinal intended his own notes for private purposes is demonstrated by a reference to Pacelli's declining command of German. Was he too tired? Or simply out of practice? These questions are less important than the fact that Pacelli's interlocutors knew him personally from the twelve years that he had spent as nuncio in Germany.

A tone of confidentiality was maintained in the first discussion. Pacelli informed Bertram and Faulhaber about the chronic illness of Pius XI, concerning which the *Osservatore Romano* was publishing nothing. The Pope, reckoned Pacelli, could survive another two years. (That prediction, expressed on January 15, 1937, was fulfilled almost to the day on January 10, 1939.) It would be unwise to attach much credibility to the memoirs of Pacelli's housekeeper and "cross," Sister Pasqualina Lehnert. Yet her report, derived from Faulhaber, that, a few months before his death in 1939, Pius XI stated that, for two years, he had been Pope only in name and that all the work was undertaken by his secretary of state is relevant to this meeting.[17] For there can be little doubt that the German cardinals, meeting Pacelli, knew that they were dealing with a figure whose role, during the illness of Pius XI, had become more central than ever.

The conversation turned on two recurrent themes: "Bolshevism" and Orsenigo. Each was a source of irritation. The nuncio's recall was mentioned by the Germans. His illnesses, like his faulty command of detail and of the German language, led to an unfavorable comparison with Pacelli. "If only [Your] Eminence were still in Berlin!" exclaimed the flattering Faulhaber. "I return there each day," replied Pacelli. "It is now that I really love Germany, because it must suffer."[18] Some might have found that declaration less than reassuring.

"Bolshevism" appeared to be the prime source of anxiety. Pacelli reported (without irony) that it was a danger in America, on account of unemployment. He insisted on this point, to which Faulhaber replied with a distinction between "religious" and "political" Bolshevism. (The Nazis presumably represented the first variety and the Communists both.) But previously the cardinal of Munich had raised an issue of concrete significance. He spoke in favor of maintaining the Concordat because it provided a "[legal] basis." The "dead man" described by Orsenigo weeks earlier was still alive and kicking in the mind of Faulhaber. This was the position that would determine the course of further discussions.

The following evening, another meeting between the secretary of state and all five members of the German hierarchy took place. Pacelli's report,[19] although fuller and more detailed than Faulhaber's notes on the same audience, omits a number of points that the cardinal of Munich recorded.[20] One of the most revealing was the Germans' lamentations about Hudal: "He believes that we are all opposed . . . on a purely ideological basis, not according to the Catholic literature, without knowledge of the difficulties out there in reality."[21] As the German hierarchy raised its voice in protest against *The Foundations of National Socialism*, it is not difficult to imagine Pacelli shifting in his chair. He was aware that Hudal had published that book in full knowledge of the most recent "Catholic literature" on the subject of the Nazis produced, by the Holy Office, in Rome. And he passed over the protest, after the Germans had been allowed to vent their wrath. Pacelli made no recorded comment, nor does Hudal's name figure in his report.

Asked to deliver a judgment on the situation in the Third Reich, the hierarchy agreed that the government and, still more, the Party regarded the Concordat as a dead letter. No one was in doubt about the hostility of the Nazis. The Church stood before a choice between life and death: "They want to destroy it directly."[22] Young people were being educated in Rosenberg's ideology, which had become the religion of the Party. So stated Pacelli's report. Faulhaber voiced the opinion that, in ten years' time, there would no longer be a Catholic youth.[23] Little did the cardinal of Munich know that he was echoing a view delivered to the Holy Office in 1934 by the man now described by Hitler as the "court theologian of the Party." [24] It cannot be determined whether Pacelli recognized that echo but, if he did, it is unlikely that his sense of irony permitted a smile.

Lament followed lament—each of them in terms familiar to the secretary of state from diplomatic correspondence. The Führer could not be exempted from responsibility and the bishops (or, perhaps, Faulhaber alone[25]) were convinced that Germany was now ruled by a "dictatorship of the Party. Even if Hitler wished, he could hardly do otherwise." Imagining the Führer helpless in the grip of this crisis, the German hierarchy placed no hope in *a counteroffensive*. Those words were underlined by Pacelli. As if to underscore the helplessness of the situation, he recorded the wish that the nuncio should intervene energetically.

What to do? *(Quid faciendum?)* asked the secretary of state. A letter from the Pope to the Führer was ruled out. Criticism was impossible: Hitler would not tolerate it, and the danger existed that the Nazis would publish a falsified version of a papal epistle in order to deceive Catholics. What both clergy and laity now needed was an encyclical making a warm appeal. The time was ripe: Public opinion was convinced of the regime's hostility to the Church, and the Party would not dare to go too far in the present state of foreign affairs.

A decisive step had been taken, accompanied by a significant silence. Pacelli, in response to the German hierarchy's request for an encyclical, said nothing about the preparations already made by the Holy Office. Was he bound by *secretum pontificium* or inhibited by the Hudal affair? The next day the cardinals and bishops were received in audience by the Pope, who had wished to index their host and who had a reputation for forthrightness. Pius XI was free, had he wished, to speak about Rome's plans; and now was the time.

Before taking the elevator to the third floor of the apostolic palace, where the papal apartments were located, the German prelates assembled in Pacelli's rooms on the morning of Sunday, January 17, 1937. The secretary of state read them his account of their discussion the previous day. Then, at ten A.M., all of them proceeded to the audience with the Pope.

Books abounded in the apartments of the ex-librarian. Splendidly presented in glass cases, they contrasted with the simple (and, at times, questionable) taste of the Pope in furniture. Pius XI was no aesthete nor, despite his sense of dignity, was he then capable of insisting on protocol. He received the German cardinals and bishops on his sickbed, like an improvised throne of pain. Clad in white, the left leg bent and the right one stretched out, the Pope greeted them with faltering voice. Pacelli faithfully recorded what was said.[26]

After accepting the report on the discussion of January 16, the Pope greeted those present and invited each of them to speak.[27] The senior member of the German hierarchy began:

CARDINAL BERTRAM: The present government and the Party that supports it are striving with every means to nullify all our ecclesiastical institutions. Our greatest and most burning anxiety is the youth. The lack of ecclesiastical freedom is unimaginably great. Everyone has the right to attack the Church; the Church does not have the right of self-defense. A fundamental point in the government's program is to do away with the influence of the confessions on public life. That means the complete disappearance of the confessions. The great legal advantages that the Concordat might have brought us are cancelled increasingly each day by a policy of *faits accomplis*.

THE HOLY FATHER: Nevertheless the bishops are not dissatisfied with the Concordat. As soon as We, for compelling motives, concluded it, We knew with what sort of people we had to deal. But We would not have believed in, or expected, such a degree of disloyalty after they had given their word. Nonetheless the Concordat is still valuable in the present circumstances, at least on the basis of law.

CARDINAL BERTRAM: The government annihilates ecclesiastical freedom. The first letter that I received in Rome was a document from the minister of education to the effect that there shall be no more Catholic kindergartens—i.e.: no more "Catholic children"!

The twisting of concepts which follows from such a policy that denies objective rights is depressing.

THE HOLY FATHER: We have never understood Christ's suffering so well as during this period. Our own suffering has taught us something precious—above all, the secret of Christ's suffering. We were to some extent illiterate in the great, holy science of suffering and pain. Now kindly God—so kindly to Us as well—has accepted us into his school of suffering. Throughout Our entire life work was Our joy and happiness. Now we have begun to make Our way in understanding the nature of pain. How many hurtful things there are at present (Germany, Spain, Russia, Mexico)! Who knows what this coincidence of Our suffering with these many great sufferings means? In any case it is an occasion, day by day, to feel more confidence in a better future. We say "day by day" because literally every day promises and brings us new, deep, and grave sufferings! But We intend to suffer for Germany, for Russia, for Spain, for Mexico, for all those parts of Christ's mystical body that suffer more than the others. It is a real *solatium mentis et corporis* [solace to the mind and the body] to be able to think so.

CARDINAL FAULHABER: The prime and hardest struggle for survival is over the confessional schools. In practice we have learnt, in daily life, what a great gift Your Holiness has made to us in the Concordat. Without this Concordat we would perhaps already be at the end of our fight. As long as we have this Concordat we can protest against the violations and denials of our rights with at least the prospect of agreement on the part of men of good will, even if it produces no immediate practical or tangible effect. We have beneath our feet a legal foundation which is important—at least in principle and in certain practical effects—despite all the violent measures.

THE HOLY FATHER: We maintain firm trust, as firm as a rock, not in men but in God. Kindly God, who has allowed all this to happen at present, undoubtedly has His purpose.

CARDINAL FAULHABER: We are profoundly grateful for the powerful diplomatic notes which [His] Eminence Pacelli continually sends to the government to defend the Church's rights and support the episcopate. We bishops receive no answer to our representations. But the Holy See's notes cannot be left without a reply.

THE HOLY FATHER: *repeatedly voices his paternal approval for the work of the cardinal–secretary of state . . . :* We continue on our path with courage and confidence. We are not pessimistic. Convey to Bavaria Our apostolic blessing.

CARDINAL SCHULTE: Recently, in Cologne and in the Rheinland, the struggle against the confessional schools has been systematically supported and advanced, as has the movement to leave the Church. But, despite all losses, the faith and loyalty of the great majority of Catholics are strong. A large, increasing, if naturally unorganized and publicly discreet, dissatisfaction with the regime is prevalent. That perhaps gives grounds for hope. Those members of the clergy who have returned after months in prison have lost none of their courage. A large part of Catholic Youth remains firm—even in the organizations. The situation is not at all hopeless.

BISHOP VON PREYSING: In Berlin the pressure from government and Party is not so strong as in the purely Catholic regions. The Catholics are a minority here, and they are less feared. The presence of the diplomatic corps counsels prudence.

THE HOLY FATHER: Bishop von Galen, We hear many splendid things about you.

BISHOP VON GALEN: I have a very faithful people and a faithful clergy. The clergy and very large sections of the people are loyal to the Church. Our great worry is young people will develop in the long run. We have to deal with an opponent who shares nothing of our fundamental ideas of loyalty and sincerity. All that he says and does is falsity and lies!

THE HOLY FATHER: Our special blessing to all Our courageous champions. Our cause will certainly triumph. That is Our firm conviction. Our cause is in God's hands. And that is better than if it were in men's hands. We are accordingly in good and kindly hands. Nonetheless the present hour is very gloomy and even threatening. But the eternally true dictum *Non praevalebunt!* [They shall not prevail!] is valid for our times and for the enemies of the Church in these times. When kindly God, with His grace, His help and His comfort, stands by us, then the final issue of this struggle cannot be so bad as it may seem to many a person of small spirit. Convey Our paternal blessing to all your "fellow-bishops," to the clergy, to the entire Catholic people of Germany, which We embrace in faithful pastoral love and for which We heartily wish the fruits of its suffering and loyalty.

Perhaps the most remarkable feature of this audience is what was not said. Pius XI made no mention of the condemnation prepared by the Holy Office, nor did anyone refer to Hudal. Yet the two issues were linked, in the minds of the Pope and Pacelli, by a bond of ill-ease. Ill-ease at the work of the Holy Office on the subject of National Socialism, which he had already ordered to be put aside, coupled with a desire to avoid the embarrassing theme of Rome's leading "appeaser," whose name the secretary of state had removed from the agenda, lent Pius XI's tone a combination of insistence and evasiveness. There were topics that the Pope wished to avoid, and others which he emphasized.

Overriding emphasis was placed on the Concordat. When a German prelate—such as Bertram, at the beginning of the audience—repeated the grounds, already familiar to the Vatican, which demonstrated that it was superseded, Pius XI hastened to defend it. He told the bishops what they were to think. Seconded by Faulhaber—profuse in his gratitude to Pacelli, the architect of the Concordat—the Pope was concerned, above all else, to avoid undermining the "legal basis" of Catholic rights that it provided so shakily.

The specter of the Concordat, or its abrogation, haunted both the Roman and the German authorities. There was not the faintest trace of the willingness, voiced in the Vatican of 1933,[28] to face the consequences of doing without it. Acknowledging the gravity of the situation, no one could imagine an alternative strategy. That is why the suggestion that a moral and doctrinal alternative might be provided by Rome was avoided—partly because of the difficulties raised by Hudal but also because the probable result of a condemnation, in the tough form prepared by the Holy Office, would have been a rupture which the authorities of the Church could not contemplate. They were neither "appeasers," in the sense of *The Foundations of National Socialism,* nor were they martyrs, those champions of the faith whom Pius XI praised publicly.[29]

The Pope was informed about the devastating effects of Nazi hostility to the Church and he was aware, from Rome's secret analysis, that the German partner to the Concordat believed in a political religion incompatible with Christianity. On the morning of January 17, 1937, Pius XI, who had already stated to the Holy Office that he "would do something," might have decided to speak out, announcing a struggle on doctrinal and moral principles which had been elaborated with care. He did not do so, nor did he even raise the possibility with the German hierarchy. Instead the aged and ailing Vicar of Christ talked about the parallels between his sufferings and those of the Savior.

———⊶∞⊷———

With Burning Concern

THE POPE HAD ANNOUNCED to the Holy Office in November 1936 that "he would do something." What he would do was left open at the audience granted to the German hierarchy in January 1937. Reading between the lines of Pacelli's report on that audience, however, it emerges that crucial decisions had already been made before it took place.

The most crucial of those decisions was negative. If Pius XI did not mention the condemnation prepared by the Holy Office, that was because he was against issuing it in the form prepared at Rome. The "Syllabus of Errors" of the twentieth century was in place when he met the German cardinals and bishops, the "grand design" elaborated in successive versions of which he had approved. The Pope was free to choose between them. More than two years before the outbreak of the Second World War, the head of the Roman Catholic Church might have damned, point by point, the heresies of National Socialism and linked them with the other "errors of the age." Yet he held back.

This is not what the textbooks tell us. It is maintained that Pius XI condemned the Nazis forthrightly in his encyclical *Mit brennender Sorge (With Burning Concern)*, of March 1937. Since the secret documents in the archives of the Holy Office have became available, opinions need to be revised.

Condemnations may differ in tone and in substance. What the

Holy Office had prepared was both detailed and wide-ranging. Its lists of propositions named no names, but the sources—in particular, Hitler—were easily identifiable. There, in "difficulties with governments,"[1] lay the danger. It was feared that the Führer, if attacked openly, would abrogate the Concordat.

The Concordat, still viewed as the Church's only "legal basis," had to be preserved at all costs. One of the costs was the moral and doctrinal stand represented by the Holy Office's list of damnable propositions (Appendix I and Appendix II). Those lists formed the "negative" part of a two-pronged strategy, to be accompanied by a "positive" encyclical, which the German bishops had requested in August 1936.[2] If the second part of that strategy was executed, the first was blurred and blunted by general references, in *Mit brennender Sorge,* to points that the Holy Office had intended to condemn specifically. Far from being a full rejection of National Socialism, that famous encyclical is a curtailed compromise. A compromise between the concerns of the German hierarchy and Roman anxieties.

The anxieties of Pius XI and Pacelli at the consequences of an encyclical were expressed at a meal following the audience with the Pope on January 17, 1937. Then the secretary of state asked whether such a document might lead the Nazis to do away with the Concordat. Schulte, the cardinal of Cologne, thought that possible. Cardinal Faulhaber of Munich disagreed. Much depended on the form and style that the encyclical took. "Polemic" must be avoided, opined Faulhaber. National Socialism and the Party should not even be mentioned. The document ought to refer to Germany, but should deal with dogma and be of a peaceful character.[3] This was the view that carried the day, for it was in line with the wishes of Pacelli and the Pope.

Faulhaber was asked to contribute.[4] No one had spoken more forcefully than he in defense of the Concordat at the audience with the Pope. Pius XI had made clear his desire to continue on that "legal basis," and the diplomatic efforts of Pacelli to maintain it had been praised fulsomely by the cardinal of Munich, who was on cordial terms with the secretary of state.

All this was consistent with one of the strategies that the Vatican had been pursuing for years. Faced with the threat of National Socialism, Rome had repeatedly urged the German bishops to take action, and the German bishops had replied by asking the Holy See to intervene. Now, after interminable consultations, the two had come together. Both of them were alarmed by Communism, and neither wanted a rupture with the Nazis. In this clinch between compatible insecurities, there was no room for "polemic."

The cardinal of Munich did not specify what he meant by that term but, had he known of the Holy Office's draft condemnation, it is more than probable that he would have regarded it as polemical. And although they would not have disowned that "negative" part of the "double document" prepared by the Holy Office, both Pius XI and his secretary of state were willing to suppress it in silence, without the knowledge of the German cardinals and bishops. Motives differed on each side, but the effect was the same: an alliance of uncertainty rather than a pact of steel.

The cardinal of Munich set to work, unaware that he had been anticipated by the Holy Office. Diligent as ever, Faulhaber wrote through the Roman nights. On January 21 he sent Pacelli "an incomplete and fully useless draft,"[5] adequate for a bishop's pastoral letter but not for a papal encyclical.[6] That description was not inaccurate. Nothing in the draft that Faulhaber delivered to Pacelli goes beyond the familiar admonitions that the German episcopate had been issuing for years, such as the pastoral letter that they had addressed to the faithful at Fulda on August 23, 1935.

Taking his cue from Pius XI's remarks on his illness during the audience of January 17, Faulhaber dwelt on the theme of suffering, which he linked to that of Christ (Colossians I, 24).[7] When the cardinal touched on the issues of neo-paganism and the cult of race or the state,[8] his tone was rather cautious than condemnatory. He warned, for example, that, while race and state deserved "a place of honor" among "earthly values," they should not be "over-valued" or deified.[9]

Diplomatic in substance and conciliatory in tone, Faulhaber was at pains to avoid "polemic," even when National Socialism and Catholicism clashed. Not that he failed to see the menace of the political religion that the Nazis were attempting to substitute for Christianity. The use of the term "trinity" to describe "a thoughtless product of human imagination," for instance, was dismissed in his draft as "an empty label" [10]; the notion of a "national God" written off as an "erroneous doctrine" *(Irrlehre),* credible only to the superficial.[11] Yet Faulhaber's aim was rather to instruct than to attack. True belief in God, in Christ, in the Church, and in the primacy of the Pope were his central concerns. His draft is less a condemnation than a catechism. Its chief purpose was to remind Catholics of the chief articles of the faith.

Such was the light in which Pius XI and Pacelli read Faulhaber's work. Coming from a leading member of the German hierarchy, this testimony to their search for consensus approximated to one-half of the "double document" recommended by the Holy Office. That is why it is important to consider how the final form taken by their encyclical differed from Faulhaber's draft. For Pius XI and Pacelli might have toughened its tone and sharpened its substance by using materials which, at Rome, lay to hand.

They did not do so. Instead they addressed the encyclical known as *Mit brennender Sorge* from its opening words, not only "to the German bishops," as suggested by Faulhaber, but also to "the other religious superiors who live in peace and communion with the Apostolic See." [12] The attention of the universal Church was being drawn to "the situation . . . in the German Reich."

That Church received a justification of Rome's policy that Faulhaber had not offered. But what was stated, at the beginning of the encyclical, corresponded to wishes that he expressed at the audience of January 17. Hammering home the point that the Concordat had been signed to the general satisfaction of the German episcopate *(zu Euer aller Befriedigung),*[13] Pacelli emphasized that previous negotiations had been resumed at the initiative of Hitler's government. Changes made to successive versions of the encyclica are revealing of that emphasis.

In a first version, composed in Italian, the text read:

When We . . . in the summer of 1933 resumed negotiations for a Concordat . . .

Pacelli crossed that phrase out and wrote instead:

> When We . . . in the summer of 1933, *at the request of the Reich government, agreed* to resume negotiations for a Concordat . . . [emphasis added].[14]

Stressing that the Nazis had instigated the Concordat only to violate it, the moral burden was placed where Rome was convinced that it belonged—in Berlin. At this level, subtler and less direct than a confrontation, Eugenio Pacelli was a master tactician.

Only the best of motives had led the Holy See to ratify the Concordat, asserted *Mit brennender Sorge.* There was no hint of Pacelli's claim that a pistol had been pointed at his brow,[15] unless in the convoluted phrase "Despite many a grave reservation, We then struggled with Ourselves not to refuse our agreement." [16] If the tree of peace planted in German soil had not produced the fruits hoped for, no one could blame the Church and its head. (No one, that is, except the National Socialists.)

Accusation mingling with self-justification, the encyclical passed to direct criticism. "Machinations," "struggle to the death," "mistrust," "disturbance," "hatred," "fundamental enmity towards Christ and the Church": All these expressions derived from Pacelli's notes to the German government. "Twisting, evasion, undermining and more or less public violation of the treaty" were the other terms used. Outspoken on issues such as the destruction of Catholic schools,[17] the encyclical insisted on the "chartered right" *(verbrieftes Recht)* of the Concordat. On that "legal basis," the Pope and Pacelli were firm.

Less firm and less specific were the passages of *Mit brennender Sorge* that dealt with matters of doctrine and morals. From the Holy Office's lists—the one containing forty-seven points, the other twenty-five—the encyclical incorporated a selection, cautiously formulated, ruling out pantheism and "the secularization of God in the world and the divinization of the world in God." Those who held such a view did "not belong to believers in God." [18] Striking, here and elsewhere, is what was not said.

The word "heresy" never appears in *Mit brennender Sorge*— "erroneous belief" *(Irrlehre)* as applied to the notion of a "national

God" or "national religion" is as near as the encyclical comes—nor does it employ the forthright language of condemnation traditional in papal censures and inquisitorial decrees. "Heretical," "immoral," "offensive to pious ears"—anathemas used so readily by the Roman tribunals of the faith—are replaced by the circumlocution "far from the belief in God and an understanding of life that corresponds to that belief." [19]

That circumlocution, uncharacteristic of Rome's hard-hitting style when dealing with errors in faith and morality, again reflects the desire, voiced by Faulhaber and shared by Pius XI and Pacelli, to avoid "polemic." In keeping with the cardinal of Munich's suggestion, the Nazis are not mentioned by name. Although the divinization of race and state are singled out as "far from belief in God," in a manner that recalls the Holy Office's lists (cf. Appendix I, 1), its teaching about the equality of mankind and the sameness of human nature (ibid. 9 ff) is hardly mentioned, despite a reference to the universal validity of God's commandments.[20]

Much of the detail, more of the substance, and all the damning tone of the Holy Office's work on National Socialism are omitted in *Mit brennender Sorge*. This encyclical, still hailed as the most courageous attack made by the papacy on Hitler and his followers, in fact marks a retreat. Retreating from the line of confrontation represented by the "negative" part of the planned "double document," Pius XI and Pacelli confined their harshest criticisms to Nazi misuse of religious language.

It was "confusing" or "false" to describe "blood and race" as a "revelation." [21] It was a "distortion" to apply the term "immortality" to the survival and persistence of a people.[22] The Church, declared the encyclical, existed for all peoples and nations.[23] Yet *Mit brennender Sorge* never mentions the head of that Church's role as a guarantor of human rights—including those of races persecuted within the Third Reich—although attention had been paid to this doctrine by the Jesuits in their work for the Holy Office.

The omission of so much of the draft condemnation from the encyclical casts the old problem of the papacy's silence in a new light. It is no longer necessary to speculate about what the head of the Catholic Church "might have said." It is a matter of fact that the Pope decided against speaking out on racism, human rights, and allied issues in the direct and detailed form prepared by the Supreme Tribunal. Emphasizing his desire to "re-establish true peace in Germany,"[24] Pius XI sacrificed on the altar of the Concordat the outright attack on the Nazis that, in 1937, Rome might have launched.

Even after that sacrifice, the encyclical remained too provocative for some. Before being sent to Germany, *Mit brennender Sorge* was shown to the Jesuit general Ledóchowski. He, whose subordinates had drafted a much tougher condemnation of National Socialism, regarded the document as "a bit hard."[25] Writing to Pacelli at the beginning of March, the "black Pope" counseled caution. He believed that the encyclical would do "great good," but recommended that some of its expressions be "toned down." "Avoid going into questions that are very difficult and subtle," Ledóchowski advised.

In that advice from a powerful confidant of the Pope is summed up another of Rome's dilemmas. The Vatican was not united in its approach to the Nazis. The strategy developed by members of the Company of Jesus differed from that of their general, who wished to be more conciliatory than even Pius XI and Pacelli (as Friedrich Muckermann rightly surmised[26]). The secretary of state faced that dilemma under the heading *Fears and Worries* in one of his drafts:

> Confronted with this state of affairs, which has continued to get worse, the Holy See could not be silent.
>
> The Pope does not want to exclude a hope, however slight, that the situation may improve.[27]

Torn between indignation and aspiration to reach a settlement, the authorities in Rome—Pius XI and Pacelli, flanked by Ledóchowski—flinched before a break. They believed that a break would have been the probable consequence of a "double document," including the Holy Office's propositions to be condemned; and that was why *Mit brennender Sorge* appeared alone, unaccompanied or followed by that list of errors. Expressed in Pacelli's terms, the encyclical was a compromise between the Holy See's sense that it "could not be silent" and its "fears and worries."

After elaborate and effective preparations to keep knowledge of the encyclical from the Nazis, *Mit brennender Sorge* was read aloud by the German bishops on Palm Sunday 1937 and hailed with almost unanimous admiration by the Vatican's sources. Faulhaber, writing to Pacelli on March 22, declared: "We wish . . . to use this document, which will make Church history, to save the Catholic faith in Germany." [28] The people had listened with great attention; the police stood by helplessly, unsure of what to do. As reports poured in from nuntiatures all over the world—most of them enthusiastic[29]—Pacelli had to balance the joy of Catholics and (he was assured) of Protestants with the hostility of the Nazis.

More significant than the protests made by the German ministry of religious affairs against this "violation of the Concordat" [30] were the warnings that Pacelli received from Orsenigo and other informants. The nuncio at Berlin, writing on April 1, foresaw a resumption of repression "from above." Exposed in its "underhand tendencies to demolish rights [guaranteed by] the Concordat," the government, believed Orsenigo, would initiate a "real anti-religious policy." [31] He did not note that that policy had been initiated long before.

Others, more perceptive or more concerned to influence the Vatican, presented different interpretations. Bonifacio Pignatti Morano di Custoza, the Italian ambassador to the Holy See, reported, on April 24, a conversation held between his colleague at Berlin, Bernardo Attolico, and the foreign minister Neurath. There the impression had been given that the Nazis did not desire a rupture with Rome, providing "the situation was not exacerbated further." Hitler, believed Attolico, was holding back on polemic. The Holy See should do the same. A "negative defense of its own positions" would mean the end of the Concordat. Life without that agreement was impossible to imagine, opined the ambassador. Negotiations were required, on a new and "more realistic basis." [32] This was the diplomatic language that Pacelli spoke and he might have seen in it confirmation of

Rome's decision not to publish its "negative defense of its own positions." Yet other sources gave grounds for skepticism.

From Romania came a letter expressing the fear that the encyclical would unite the enemies of the Church[33]; Hitler was revered by the 800,000 Germans in that country. On April 30, 1937, Pacelli responded, via the nuncio, in a rare tone of tartness—not only his but also that of Pius XI:

> The August Pontiff was profoundly sorrowed to learn that the German population in Rumania, including the Catholics, admire Herr Hitler as a hero, *despite his hatred for the Church,* and consider the Nazi doctrines condemned in the recent encyclica compatible with the Catholic faith [emphasis added].[34]

That letter was written shortly after Pacelli had received a dispatch from Amleto Cicognani, the nuncio at Vienna, who reported, on April 24, that the Austrian minister of the interior (and Nazi sympathizer) Glaise-Horstmann had asked Hitler why he was waging war against the Church. The Führer exploded in anger. Violent in gesture and tone, he ranted against the encyclical and threatened: "I won't throw any bishop into prison . . . but I will heap disgrace and shame on the Catholic Church, opening unknown monastic archives and having the filth contained in them published! . . . [35] It was wrong, concluded Cicognani, to suppose that hatred of the Church was limited to Hitler's entourage, not his person. Pacelli responded, on April 28, with diplomatic measure: "To tell the truth, the feelings of violent hostility toward the Church on the part of the present chancellor of the German Reich have been well known here for a long time." [36]

So much for Hudal's distinction between the "conservative Catholic" Führer and left-wing extremists. Pacelli did not believe in this illusion. Yet he, like others, continued to hope for an "improvement" from Hitler. Rome's attitude was divided between realism and wishful thinking.

• • •

On March 17, 1937, the cardinals of the Holy Office had met to consider what they should do about their draft condemnation of Communism. Informed that the Pope was preparing one, they decided to wait for his encyclical. Pius XI approved their decision on March 18. A day later, on the nineteenth, appeared *Divini Redemptoris,* which censured "atheistic Communism." [37] Coordination of strategy was not the Vatican's strength; in November 1936, the Pope had merely announced that he would "do something." [38]

That "something" reaffirmed Tardini's principle of not favoring any side but striking both—meaning that, if the Nazis were criticized in *Mit brennender Sorge,* the Communists were anathematized in *Divini Redemptoris* (for the second time in a year, after *Dilectissima nobis* of March 19, 1936). "Equilibrium" was maintained at the price of repetition, yet the two encyclicals were distinct and separate—not integral—parts of a syllabus aimed at all the "errors of the age." And this created confusion about which strategy was being followed.

It was noted, in the Holy Office, that there was no difference between its own work on Communism and the papal encyclical on the same subject.[39] They differed only in style. The commission's draft was worth retaining, although modifications were recommended— some of them with inadvertent humor. It was suggested, for example, to condemn the proposition: "Man is led by natural necessity into Communist society in which, when every source of inequality is abolished, together with private property, that fact alone removes grounds for disputes and oppression among men, and there will be a paradise on earth."

That proposition ought to be altered, it was objected because, as it stood, it recalled the communal life of the apostles and the religious orders. (The Church might condemn the "Bolsheviks," but not them!) Should, elsewhere in the document, the expression "the *servitude* of marriage" be replaced by "the *duty*"? Or was *"bond"* a happier choice? So the discussion wore on. By the beginning of April, the Holy Office was wearying of this task and, on the first day of that month, it decided to prepare a comparison between its draft on racism, "hypernationalism," and totalitarianism with *Mit brennender Sorge.*[40]

Divided into three columns, this document reveals the many and major differences between the papal encyclical and the condemnation planned by the modern inquisitors (Appendix III). Perhaps the most significant difference to emerge from the comparison is highlighted by the blank spaces. Most of them refer to racism, about which the Holy Office had been voluble and the Pope, by comparison, reticent. Here was the lacuna which, during the spring of 1937, the authorities of the Vatican could not ignore.

They addressed it in May, at what was to be their final discussion of the "Syllabus." [41] That was the term still used, because the intention of publishing a condemnation of "racism and Communism" together had not been abandoned. The cardinal-secretary of the Holy Office, Sbarretti, made a shrewd observation:

After the encyclical on the situation of Catholicism in Germany, *there no longer exist reasons for considering it advisable to exclude the propositions on racism* and, after the encyclical on Communism, *many have dared to say that the Church has taken the side of the authoritarian regimes against the proletariat* [emphasis added].

Why had it been thought "advisable to exclude the propositions on racism" that had formed a core of previous drafts? Only one motive had been given in earlier discussions, and that was "difficulties with governments." [42] Hitler's was the government at which the condemnation of racism by the Holy Office was aimed, and the "difficulties" expected from Germany were the reason why *Mit brennender Sorge* was toned down on that subject. Rome knew, from Cardinal Faulhaber's audience with the Führer, that the racial laws were at the forefront of Hitler's mind[43]; and Pius XI accordingly chose the path of discretion.

If *Divini Redemptoris*, by contrast, was direct, with no blows excluded, that was because reconciliation with "atheistic Communism" was inconceivable. While the politics of condemnation had their nuances, they were lost in those who thought that "the Church had taken the side of the authoritarian regimes." That view, expressed so sweepingly, was not wholly accurate. The fact was that, in 1937, the Supreme Tribunal of the Catholic Church had compelling reasons of doctrine and morality to damn Nazism and Communism with equal force, but Pius XI and Pacelli—who had no sympathy for the Führer and knew that he had none for them—chose not to do so because they remembered his appeal, or his menaces, delivered to Faulhaber at Obersalzberg.

Rome's view of the similarity between the Communists and the Nazis had been sensed by Hitler's designated successor, Hermann Goering. Portrayed as a "moderate" by Vatican sources, he was to observe, in a conversation with Count Massimo Magistrati, counselor at the Italian embassy in Berlin, that, on meeting Pius XI, he had formed the "vague impression" that the Pope scarcely distinguished between Bolshevism and National Socialism.[44] That impression might have been confirmed by Pius XI's remark to Bishops Preysing and Galen during their audience with him on January 23, 1937: "In purpose and method National Socialism is nothing but Bolshevism. I'd say that to Herr Hitler."[45] Yet Rome continued to respond to approaches from Germany. To the proposal that the conflict could be settled, if the Vatican did not oppose Hitler's plans to annex Austria, Pacelli replied, on March 20, 1938, with overtures for an agreement and "pleasurable memories" of Goering's visit to the Vatican.[46] Behind the scenes, the diplomatic lines of communication continued to function after *Mit brennender Sorge,* as its authors intended.

The Holy Office was unaware that this was the policy being followed by Pius XI and Pacelli. Pressing ahead in the belief that its "Syllabus" would be issued, it discussed racism further. Undaunted by his recent setbacks, Hudal took part. He wanted more to be said on the "religious" aspects of racism—especially on the idea, embraced by Mussolini and others, that Christianity was not universal but a faith particularly suited to the mentality of the Italians. And as he held forth, without embarrassment, on subjects that he had sought to reconcile with Nazi ideology, a cardinal of the Roman Church made a speech that raised the hackles of Hitler.

"How can a nation of 60 million people, intelligent people, submit in fear and servitude to a foreigner, an Austrian paper-hanger, and . . . a bad one at that?" asked Cardinal George Mundelein of Chicago on May 18, 1937. His reply was that the Germans must have had their brains removed. Mundelein's words, addressed to an audience of diocesan priests, were not intended to be published and, when they were, they caused a furor in Germany.[47] Pacelli's refusal to disown or correct Mundelein led to rumors that the Concordat would be abrogated by the Nazis.

Throughout May and June alarming dispatches were forwarded to the secretary of state. A report on Goebbels's tirade of May 28 threatening measures against Catholics appeared, the following day, in the *Völkischer Beobachter* and was sent to Rome.[48] The nuncio at Vienna interpreted that speech as the prelude to a "religious struggle . . . conducted in grand style"[49]; Orsenigo advised that the populace was critical of Mundelein and that the government planned to isolate the Roman Church, reducing it to a form of "bureaucratic piety like Protestantism."[50] Attolico, the Italian ambassador in Berlin, asserted that the cardinal of Chicago had caused "a very acute phase" in the relations between Germany and the Holy See by insulting Hitler. The Third Reich, which had wished to avoid a break with Rome, would now push its persecutions to the extreme in order to emasculate the Concordat. Any reaction by German Catholics would be counterproductive. The Vatican should not rely on young people, indoctrinated by Nazi ideology. Pacelli was held responsible by the government for the current crisis.[51]

The cardinals of the Holy Office met again in the midst of that crisis. At a congregation held on June 2, 1937, from which Pacelli was absent, they resolved to postpone their syllabus *sine die* (without limitation of time). On June 4 the Pope approved their decision with the following words, recorded in the minutes of the Congregation: "Considering the present grave situation, let us wait; when it becomes calmer and the storms of this moment have passed, we can resume the study."

Calm was never restored, and the storms became more violent. Swept away by their fury, the Syllabus aimed against racism and other "errors of the age" became a ghost that haunted the archives of the Holy Office, until it was transported to America in secret.

• • •

On June 20, 1937, Ottaviani, the assessor of the Holy Office, came to the apostolic palace for his weekly audience with Pius XI. Ottaviani brought with him a decree banning a book on racism by G. Cogni.[52] The work had been denounced by Hudal, who feared (or claimed to fear) that Italian youth would be corrupted by ideas imported from the Third Reich. A plan for racial laws on the German model had already been made by a member of the German community at Rome, he declared. Hudal maintained that he had sent a copy to the Secretariat of State (where no trace of the document remains). The Church should act immediately to condemn such errors. Otherwise, underlined Hudal, it would be *too late*. The opportunist was seeking to redeem himself where previously he had erred.

Pius XI was in one of his recurrent moods of impatience. Not waiting to hear what Ottaviani had to say, the Pope snapped: "It is obviously necessary to do more and better; for ages they have been coming to me and saying such things, but they do nothing. Let them start to waffle less and *do* something."

In the light of Pius XI's declaration on June 4, these words assume an unintended irony. Two weeks later, ironies multiplied. Referring to the Pope at the consecration of the basilica at Lisieux on July 18, 1937, Pacelli poured scorn on those "teachers of impiety . . . who have not been able to bind with chains the words and the pen of that intrepid old man." On the twentieth of the same month, in Notre Dame de Paris, the secretary of state declared that the Church "condemned injustice, wherever it is to be found."[53] "Wherever" included Berlin, which the policy of the Roman and German hierarchies had spared the full sting of the inquisitorial lash. Naturally Pacelli did not say so. But he did make, in the same speech, a revealing observation on this discrepancy between rhetoric and silence: "It is at times of crisis that one can judge the hearts and characters of men."[54]

The Excommunication of Hitler

DURING THE LAST YEARS of Pius XI's life, there were, or appeared to be, signs that his position toward National Socialism was becoming tougher. The Pope knew that Hitler hated and persecuted the Church. A baptized Catholic, the Führer held and imposed views that the Holy Office judged heretical. These were grounds for expelling him from the community of the faithful, to which—nominally—he belonged. Yet, on the evidence available in the Vatican, no member of the Church, priest or layman, made that proposal. It came instead from Hitler's ally, Benito Mussolini.

On April 10, 1938, Tacchi-Venturi reported to the Pope that the Duce had said to him three days previously:

> It would be appropriate to be more energetic, without half-measures, but not immediately . . . waiting for the most opportune moment to adopt more dynamic measures—for example, excommunication. It is important to avoid believing that Hitler is a temporary phenomenon, because this man has won great successes for Germany. There is no other means of preventing him but war; and no one wants war . . . [1]

No one included the Vatican, indebted to Mussolini for help behind the scenes. The two Romes collaborated. Their "marriage of convenience" [2] had lasted for seven long years, after the Pope, in 1931, yielded to Fascist demands to dissolve some Catholic youth organizations and to restrict the activities of others. But that had been no more than a tactical retreat.

Catholic Action had reorganized and was expanding. To Fascist claims that its role was political, Pacelli had replied with a denial in September 1936. At the beginning of 1938 he found it necessary to remind Mussolini of that organization's patriotism and of Catholics' support for the Abyssinian war.[3] The argument did not impress the Duce, who regarded the independence of Catholic Action from the Party as a threat.[4]

Increasingly dissatisfied with his failure to bring the Church behind the regime, Mussolini inveighed against priests and Christianity, repeating his belief that the Italians were anticlerical.[5] By October 6, 1938, he was declaring, at the Fascist Grand Council, that "this Pope is a bane to the Catholic Church."[6] Ten days later, in the same formal setting, he referred to the Vatican as a "ghetto."[7] And on December 14, the Duce expressed, to Ciano, his hope that Pius XI would die soon.[8]

Yet even then, at the height of his hostility, Mussolini did not wish to provoke a crisis with the Holy See. Their "marriage" still had its uses, despite the chasm of belief that divided the two Romes. The one knew that the other represented a political religion incompatible with Catholicism. A list of Fascism's errors had been drawn up, chiefly based on the writings of the Duce, but had not been issued. As with Hitler's Germany, so with Mussolini's Italy, the Vatican stood poised between condemnation and conciliation. So it was that the two Romes, outwardly amicable and inwardly hostile, continued to play their "double game" with one other.

On March 16, 1938, Pacelli wrote to the Duce thanking him, in the name of Pius XI, for his interventions with Hitler to check the religious repression that had been intensified since the appearance of *Mit brennender Sorge*.[9] As weeks passed, and Italy moved closer to Germany, however, the "marriage of convenience" began to feel the strain. The imminent visit to Rome by the Führer, on May 3–9, was of concern to the Vatican. Pacelli noted that Pius XI was opposed to decorating religious buildings for the occasion on the grounds that ". . . the Holy See wonders whether so extreme an apotheosis of such a confessed enemy of the Catholic Church and the Christian religion is not contrary to the first article of the Concordat and to good sense." [10] So read the secretary of state's note on his audience with the Pope on March 24, 1938. Pacelli added the observation that Pius XI doubted Mussolini's sincerity.

Sincerity was not the most salient quality of any of the participants in this war of nerves. To the overtures of the Nazis for an alliance the Fascists responded evasively. Hesitating to commit themselves politically, they were prodigal in ceremonies, speeches, and banquets when Hitler visited Rome. He reveled in the pomp—especially the military parades in his honor, with Italian troops mimicking, in their new *passo romano*, the goose step. His hosts shuddered. Victor Emmanuel III ("King Nutcracker," in the Führer's quip) was, as head of state, obliged to offer hospitality at the Quirinal. There Hitler caused scandal by demanding a woman at one in the morning. That demand was not made for services that a self-respecting tyrant might have required, but because he could not sleep unless, with his own eyes, he had seen her remake his bed. [11] The royal household sneered but failed to spoil the Führer's visit. Impressed by the spectacle of one hundred submarines vanishing beneath the waves, then reappearing simultaneously, at Naples, Hitler was entranced by the "magic of Rome."

Less enchanting was the reaction from Pius XI. The Pope withdrew to his summer residence at Castel Gandolfo, ordering the Vatican museums to be closed, but announced, in a letter to the curial cardinals, that he was prepared to return and meet Hitler, providing that the Führer first announced publicly, in a communiqué to be agreed before any audience with Pius XI, that he would change his religious policy. [12]

Such were the hopes, tenuous but tenacious, that the Vatican continued to nourish. They explain why, in March 1938, Pacelli was still willing to "negotiate," via the Italian ambassador Pignatti, for a settlement with Goering, whose visit to the Vatican was "remembered with pleasure." [13] Moderation remained the watchword that concealed muddle on both sides. On May 2, 1938, for example, Ciano told Orsenigo that he admired the Church's restraint in not adopting "extreme sanctions," such as excommunication.

Unaware that he was contradicting the advice given by his father-

in-law three weeks earlier, Ciano probably realized that he was playing a card that, at least with the pliant nuncio at Berlin, was bound to
turn up trumps. Orsenigo responded that "the Holy See did not want
to be the one to sever the last thread" while speculating on a coolness
between Hitler and Mussolini that could be turned to the Vatican's
advantage.[14]

That advantage, for Pacelli, was difficult to calculate. Linked by
bonds of apparent trust and actual suspicion with the Italian government, the Holy See received different opinions from leading Fascists
about how it should act toward Hitler. Francesco Borgongini-Duca,
the nuncio to Italy, reporting to the secretary of state on June 15,
1938, relayed Ciano's desire to establish peace between Germany and
the Catholic Church. Would it not be the case, the Italian foreign
minister had suggested, to "give way a little . . . from the line of absolute intransigence?"

Mussolini's government would help, but it was impossible for it to
compromise the Rome–Berlin axis, Ciano added.[15] He did not divulge
that that axis was hardening into an alliance that would lead to the
racial laws that aligned Fascism with German anti-Semitism.[16] Pius
XI had been aware of that menacing possibility since 1937.[17] In that
year he had expostulated angrily that there was too much "waffling"
on the subject. Something, he had repeated on June 20 should be
done. What the Pope now did was to issue an instruction.

A copy of that instruction was transmitted to Pacelli, on April 13,
1938, by Ernesto Ruffini, the secretary of the Congregation for Seminars and Universities. During a vacation in its prefecture, the Pope
had assumed command. It is true that Pius XI attached great importance to education,[18] but that was not the only reason why he chose to
issue his instruction as head of this relatively minor congregation.

The Supreme Tribunal had pointed out the Pope's omissions, especially on the subject of racism (see Appendix III), in *Mit brennender Sorge* and had roused his impatience. To Pius XI, it appeared that
the modern inquisitors' hot air about condemnations was ill-suited to
the chill atmosphere in which the Vatican had to operate. Yet the

Holy Office—whose secretary, Cardinal Sbarretti, had written, almost certainly at papal prompting, to the Congregation for Seminars and Universities about the Nazis on November 23, 1937[19]—was the only department of the Curia that had studied racism. That problem, for Rome, was fundamental to the policy of the Führer, to whom the Pope wished to signal disapproval but whom he hesitated to attack directly. So it was that, shortly before Hitler's state visit, Pius XI decided to intervene, using the Holy Office's material but in a form more discreet than its draft condemnation. Explicit reference to Germany was to be avoided.[20]

Referring to his Christmas message of the previous year, which had dealt with the persecution of the Church in the Third Reich, the Pope deplored "most pernicious doctrines counterfeited with the false name of scholarship" that aimed to "subvert true religion," and ordered the rectors of Catholic universities and seminars to have their staffs refute eight points that he described as "ridiculous" (see Appendix IV).

That enterprise, as the Pope envisaged it, was to be interdisciplinary. Teachers of biology, history, philosophy, [Catholic] apologetics, law, and ethics were to join forces and attack eight "ridiculous dogmas." All but one of them derived from the Holy Office's lists of propositions to be damned[21]; and the sole exception referred to an issue discussed there in July 1936.[22] The list included little more than a sixth of the points assembled in Hürth's and Rabeneck's first draft (Appendix I) and less than a third of those contained in Hürth's and Chagnon's revision (Appendix II). Pius XI's list represented a selection of the Holy Office's material, placing emphasis on the ideology of blood and race, followed (at the end) by the absorption of the individual into the state. No mention was made of anti-Semitism, although, in the dossiers of the Holy Office, the Catholic doctrine of mankind's unity had been connected with a defense of the Jews.[23] At those issues, the Pope stopped short.

Germany remained at the forefront of Pius XI's thoughts; Italy did not yet provoke the same alarm. In February 1938, Mussolini had denied that his government was about to embark on an anti-Semitic policy. The *Manifesto of the Racist Scientists*, claiming that the population and civilization of Italy were of Aryan origin and that the Jews were excluded from the "pure Italian race," was not to appear until July 14 of that year; and, while there were Catholic anti-Semites, Italy lacked the same tradition of hostility to the Jews that the Nazis were able to exploit.[24] National Socialism was the instruction's main target. The letter was published, in the *Osservatore Romano*, on May 3, 1938—the first day of Hitler's state visit to Rome.

Pius XI made no secret of his displeasure at the Führer's presence. In a speech, printed in the same newspaper on May 5, he deplored the "sad fact" that, on the day of the Holy Cross, "the sign of a cross" [the swastika] had been displayed at Rome which was "not the cross of Christ." Neo-paganism was not the only issue. It is clear that, in 1938, the Pope was thinking afresh about the issues, including anti-Semitism, addressed by the Holy Office; and some have detected a change in Pius XI's attitudes during this last year of his life, when the Pope did speak out about the Jews.[25] The *Manifesto of the Racist Scientists* was later condemned as contrary to the faith; and Pius XI stated, in tears, to Belgian pilgrims on September 6, 1938: "Anti-Semitism is inadmissible. Spiritually, we are Semites." [26]

There is no denying that such a statement marked a new departure in the Vatican, both publicly and behind the scenes. Yet the *Osservatore Romano*, reporting the Pope's speech, omitted both those sentences and his other references to anti-Semitism.[27] What the Vatican's newspaper refrained from publishing was not intended to be diffused as a papal pronouncement. Understatement was the key to his strategy.

So too with the instruction, chiefly on the same subject of racism, that Pius XI issued in April in his capacity as Prefect of the Congregation of Seminars and Universities. The Pope meant the document as criticism, but at a lesser level of solemnity than a decree by the Holy Office. He did not speak, in his universal voice, as the "father of all" but rather addressed a letter to Catholic rectors. A call for intellectual mobilization against racism may have caused a stir within orthodox institutions,[28] yet it was intended, and received, more discreetly than a public condemnation.

Internal opposition increased the Pope's caution. Voices of alarm were raised within the establishment that he might browbeat them, but he did not dominate as completely as has been supposed. A note on the copy of the text of Pius XI's instruction was made in the Secretariat of State. It contains this observation: "... The opening of the circular ... does not seem happy. On the one hand, it gives the impression that the theses are reactions ... to the persecution; on the other it appears to trespass on the territory of the [Congregation] for E[xtraordinary] E[cclesiastical] A[ffairs]." [29]

Noteworthy, here, is the assumption that a papal document dealing with such matters infringed on the competence of the Vatican's "political" department of "foreign affairs." The observation, made by a collaborator of Pacelli's, would hardly have been imaginable had Pius XI chosen to issue a decree from the Holy Office. There his authority, in matters of doctrine and morals, was firm. In his role as prefect of the Congregation for Seminars and Universities, it appeared less unassailable.

The components of the curial machinery were ill-coordinated. The Pope used the Vatican's departments as he pleased. Papal interventions by one might be regarded by members of others as trespassing on their territory because only Pius XI, flanked by Pacelli, knew the lay of the land and how its borders might be maintained or changed. No major change was marked by the instruction of April 1938. Like the papal encyclical of the previous year, it was restrained in form and limited in substance. Having withdrawn National Socialism from the Holy Office in 1937, the Pope continued on the course initiated by *Mit brennender Sorge,* as his secretary of state had recommended. [30]

Pius XI did not become tougher in the last year of his life. He stuck fast to his previous policy: a compromise between the urge to speak out and the desire to preserve the Concordat. That compromise, imperfectly understood within the Vatican, left its bureaucracy at cross-purposes. The strategy of confrontation shelved for more than a year, it was understandable that an official in the Secretariat of State regarded as "unhappy" anything that recalled it. The diplomats were nervous. Reactions from Germany confirmed, in the violence of their polemic, that their concern was not unfounded. [31]

• • •

In this context—less of newfound courage than of old doubts and hesitancies—occurred one of the most curious episodes from the end of Pius XI's pontificate. On June 22, 1938, at Castel Gandolfo, the Pope received in audience the American Jesuit John La Farge, an expert on racism, and ordered him to prepare an encyclical on that subject, paying particular attention to the problem of anti-Semitism.[32] La Farge collaborated in Paris with German Jesuits Gustav Gundlach and Heinrich Bacht, assisted by a French member of the order, Gustave Desbuquois, between July and September 1938. Delivered to the Jesuit general Ledóchowski, whom Gundlach suspected of delaying their transmission to the Pope, the drafts reached the Vatican shortly before Pius XI's death on February 10, 1939, but were not published until decades later.

Here, it has been argued, is evidence that the Pope was preparing to strike out with new firmness. We now know, however, that Pius XI was returning to an issue that had been first shelved, then dealt with selectively, by himself. This time circumventing the Holy Office, he summoned the Jesuits. Members of that papal "secret service" were perhaps more reliable, and certainly less irritating, than modern inquisitors.

By commissioning from the Jesuits drafts of this encyclical, Pius XI was by no means committing himself to publish it. In the light of the Fascists' anti-Semitic measures, he was addressing the same problems that had been studied at Rome in the mid-1930s—possibly, in 1938, with an uneasy conscience. We cannot know whether, had he lived, the Pope might have made bold to issue a condemnation that might have meant conflict not only with Germany but also between the two Romes. Yet there are strong grounds for doubt. The "storms" had not passed; the clouds were darkening. Anti-Semitism was one of a complex of problems posed both by National Socialism and by Fascist totalitarianism, on which Pius XI had compelling reasons for forthrightness as early as 1936—and on which he had held back until his death on February 10, 1939.

Holding back had become a trait of Vatican policy long before Pius XII became Pope on March 2, 1939. This helps us to understand his notorious silences. They are attested from the outset of his reign. If his secretariat noted, on March 5–6, that, in a discussion with the German cardinals held shortly after his election, the question of an encyclical on racism and nationalism might have been broached,[33] it was consistent with the example set by his predecessor that Pius XII brushed it aside. Mute on the subject of the violence against Jews during the *Reichskristallnacht* of November 9–10, 1938, about which it was informed,[34] the Vatican considered breaking off diplomatic relations with Nazi Germany but again chose not to take such a step. The reason why was stated clearly by Pius XII in his second meeting with the German cardinals on March 9, 1939: "If the government breaks off relations, good—but it would not be clever if the break comes from our side."[35]

"Cleverness," in this sense, had been defined by the Pope during the first audience on March 6. "Cleverness" meant "doing one's best" to improve relations. Should "war" between the Holy See and the National Socialists come, then "we will defend ourselves. But the world should see that we have done everything to live in peace with Germany."[36] The alternative was an encyclical. That, Pacelli objected, would require "much time."[37]

What he did not say was that drafts of condemnation had been prepared, three years earlier, under his predecessor. If Pius XI had neither mentioned nor published them, nor would Pius XII. The scene in the apostolic palace of March 1939 matched, in its heavy silences, that of January 1937. The strategy of Eugenio Pacelli was formed before he mounted the throne of St. Peter.

On June 11, 1940, the French cardinal Eugène Tisserand—one of the scholars whom Pius XI had elevated to the Sacred College and who had voted against Pacelli at the conclave of the previous year—wrote to Cardinal Emmanuel Suhard of Paris:

> I have asked the Holy Father insistently, since the beginning of December [1939], to issue an encyclical on the duty of the individual to obey the dictates of his conscience, because this is a vital point of Christianity . . . I fear that history will have grounds to reproach the Holy See for a policy that suited its own ends and not much more. This is extremely sad, especially when one has lived under Pius XI.[38]

Despite Tisserand's denials that he meant to criticize Pius XII,[39] this letter is often quoted to support a contrast between that "timid and indecisive" Pope and his "intrepid" predecessor. That contrast is depicted, for some, by their coats of arms: Pius XI's emblazoned with a valiant eagle, Pius XII's with the dove of peace. Neither bird will bear the weight of meaning attributable to it in reality. More accurate, perhaps, as a symbol for the strategy of both popes would be an ostrich with its head in the sand.

On that sand should be inscribed the word "concordat," which Pius XII defended adamantly during and after the Second World War. That, for him, remained the linchpin of political reality—even when the brutal facts of Nazi rule clashed with the legal and diplomatic subtleties of his vision. Pius XII was sustained in his faith in the Concordat by his experience with Pius XI. From that it does not follow that either of them can be described as "Hitler's Pope." They knew, on doctrinal and moral grounds, that National Socialism was incompatible with, and opposed to, Christianity. If each of them flinched from an outright condemnation of the Nazis, that was because they wished to avoid (in Pacelli's expression) a "war" between them and the Church.

Neutrality or, as he preferred to call it, impartiality was one of Pius XII's objectives. Yet he was not consistent on this point. A pope who acted as an intermediary between the British government and German conspirators against Hitler in 1939–40[40] might claim to be above taking sides but, secretly, he ran a risk that is out of keeping with his public personality. Secrecy, for him, was fundamental. Publicly cautious to the point of timidity, Pius XII ventured further only behind the scenes. And then he acted alone, without consulting his secretary of state.

In this episode, Pacelli revealed both a degree of courage and its limits. He thought in terms of his responsibilities to an institution that he had served devotedly as nuncio and secretary of state and for which, as pope, he would have to answer to God; and he was unprepared to launch an open offensive. More than caution lay behind this policy. In all the high offices he held, Pius XII regarded himself as a realist. Realism, for him, excluded flights of fancy. Calculating his options, he chose those that exposed him least. His entire career, before he became pope, is distinguished by its lack of evident mistakes. They had been avoided by never being seen to strike out on his own; and none of his ideas, as expressed in the documents dealing with Germany produced in the course of nine years' "apprenticeship" to become Pius XI's successor, reveals the slightest trace of originality or independence.

Neither independence nor originality was required from the man groomed, by the imperious but indecisive Achille Ratti, to become the next head of the Church. A meticulous executor of orders, Eugenio Pacelli valued predictability more highly than imagination. If he had a taste for bold orators, like Cicero and Bossuet, he imitated only the more conventional of their classic qualities in his own pedestrian prose. As with the style, so with the man. Precedents set his standards of conduct, and the precedents that Pius XII learned from Pius XI, on the issues posed by National Socialism were opportunism and restraint.

Those lessons were all the more formative because they were imparted by a personality who seemed to lack Pacelli's self-control. Impulsive and irascible, Pius XI was capable of outbursts and tears. Nonetheless he, the pope of overt emotions that his successor refrained from displaying, was not willing to take the steps which, in 1937, might have required the Church to weather worse "storms." Faced with the choice between a condemnation that, in the final form prepared in the Holy Office's "grand design," would have brought Rome into conflict not only with the Nazis and the Communists but also with the Italian Fascists, Pius XI backed down.

That decision sums up the Vatican's sense of wisdom. If it was unwise to damn the "heresies of the age" together in March 1937, it became more so when the storms waxed more tempestuous later. The notorious silences of Pius XII were a consistent development from Pius XI's no less notable reticence.

The notion of consistency, here, does not imply that the two popes had no choice. They did, but decided against exercising it to declare "war" on the Nazis and the Fascists. Neither Pius XI nor Pius XII was a coward, and both believed that they were displaying wisdom. That is the term which raises difficulties, trenchantly formulated by the British historian Owen Chadwick: "There may be moments . . . when wisdom is not the first quality on demand, when what a moral situation needs is an explosion and let wisdom be damned." [41]

The first quarter of 1937 was one of those moments. An "explosion," in the form of a full and open condemnation of all that Rome considered wrong, might have hindered Mussolini's anti-Semitic measures and admonished Roman Catholics that the policies and practices of Hitler's regime were incompatible with the teaching of the Church. That Church did not hesitate to damn (twice, in two years) atheistic Communism in forthright terms. Why then did it hold back on the Nazis and the Fascists? Not only because they were regarded, by Rome, as allies against the "Bolsheviks," but also because the Vatican had signed concordats with Germany and Italy.

On that "legal basis," so fragile yet so cherished, the leadership of the Church continued to pin its hopes against hope. The alternative, a condemnation, had been provided by the Holy Office at the end of 1936. Yet Pius XI and Pius XII, considering the effects of the "explosion" that it would be bound to produce, were advised that the German people, backing Hitler, would not resist his regime; and, as they looked to the Catholic hierarchy in the Third Reich, they found scant support for boldness.

Decent, honorable patriots, with a profound reverence for authority, few of the German bishops had the stuff of heroes. They protested and they preached, while assuring the Führer of their loyalty; and if they nurtured illusions, they were less dim or deluded than papal nuncio Orsenigo. Such were the collaborators on whom Pius XI and Pacelli had to rely. And the Vatican, which shared the Germans' hesitations, believed that, in the case of an "explosion," its first victims might be members of the episcopate in the Third Reich still seeking to shelter beneath the inadequate protection of the Concordat that Rome had signed.

Rome had signed but was not satisfied with the consequences, which limited its options more severely than had been foreseen. A desire to assert greater freedom is detectable: an uneasy edging at barriers imposed by prudence. Pius XI, in 1938, felt the need to return to the condemnation of racism from which he had retreated. Why the

Pope was dissatisfied with his abandonment of this part of the Holy Office's "grand design" is not difficult to see. His decision may have been in keeping with the legal and political equilibrium that he and Pacelli wished to maintain, but it was more difficult to square with Pius XI's stated principles, especially his praise of martyrdom.

Invitations to Heroism was the title given to three volumes of the Pope's collected addresses on that subject published, not long after his death, in 1941.[42] Filled with stirring rhetoric about Christians' duty to offer up, in the name of the faith, their blood, and their lives, these books present an invitation that their author declined. It was during Pacelli's reign that *Invitations to Heroism* appeared—despite the gap that yawned, in the pontificate of Pius XI, between reality and rhetoric.

The heroic and authoritarian rhetoric favored by the papacy asserted an ideal at variance with the real conditions of its existence. One of those realities, seldom appreciated, was lack of firmness in its rule over the Church. Vacillating in its own policy toward the Third Reich and rather hindered than helped by its feeble representative at Berlin, Rome consulted with a German hierarchy that often seemed unsure of its own mind. In the face of hesitancy on the part of its interlocutors, the Vatican chose to hide its hand, reluctant to compel them to a course that an official had at Rome launched, then attempted to undermine. Inside and outside the curial establishment, its apparent masters exercised imperfect control.

Centralization was the theory, but dispersion the practice. Dispersed in various departments, authority had only a nominal focus. The Pope, seconded by his secretary of state, appeared to rule supreme. Yet, in fact, he merely reigned over an intricate structure of ill-coordinated departments whose members had, or could claim with relative impunity, opportunities for their own initiatives. The "monolithic Vatican" is little more than a myth; and the precariousness of papal governance is illustrated by the case of Alois Hudal.

The "court theologian of the Party," after publishing *The Foundations of National Socialism*, was not dismissed by Rome. Nor was his book indexed, although it had attempted to subvert a policy being developed by the Holy Office. Remaining in his post of consultant, Hudal did not behave as if he had been disavowed. Thick-skinned, obtuse, and arrogant as ever, he went on without realizing that he had been marginalized. The subtlety of the secretary of state was lost on the rector of the Anima. And Hudal, to the irritation of his superiors, continued to proffer them unwanted advice.

On November 2, 1938, for example, he addressed a long memorandum to Pius XI on the situation of the Church in Austria after the Anschluss.[43] The problem, as Hudal saw it, lay in the ecclesiastical leadership. Too old, too slow, too feeble, the bishops needed "new methods and a new Führer." [44] The nuncio at Berlin was ineffective and remote. Hostility to Rome was widespread, under the influence of the "radical wing" of the Nazis, which was portraying Christianity as senile. The Concordat had been written off as a dead letter. Hudal argued that what Austria required was a papal legate who should be a native Austrian (no foreigner) and an archbishop as coadjutor, with the right of succession, to Cardinal Innitzer of Vienna. "A strong personality is needed," announced Hudal; "only an entirely independent man could risk a struggle today." [45]

Plainly referring to himself, he was not content with one memorandum; another followed two days later.[46] The "combative attitude" of the German bishops was mistaken.[47] The Nazi "radicals," such as Goebbels and Rosenberg, were in the ascendant; and the Führer, "as I know from the immediate circle of his friends," was filled with hatred toward the Vatican because the Pope had closed its museums when Hitler visited Rome.[48]

All this was dangerous for Catholicism. The Church had to find an accommodation with the "historical phenomenon" of National Socialism "which will last for a long time." [49] The solution was to survive, avoiding at all costs a struggle against Fascism, which would merely strengthen the hand of Rome's enemies in Germany. A modus vivendi was the answer, followed by a new but more modest concordat. There was no point in combating Hitler, who was "rightly" surrounded "with the aura of German history's national hero." [50]

Hudal then outlined a "program" for that modus vivendi.[51] It amounted to a capitulation—specifying, for instance, that priests who overstepped the limits of their religious functions should be prosecuted not only by the lay but also by the ecclesiastical authorities. That was what Hudal meant, in October 1938, by changing the "purely negative and aggressive policy of the Church." When his views were submitted to the judgment of Cardinal Schulte of Cologne and Bishop Bornewasser of Trier (both, then, at Rome), they were dismissed as the delusions of one who was wholly out of touch.[52]

Sustained in his dreams of influence only by contacts with German diplomats, Hudal had already severed most of his links with reality. That, however, did not prevent others from taking his fantasies half-seriously. On March 3, 1943, Goebbels noted in his diary that the Pope, intending to negotiate with the Nazis, was about to send "one of his intimate cardinals incognito to Germany."[53] That "cardinal" was titular bishop Hudal, whose pretensions but not whose rank had reached Goebbels's ears; and the reference was to yet another attempt to make peace between Rome and Germany undertaken, on no authority but his own, by the rector of the Anima, together with an officer of the SS.[54]

Held at arm's length by the Vatican,[55] Hudal was only consulted in 1943, when the links that he cultivated with the German high command in occupied Rome could be exploited. An outsider for the central authorities of the Church, he had drawn closer to the generals leading the forces of the fatherland. One of the two Romes crumbled when Mussolini was voted out of the office on July 24, 1943; and, from September 11, martial law was imposed on the Eternal City by its occupiers. There, amid an atmosphere of tension in which telephones were tapped and strikers might be shot, Hudal thrived. At last he might act as a mediator and, on October 16, 1943, his ambition was briefly achieved.

The Pope's nephew, Prince Carlo Pacelli, had him relay a message to General Reiner Stahel, military governor of Rome, that the deportation of Jews from the Holy City had to be stopped, if a protest from Pius XII was to be avoided.[56] As a channel of communication with the Nazis, Hudal had his uses but, limited to that episode, they had to be reinvented after the war, when he became active in the Austrian section of the Pontifical Commission for Prisoners and Refugees. There he helped a number of war criminals, including Adolf

Eichmann, to flee Europe to South America, equipped with false documents.[57]

This has been taken as proof that Pius XII wished to assist ex-Nazis by allowing Hudal to "be in touch" with them.[58] The Pope allowed nothing of the kind. Hudal had no further dealings with him; and efforts to ingratiate himself with the papal secretary, Father Robert Leiber, were rebuffed. Left to his own devices at the Anima, before being removed, under Allied pressure, in 1952, the "brown bishop" spent his old age composing embittered memoirs and providing Rolf Hochhuth with material for *The Deputy*, so formative of Pius XII's negative image.[59]

From *The Deputy* to *Hitler's Pope*, the path was direct. It had been smoothed by the "insider" knowledge of Alois Hudal, whose motive was revenge. Having regarded himself as an alternative, or rival, to Pacelli—that model of curial success—the failed "court-theologian of the Party" could not come to terms with a fate that consigned one of them to the throne of St. Peter and the other to exile at Grottaferrata. Rancor substituted for reality, Hudal assigned to Pius XII qualities that were his own: ambition, ruthlessness, and deviousness behind the scenes.

Incapable of learning from his experience, the "brown bishop" was then left alone with the only cause that gave him comfort. Comfort was found, by Hudal, in recounting his role as intercessor on behalf of Nazis in flight from their "persecutors." In a passage of his memoirs that hovers between pathos and bathos,[60] he told the tale of the death, in his arms, of Otto Gustav von Wächter, former officer of the SS, Nazi vice-governor of Poland, and participant in the murder of Dolfuss. Before expiring in the Roman hospital of Santo Spirito on July 14, 1949, Wächter expressed his regret that the Party had failed to reach an understanding with the Catholic Church. The dying convert to Hudal's cause lent it enduring legitimacy, in his own eyes. As its stalwart defender to the last, this duplicitous maverick wished to be remembered.

A maverick might be tolerated in the Vatican ruled by the hesitant hands of Pius XI and Pius XII. Scandal, like conflict, was to be avoided. Both alarmed the highest authorities of the Church. They sidestepped confrontation; and the cumbrous machinery of the Curia was ill-equipped to regulate the different and, at times, incompatible strategies developed by members of its separate departments.

Separation or division between components of the Roman bureaucracy was a tactic used to maintain papal primacy. Pius XI employed that tactic when he withdrew from the Holy Office the issues posed by National Socialism and dealt with them in the Congregation for Seminars and Universities and in private consultation with the Jesuits. Such moves did not amount to a grand strategy. The only grand strategy toward the Nazis that Rome possessed was that of the Holy Office.

When that strategy was rejected, or radically modified, the Vatican did not have another to put in its place. It clung to the Concordat because the order that it understood was that of law and tradition. Faced with those revolutionary criminals, Hitler and Mussolini, Rome huffed and puffed. It protested and appealed to rules that the dictators flouted, unless they served their political purposes. Within the limits set by politics, the leadership of the Church spoke out. But uncertainty prevailed, and the planned condemnation was suppressed.

Suppression meant safety. The German threat had to be weighed against Italian perils, and both played off against the "Bolshevik" menace. The stakes were high in this "double game," and neither Pius XI nor Pius XII was a gambler. So it was that they chose, not once but repeatedly, to hide their hands. Despite the malice with which Mussolini attempted to stack the Vatican's pack, the excommunication of Hitler—like much else—was never on the cards.

Appendix 1

*The Holy Office's First Proposed Condemnation
of National Socialism (1935)*

*Elenchus Propositionum de Nationalismo,
Stirpis cultu, Totalismo*

I. DE NATIONALISMO
Nationalismus idololatricus

1. Natio vel status, quamquam nomine numinis non appellatur, est
    verum numen, cui ideo praeter civilem etiam religiosus cultus de-
    betur.

    Status autem ipse est deus, prout Deus in unaquaque natione
    formam et indolem nationi propriam assumit et in ea sese mani-
    festat.

2. Numina nationalia, religiosa mysteria ac ritus, festa religioso-
    nationalia, quae proavi pagani, ut numen nationis colerent, olim
    habebant, legitimo iure redintegrantur tamquam huius numinis
    symbola religiosi cultus, adaptanda quidem ad hodiernum cogi-
    tandi sentiendique modum.

    Hic religiosus patriae cultus cultui christiano substitui aut
    saltem ei aequiparari et una cum eo exerceri potest.

    Hic cultus nihil habet neopaganismi aut cuiusdam idolola-

SOURCE: ACDF, R.V. 1934, 29; Prot. 3373/34, vol. 1, fasc. 3 b (01. Mai 1935), 16–26

Appendix 1

The Holy Office's First Proposed Condemnation
of National Socialism (1935)

List of Propositions [to be Condemned]
on Nationalism, Racism, Totalitarianism

I. ON NATIONALISM
Idolatrous Nationalism

1. The nation or state, although it is not called divine, is a true divinity, to which therefore not only civil respect is due but even religious worship.

    Moreover the state is a god, just as God in each nation takes on the form and character suited to that nation and manifests Himself in it.

2. National divinities, religious mysteries and rites, religious-national festivals that pagan ancestors once held to worship the divinity of the nation are to be reestablished by due process of law, just as the symbols of this divinity are to be objects of religious worship, adapted to modern forms of thought and feeling.

    This religious cult of the fatherland is to be substituted for the Christian religion or at least made equivalent to it and may be practiced together with it.

    This cult has nothing in common with neo-paganism or any

SOURCE: ACDF, R.V. 1934, 29; Prot. 3373/34, vol. 1, fasc. 3 b (01. Mai 1935)

triae nationalis, sed est spontanea manifestatio spiritus nationalis
sinceri, qui naturali necessitate in cultum religiosum prorumpit.

Nationalismus immoderatus

3. Natio statusque, contra atque religio christiana docet, non subest
   uni vero Deo, omnipotenti creatori caeli et terrae, neque eius legibus, neque ullo modo tenetur ad Deum colendum; sed ipsa sibi
   est suprema lex, ultimus atque unicus finis.

   Est igitur Natio plenissimo sensu sui iuris, omni ex parte in-
   dependentis atque illimitati.

Suprema norma generalis

4. Civitas natioque ad nihil omnino attendere debet nisi ad se ipsam,
   propriam gloriam atque omnimodam prosperitatem sine ullo re-
   spectu ad aliquod ius privatorum aut ad ius vigens inter gentes.

Norma oeconomica

5. Axioma illimitatae "curae et amoris sui" maxime valet et usui
   esse debet in re oeconomica commu, quam status agens cum aliis
   statibus tractare nequit secundum sic dictas leges iustitiae, aequi-
   tatis et caritatis, quae a vera et dira rerum condicione sunt alienis-
   simae.

Expansionismus

6. Propria gloria et potestas est sufficiens ratio, cur natio proclamet
   et sequatur principium "expansionismi", aliasque nationes
   earumque territorium sive ex parte sive ex toto sibi subiciat, ar-
   reptis etiam armis et vi.

Militarismus

7. Gloria, quae ex victoria armis obtenta maior censetur, est etiam
   sufficiens ratio, cur status, quando conflictus inter nationes oritur,
   provocet ad bellum et arma, spreta pacifica compositione, qua
   conflictus solvi et proprio iuri satisfieri potest.

form of national idolatry. It is a spontaneous manifestation of sincere national feeling that, impelled by nature, finds expression in religious worship.

Exaggerated Nationalism

3. The nation and the state, contrary to Christianity's teaching, are not subject to the one true God, the omnipotent creator of heaven and earth, nor to His laws, nor are they in any manner required to worship God. The nation is the supreme law for itself, the final and sole end.

   That is why the nation is, in the fullest sense, a law unto itself, independent and unlimited in every respect.

The Supreme General Standard

4. The state and nation should pay no attention to anything except itself, its own glory, and general well-being, with no reference to any private or international law.

Economic Practice

5. The rule of unlimited "love and concern for oneself" is of the utmost validity and should be applied in economic affairs that the state conducts with other states, in which it cannot act according to the so-called laws of justice, fairness, and charity, which are wholly alien to the true and terrible reality.

Expansionism

6. Its own glory and power are sufficient reasons for the nation to proclaim and follow the principles of "expansionism" and to subject other nations and their territory to itself in whole or in part with armed force.

Militarism

7. The glory obtained by victory in armed struggle is considered greater, and is indeed sufficient reason for the state, when a conflict arises between nations, to provoke wars and armed conflicts, in contempt of peaceful negotiations capable of resolving the conflict and satisfying its own claims.

Fanatismus nationalis

8. Non solum sincerus atque flagrans patriae ac propriae nationis amor, sed praeterea fanatismus nationalis est promovendus, qui omnes alias nationes contemnens infra se ducat, neque aliam habeat sentiendi agendique mensuram nisi propriae nationis gloriam et super alias nationes dominatum.

II. DE STIRPIS CULTU
Natura et dignitas humana

9. Natura humana non est essentialiter eadem in omnibus hominibus; sed genus humanum, quod nunc terram inhabitat, constituitur stirpibus (ital. *razza,* gall. *races,* german. *Rassen*) tantopere inter se differentibus, ut earum infima magis distet a stirpe suprema, quam distet a suprema brutorum specie quae proxime ad hominem accedit.

10. Genus humanum, quod constat stirpibus tantopere inter se differentibus, non est origine unum, descendens a protoparentibus numero iisdem.

11. Genus humanum animalia bruta non superat inprimis anima spirituali et immortali, sed generositate sanguinis innataque indole stirpis, quod est ultimum fundamentum ac fons omnis ingenii et virtutis.

Neque elevatio hominis in ordinem supernaturalem quidquam probat contra hanc sanguinis et stirpis absolutam praevalentiam neque eam ullo modo immutat.

Religio

12. Religio neque ex rei natura neque ex lege divina positiva est una, eaque essentialiter eadem pro omnibus hominibus, sed indole sanguinis et stirpis recte et iuste efformantur religiones stirpeae, singulae pro singulis stirpibus, quae non in solis accidentalibus inter se et a religione christiana discrepent.

13. Religio stirpea religioni christianae substitui debet.

14. Religiosa dogmata stirpis—idest ideae religiosae quae cum indole stirpis inseparabiliter iunguntur—mysteria cultus totusque externus cultus religiosus stirpi proprius, quantumvis a religione christiana differant, pro veris et honestis habenda sunt. Congru-

National Fanaticism

8. Not only a sincere and ardent love of the fatherland and one's own nation but, in addition, a national fanaticism are to be encouraged in contempt for all other nations that it considers inferior to itself, nor is there to be any standard of thought and action except the glory of one's own nation and its dominion over others.

II. ON RACISM

Human Nature and Dignity

9. Human nature is not essentially the same in all people, but mankind, which now inhabits the earth, is composed of races (Italian *razza*, French *races*, German *Rassen*) so different from one another that the lowest of them is even further from the highest race than it is from the highest kind of animal that most closely approximates to man.

10. Mankind, which consists of races so different from one another, is not one in origin or descent from the same common ancestors.

11. Mankind is not superior to brute beasts primarily through its spiritual and immortal soul but by nobility of blood and its inborn racial character, which is the final basis and source of all intelligence and virtue.

    Nor does the elevation of man into a supernatural order constitute any proof against the absolute preeminence of blood and race, nor does it alter it in any way.

Religion

12. Neither by its nature nor by any positive divine law is religion one and essentially the same for everyone, but racial religions are with absolute correctness formed from the character of blood and race, one for each race; and they do not differ from one another and from the Christian religion in mere matters of chance.

13. The religion of race should replace the Christian religion.

14. The religious dogmas of race—i.e.: the religious ideas that are inseparably combined with the character of the race—the cultic mysteries, and the entire outward forms of religious worship suited to the race are to be considered true and respectable, although they are different from the Christian religion. For they

unt enim cum suprema honestatis norma, quae est indoles et instinctus Stirpis.

15. Fideles religioni stirpeae adhaerere aut exterius saltem eius
consociationibus nomen dare possunt, cohibito, si ipsis necessar-
ium videtur, assensu interno in religiosas ideas et ritus quos falsos
putant.

   Neque offendit contra religionem christianam fideles active
partem habere in religionis stirpeae ritibus, festis et conventibus
religiosis.

   Passiva vero assistentia eis non solum semper est licita, sed
positive expedit, ut ad sincerum suum stirpis amorem et ad gen-
uinum eius spiritum manifestandum et fovendum cultui stirpeo
passive assistant.

16. Religio christiana saltem adaptari debet indoli stirpis ea ratione,
ut in religione christiana quaedam eliminentur, alia addantur,
alia immutentur, etiam quod ad sic dicta substantialia religionis
christianae.

   Falso asseritur religionem christianam—quod attinet ad res
fidei et morum, ad substantiam cultus, ad substantiam regiminis
interni et externi—constituere aliquod unum indivisibile et im-
mutabile, absoluto valore praeditum, ac supremae legi stirpis et
sanguinis subtractum.

Instinctus stirpis

17. Ordo iuris, ordo oeconomicus necnon ordo totius vitae socialis
regulam ultimam et supremam non habent; universalia principia
[non] ex rerum natura aut ex revelatione divina petita et lumine
rationis aut fidei certo cognita, sed instinctu stirpis.

   Instinctus stirpis perfecte evolutus falli aut fallere non potest
habetque valorem absolutum et est iuris inveniendi fons omni exceptione et probatione maior.

   Instinctum stirpis examinare principiis universalibus aut ver-
itatibus revelatis, est invertere ordinem rectum. Nam e contra:
principia universalia et veritates revelatae examinari et diiudicari
debent instinctu stirpis.

correspond to that supreme standard of respectability that is the character and instinct of the race.

15. Believers in the religion of race may adhere to it or, at least, subscribe to its organizations in outward forms, if it seems necessary to them when their inner assent to religious ideas and rituals that they consider false is not forthcoming.

    Nor is it an offense against the Christian religion if one of the faithful takes an active part in the rites of race, in its festivals and religious gatherings.

    Passive participation is not only always allowed but a positive advantage in encouraging sincere love of the race and revealing and fostering its true spirit.

16. The Christian religion should, at the very least, be adapted to the character of the race in such a way that some elements of the Christian religion are eliminated and others added or altered, including the so-called points of substance in the Christian religion.

    It is wrong to assert that the Christian religion—as far as matters of faith and morality, the core of worship, and the substance of internal and external control are concerned—amounts to a single indivisible and unchangeable entity, endowed with absolute value and dispensed from the supreme law of race and blood.

The Instinct of Race

17. Legal and economic organization and the regulation of all social life have no final and supreme standard; universal principles are not to be sought from nature or divine revelation and are certainly not understood by the light of reason or of faith, but by the instinct of race.

    A perfectly developed instinct of race is incapable of being deceived or deceiving, possesses absolute value, and provides a source for formulating law that is above any exception or test.

    To examine the instinct of race according to universal principles or revealed truths is to invert the correct way of proceeding. On the contrary: universal principles and revealed truths should be examined and assessed according to the instinct of race.

Stirps: supremum bonum

18. Bonum stirpis hac in terra nullo alio bono vincitur; sed ipsum omnia alia bona vincit semper et in omnibus.

Conservatio et propagatio stirpis

19. Quaelibet sanguinis permixtio cum stirpe aliena eaque deteriore, inprimis vero permixtio stirpis ariae cum stirpe semitica, iam ratione solius permixtionis est scelus maxime nefarium contra naturam et gravem culpam in conscientia denotat.

20. Omnes, de quibus timeri potest ne proles manca ex eis oriatur, licet caeteroquin sint matrimonii capaces, a fertili matrimonio ineundo aut utendo arceri et, etiam inviti, sterilizari possunt; proles vero ex huiusmodi parentibus iam concepta removeri potest directa abortus procuratione.

    Hi agendi modi non solum contra Dei et naturae legem non offendunt, sed eidem maxime conformes sunt.

21. Bonum stirpis praevalet etiam prae bono matrimonii, intra cuius limites honestus facultatis generativae usus non est coartatus; sed qui ex legibus biologicis praevidentur prolem sanam et stirpeam generaturi prolem etiam extra matrimonium recte et licite generant.

22. Qui sanitate plena necnon perfecta indole stirpis gaudent statum matrimonialem anteponere debent statui virginitatis, etsi ex amore virtutis assumpto. Quod si nihilominus statum virginitatis assumunt, directe offendunt contra naturae ordinem et intentionem, atque inhonestum quid agunt.

23. Auctoritas publica omnes qui, etsi propter Deum, a matrimonio abstinent iusto iure facit cives iuris minoris eisque apte et licite specialia onera atque tributa in favorem eorum imponit qui prolem generando stirpi inserviunt.

The Race: Supreme Good

18. The good of the race, on this earth, is surpassed by no other good but surpasses all other goods always and in every respect.

Preservation and Propagation of the Race

19. Any mixture of blood with a foreign and inferior race, in particular a mixture of the Arian with the Semitic race, is, by reason of that mixture alone, a most heinous crime against nature and marks a grave fault in the conscience.

20. All people about whom there are grounds to fear that they may produce imperfect offspring may be prevented from embarking on or conducting a marriage that could be fertile, although they are otherwise capable of marrying; and they may be sterilized, even against their will. Children conceived by parents of this kind may be removed by the direct intervention of an abortion.

    These practices are not only no offense against divine and natural law but wholly in keeping with it.

21. The interest of the race takes precedence over even the right to marriage. Within these limits there is no restriction on the honorable faculty of procreation; but those whom biological laws foresee will produce healthy offspring for the race are entirely within their rights if they have children outside marriage.

22. Those fortunate to enjoy full health and a perfect racial character should prefer the state of marriage to that of virginity, even if they have chosen it from love of virtue. Should they nonetheless decide to be virgins, they offend directly against the order and intentions of nature, and commit a dishonorable act.

23. The state authorities rightly demote those who abstain from marriage, even if it is for the sake of God, to second-class citizens and, by measures that are appropriate and justified, impose on them special burdens of taxation to the advantage of those who serve the race by producing children.

Educatio iuventutis

24. Primarius finis et suprema regula educationis est evolutio et cultus innatae indolis stirpis; ideo in educatione primum locum tenere debet educatio et efformatio corporis, quia in corpore et sanguine indoles stirpis recondita est.

    Educatione nihil rationabiliter intendi nihilque obtineri potest, nisi quod in sanguine et indole stirpis habetur. Neque educatio religiosa et gratia supernaturalis hunc naturae limitem in educanda iuventute excedere valet.

25. Educandi primum at principale ius est penes eum penes quem est primum et principale ius providendi stirpi, idest penes Rempublicam, non vero penes Ecclesiam nec penes parentes.

26. Iuventus educanda non inprimis imbui debet spiritu religioso, amore et timore Dei, sed spiritu et amore stirpis, et quidem ita ut nihil iam hac in terra magis aestimet atque curet quam stirpem et statum, indoli stirpis superstructum.

Ius absolutum ad statum stirpeum

27. Unitas stirpis et sanguinis tribuit absolutum et illimitatum ius adunandi omnes, qui vinculo eiusdem sanguinis et stirpis inter se uniuntur, in unam societatem politicam seu unum statum stirpeo-nationalem; et hoc quidem infringendo quodlibet aliud ius, etsi titulo vel maxime legitimo quaesitum.

28. Adunatio in unam societatem politicam etiam armis et bello peragi potest. Est enim ius sanguinis fortius quolibet alio iure; neque in praesenti rerum condicione coadunatio politica sine vi et armis obtineri potest.

Finis Reipublicae stirpeae

29. Respublica stirpeo-nationalis non habet alium finem aliamve regulam supremam agendi atque bonum stirpis, idest: stirpem conservare, evolvere atque ad apicem perfectionis perducere.

The Education of Youth

24. The chief end and supreme principle of education is the development and promotion of the innate racial character; that is why physical training ought to play the primary role in education, for the character of the race is secreted in the body and in the blood.

    Nothing can be reasonably aimed at by education, and nothing can be obtained, except what is contained in the blood and character of the race. Nor can religious education and supernatural grace overcome this natural limit in the upbringing of young people.

25. The first and chief right to educate belongs to that institution which has the first and chief right to make provision for the race, i.e.: the state, neither to the Church nor the parents.

26. As to the education of young people, they should not, in the first place, be imbued with religious sentiments or with love and fear of God but with a feeling of affection for the race, so that they regard nothing on this earth with more respect than the race and the state built on the basis of racial character.

Absolute Rights of the Racial State

27. The unity of the race and the blood attributes an absolute and unlimited right to unite everyone who is linked by the bond of the same race and blood into a single political society or a single racial-national state; and it may do so by infringing any other law, however legitimately it has been enacted.

28. Unification into one political society may be carried out by armed struggle. The law of blood is more powerful than any other law, and in the present political situation, unification cannot be obtained except by force of arms.

The Aim of the Racial State

29. The racist-nationalist state has no other aim or guiding principle than the good of the race, i.e.: to preserve the race, develop it, and lead it to the heights of perfection.

Ordo praevalentiae inter stirpes

30. Ex institutione naturae habetur inter stirpes ordo quidam praevalentiae, qui per ipsam naturam exsecutioni mandatur et servatur: sic dicta "pugna selectiva", quae inter viventia viget, atque "vi fortiore", qua una stirps prae alia pollet.

Ipse et solus hac in pugna felix successus, etsi fuerit fera vi, fraudibus necibusque obtentus, tamen ex iure naturae tribuit ius dominatus aliarum stirpium, estque peremptorium argumentum imperii per ipsam naturam stirpi victrici attributi.

Ordo praevalentiae inter individua

31. Eodem modo "pugnae selectivae" et "vis fortioris" constituitur per ipsam naturam ordo praevalentiae inter individua eiusdem stirpis et status stirpeo-nationalis.

Qui alios quibuscumque tandem mediis vicerit, ex institutione naturae ipso facto obtinet et habet ducatum regimenque super alios, et debetur ei subiectio absoluta et illimitata.

Forma regiminis

32. Legi et viae, quam natura in seligendis stirpibus et individuis sequitur, nulla correspondet in statu regiminis forma nisi unius hominis absolutus et illimitatus ducatus.

Quaecumque alia regiminis forma ab ordine naturae plus minus recedit.

The Hierarchy of Dominance Among Races

30. Nature has established a hierarchy of dominance, which is, by a natural process, enforced and maintained: in the so-called "battle of selection," which prevails among living beings, and with the "force of the stronger," through which one race is more powerful than others.

    Only success counts in this struggle, even if it is achieved by brutal force, by fraudulence, or by slaughter, for it gives the right, as a law of nature, to dominate other races and is a compelling argument in favor of assigning a *Reich* to the race that is victorious by nature.

The Hierarchy of Dominance Among Individuals

31. In the same manner as a "battle of selection" and "force of the strongest" there is established, by nature, a hierarchy of dominance between individuals of the same race and racist-national state.

    By whatever means it wins victory over others, it obtains and possesses, by nature's provision, effective leadership and government over them, and to it is due absolute and unlimited subjection.

The Form of Government

32. Nothing but the absolute and unlimited leadership of one man is the form of government in the state that is in keeping with the lawful path that nature follows in selecting races and individuals.

    Any other form of government is more or less a contravention of nature.

III. De Totalismo
Existentia Totalitatis

33. Totalitas status nationisve est factum et ius omni exceptione et probatione maius.

34. Doctrina saepius a Summis Pontificibus proposita de "subsidiaria" activitate status est error maxime fundamentalis, etiamsi haec subsidiaria activitas intelligitur de subsidio maioris efficientiae et dignitatis, quo insufficientia privatorum superetur.

    A totalitate, quam status ex iure naturae habet, res et conceptus activitatis subsidiariae sunt aliena.

Essentia Totalitatis

35. Statui ex principio totalitatis competit totale ius et totalis potestas, idest: ius extensione et comprehensione illimitatum et absolutum, quo omnia, quae quocumque modo hominum in societate civili consortium tangunt, tota et totaliter sibi subiecta habet.

36. Ob totalitatem status in societate civili nulli personae physicae vel morali nullique hominum associationi privatae ulla agendi libertas ullumque ius competit, nisi quod status ex autolimitatione totalitatis suae eis concedit.

    Ideo, etiam quod ad conscientiam pertinet, in societate civili omnia prohibita sunt et prohibita praesumi debent quae non expresse declarata sunt licita.

Ecclesia et Status Totalis

37. Ecclesia quoque totalitati status subiecta est tam de facto quam de iure.

38. Ecclesiae non competit ex iure nativo et divino plena independentia a societate civili nec quoad finem suum proprium plenitudo potestatis.

    Ecclesia eam tantummodo habet in societate civili licentiam docendi, regendi, cultusque exercendi quam respublica totalis ei concedit et quamdiu eam exercere sinit.

III. On Totalitarianism
The Existence of Totalitarianism

33. The totality of the state or nation is a fact and a law greater than any exception or proof.

34. The doctrine, frequently enunciated by the popes, of the "subsidiary" activity of the state is an absolutely fundamental error, even if this subsidiary activity is understood to refer to the provision of greater efficiency and dignity by which the inadequacy of private individuals is overcome.

    The totality that the state possesses by nature's law is incompatible with the theory and practice of subsidiarity.

The Essence of Totalitarianism

35. According to the principles of totalitarianism, total rights and total powers belong to the state, i.e.: absolute rights without limit of extent or scope, by which everything that in any way affects people's lives in civil society is wholly and completely subject to them.

36. On account of the totalitarian nature of society, no freedom or right of action is conceded in civil society to any physical or moral entity or private association, except what the state allows to them by limiting its own totality.

    It follows that, as far as the conscience is concerned, everything in civi society is prohibited and should be assumed to be prohibited that is not permitted explicitly.

The Church and the Totalitarian State

37. The Church too is subject to the totalitarian state both as a matter of fact and as a matter of law.

38. The Church has no natural or divine right to full independence from civil society, nor does it have full sovereignty as regards its own aims.

    The Church has only that permission to teach, organize, and practice worship in civil society that the totalitarian state concedes to it and for the period during which that permission is granted.

39. In specie Ecclesiae neque officium neque ius est docendi urgendique principia moralia quibus vita civilis, et maxime vita politica necnon oeconomica subsit.

Ecclesia ita agendo limites suae competentiae excedit et competentiam status invadit. Solius status est ex plenitudine potestatis suae, etiam quod conscientiam spectat, statuere ethicam politicam de eaque iudicare.

Individuum et Totalitas Status

40. Singulis hominibus hominumque societatibus privatis neque ex divino neque ex naturae iure ulla sunt iura, quae habeant antecedenter ad statum vel independenter ab eo, et quidem non solum, is ad iurium exercitium attenditur, sed etiam quod ad eorum originem et nudam existentiam attinet.

41. Errarunt Summi Pontifices vindicando hominibus iura, quae eis, quoad eorum originem et substantiam non primo competant ex concessione status, sed immediate ex iure sive divino positivo sive naturae; ita inter alia: ius vitae et integritatis membrorum, ius verae religionis et finis supernaturalis; ius mediorum quae ad vitam sive naturalem sive supernaturalem necessaria sunt; praeterea, suppositis supponendis: ius connubii fertilis in eoque ius procreandae et educandae prolis, ius vitae coelibis, ius famae, ius proprietatis privatae, ius contrahendi, ius coalitionis.

Ordo oeconomicus et Totalitas Status

42. In re oeconomica singulis hominibus vel privatis hominum associationibus ex iure naturae nulla omnino competit agendi libertas nullumque ius, sed solius status est vi totalitatis suae non solum privatorum activitatem ad bonum commune temperare et dirigere, sed etiam singulis primo concedere, ut in re oeconomica omnino quid possint, quantum possint et quo modo.

Vi totalitatis status auctoritas publica potest nutu suo et illimitate socialisare bona productiva necnon subditos onerare tributis aliisque oneribus quantis vult.

39. In particular, the Church has neither the duty nor the right to teach and insist on moral principles upon which civil and—especially—political and economic life is based.

 By behaving in this manner the Church exceeds the limits of its competence and invades the competence of the state. It is the right of the state alone, from the fullness of its power, even in regard to the conscience, to determine political ethics and make decisions about them.

The Individual and the Totalitarian State

40. Single individuals and private associations of people have no rights, either by divine or natural law, which are prior to the state or independent of it, and not only is the exercise of rights decided upon by the state but even their origin and simple existence.

41. The popes have been mistaken in claiming for mankind rights which, as far as their origins and contents are concerned, they do not acquire in the first place by a concession of the state but directly, by positive divine or natural law, among which are the right to life and to physical intactness, the right of true religion and its supernatural aims, the right to those means that are necessary for natural or supernatural life. In addition, let us assume the right to a fruitful marriage and, within it, to procreating and educating offspring, the right to the celibate life, the right to a good reputation, the right to private property, the right to draw up contracts, the right to form associations.

Economic Organization and the Totalitarian State

42. In economic affairs individuals or private associations have absolutely no rights or freedom of action on the basis of natural law. It is the sole right of the state, by force of its totality, not only to control and direct the actions of private citizens to the common good but also first to concede to individuals what they may do, in economic matters, how far, and in which manner.

 By force of its totality the public authorities of the state may, of their own will and without limit, socialize productive goods and burden its subjects with taxes and other impositions as it wishes.

Educatio iuventutis

43. Status vi totalitatis habet exclusivum ius idque absolutum educandae iuventutis.

    Status ex sese statuit quis sit finis educationis et quae sint media ad finem. Finis est autem ipse status eiusque universale servitium.

    Pleno iure status exigit, ut prae omni alia re educatione iuventus inflammetur fanatico spiritu nationalismi sive puri sive stirpei.

    Statui vi totalitatis competit monopolium scholarum; scholae privatae—prae caeteris autem sic dictae "religiosae"—pugnant contra nativum ius totalitatis Status ideoque removendae sunt.

    Ecclesiae et parentibus ex iure naturae aut divino nulla est pars in iuventute educanda, sed eam solummodo habet partem, quam status eis concedit et quam eos non nisi cum omnimoda dependentia a statu agere permittit.

Vita politica et Totalitas Status

44. Status vi totalitatis in civitate regenda, et maxime in vita atque activitate politica, exemptus est a legibus Dei et naturae servandis. Sibi ipse est fons omnis iuris et suprema et unica regula.

45. In specie status in "bono publico" circumscribendo nulla lege divina aut naturae, nullisque hominum privatorum aut aliarum nationum iuribus coarctatur. Bonum commune est quod ipse tale statuit, estque illimitata gloria et universalissimum emolumentum propriae nationis vel stirpis.

The Education of the Young

43. The state, by force of its totality, has the exclusive and absolute right to the education of the young.

    The state itself decides what the aim of education is and which means should be employed to that end. The end is the state itself and its universal service.

    The state demands with full rights that, above all else, in education, youth should be inflamed by a fanatical spirit of nationalism either pure or racial.

    The state, by force of its totality, has a monopoly over the schools. Private schools—above all, the so-called "religious" schools—are in conflict with the natural rights of the totalitarian state and are therefore to be abolished.

    The Church and parents do not have, either by divine or natural law, any role in educating the young, except that which the state concedes to them and which it allows them to exercise only in complete dependence on the state.

Political Life and the Totalitarian State

44. The state, by force of its totality, is dispensed from observing the laws of God and nature in ruling the community and, particularly, in political life and activities. It is its own source of law and supreme, sole standard.

45. In particular the state, in limiting "the public good," is not restricted by any divine or natural law or the rights of private persons or other nations. The common good is what the state decides it to be: limitless glory and the most general enrichment of one's own nation or race.

46. Quae ad bonum commune defendendum vel promovendum per auctoritatem publicam fiunt ex sic dictis "necessitatibus politicis", eo ipso amittunt, quodcumque forte in se habent inhonesti, et vi totalitatis status evadunt licita et gloriosa.

    Peragi recte et licite possunt, ut necessitatibus politicis satisfiat, (etiamsi nulla praecesserit culpa aut saltem nulla tanto malo digna): unius vel multorum directa occisio, vulneratio, percussio, incarceratio, expulsio, expropriatio, diffamatio et calumnia, et alia huiusmodi.

47. Auctoritas publica vi totalitatis status exigere potest absolutum subiectionis et fidelitatis iuramentum, reiecta etiam illa conscientiae clausula "salva lege Dei", licet haec implicite tantum adiecta fuerit et subintellegatur.

46. Whatever is done on public authority to defend or further the common good on account of so-called "public emergencies," by that fact alone, legitimates any act that may perhaps be considered wrongful and, by the force of the totalitarian state, makes it acceptable and glorious.

     To meet public emergencies there may be performed with absolute correctness (even in cases when the suspect is not guilty or his guilt does not deserve such severity) the direct murder of one or many, woundings, beatings-up, imprisonment, expulsion, expropriation, defamation and calumny, and other things of this kind.

47. The public authorities, by force of the totalitarian state, may demand an oath of absolute subjection and fidelity, rejecting even the clause of the conscience "saving God's law," even if this was only added implicitly and hinted at.

Appendix II

The Holy Office's Revised Condemnation (1936)

Razzismo, Nazionalismo, Comunismo, Totalitarismo

I. DE "RASSISMO" SEU DE FALSO CULTU STIRPIS

1. Stirpes hominum indole sua nativa el immutabili adeo inter se differunt, ut earum infima magis distet a suprema hominum, quam distat a suprema specie brutorum.
2. Vigor stirpis et puritas "sanguinis" quolibet medio conservanda et fovenda sunt; et medium quodcumque ad hoc utile et efficace [*sic*] eo ipso est honestum et licitum, uti ex. gr. sterilizatio ad praecavendam prolem mancam et directa procuratio abortus.
3. Ex "sanguine," quo indoles stirpis continetur, promanant tamquam ex potissimo fonte omnes qualitates intellectuales et morales hominis.
4. Finis praecipuus, nisi unicus, educationis est: provehere indolem stirpis excolendo corpus idemque efficiendo validum et formosum, atque inflammare animum flagranti amore propriae stirpis, tamquam summi boni.

SOURCE: ACDF, R.V. 1934, 29; Prot. 3373/34, vol. 4, fasc. 13 (October 1936)

Appendix II

The Holy Office's Revised Condemnation (1936)

Propositions [to be Condemned] on Racism, Nationalism, Communism, Totalitarianism

I. ON "RACISM" OR THE FALSE CULT OF RACE

1. The races of mankind are so different from one another through their innate and unchangeable character that the lowest of them is more different from the supreme race of men than from the highest species of animal.
2. The strength of the race and the purity of "blood" are to be preserved and fostered by any means whatsoever; and any means that is useful and effective to this purpose is thereby respectable and permissible—for example, that sterilization may be employed to avoid defective offspring, and abortion may be procured directly.
3. From "blood," in which the character of the race is contained, all of mankind's intellectual and moral qualities spring, as if from a mighty fountain.
4. The chief, if not sole, aim of education is to develop the character of the race by taking care of the body and making it strong and handsome, and to fire the mind with burning love of one's own race, as though it were the highest good.

SOURCE: ACDF, R.V. 1934, 29; Prot. 3373/34, vol. 4, fasc. 13 (October 1936)

5. Religio christiana legi stirpis subicitur; quapropter quae in religione christiana ab indole stirpis aliena censentur eliminari aut mutari debent, uti ex. gr. doctrina de peccato originali, de redemptione, de cruce Christi, de humilitate et mortificatione exercenda.

6. Enitendum est, ut religio christiana e vita publica penitus elabatur; idcirco e medio tollendae sunt catholicae ephemerides, scholae, associationes quaecumque.

7. Fons primus et regula summa universi ordinis iuridici est instinctus stirpis.

8. "Pugna selectiva" et "vis fortior," si fuerint fortunatae, eo ipso victori dant ius dominandi.

II. De Hypernationalismo

9. Natio ipsa sibi est suprema norma, neque in bono proprio prosequendo ullum vereri tenetur ius aliarum nationum, familiae vel hominis privati.

10. Bonum nationis est finis supremus hominis; individui non sunt, nisi per nationem et propter nationem.

11. Ne illa quidem expansionismi nationalis forma reprobanda est quae docet alienas nationes, vi quoque et armis adhibitis, subici earumque territoria occupari posse etiam ad meram propriae nationis gloriam et potestatem augendam.

12. Cultus belli fovenudus [*sic*] est, et legitime ad arma provocatur, ut natio heroicae fortitudinis exercendae et gloriae militaris obtinendae facultatem habeat.

13. Nationi debetur cultus vere proprieque religiosus.

III. De Communismo

14. Nihil existit nisi materia quae, suo motu, continuo perficitur donec fiat (ita ut fiat vel et fit) vivens, sentiens, cogitans.

15. Unica societatis humanae ratio est in labore productivo communi, sicut unicus eius finis est in felicitate terrestri.

5. The Christian religion is subject to the law of race. For that reason such things in the Christian religion that are considered incompatible with the character of the race should be eliminated or altered as, for example, the doctrines of original sin, of redemption, of Christ's cross, of humility, and the practice of mortification.

6. An effort must be made to eliminate Christian religion from public life. That is why all Catholic periodicals, schools, and associations should be abolished.

7. The prime source and highest principle of all legal organization is the instinct of race.

8. "The battle of selection" and the "stronger force," if successful, by that fact give the victor the right to dominate.

II. On Hypernationalism

9. The nation is the supreme standard to itself and, in pursuing its own good, it need not respect any rights of other nations, of the family, or of private individuals.

10. The good of the nation is man's supreme aim; individuals do not exist, except through the nation and for the nation.

11. No condemnation is to be voiced of even that form of national expansionism which maintains that foreign nations can be subjected and their territories occupied by force of arms for the unvarnished purpose of increasing the nation's power and glory.

12. The cult of war is to be encouraged and it is legitimate to provoke armed conflict in order to provide the nation with an opportunity of putting its heroic strength to trial and of winning military glory.

13. A religious cult, in the strict sense of the term, is due to the nation.

III. On Communism

14. Nothing exists except matter, which, by its motion, is constantly perfected until it becomes (so that it becomes or is) living, feeling, thinking.

15. The only purpose of human society is in common productive work, just as its sole purpose lies in earthly happiness.

16. Labori productivo communi singuli homines, quolibet bono privato posthabito, totaliter, etiam per coactionem addicendi sunt.

17. Moralitas est merus reflexus conditionum socialium.

18. Promovenda est omnibus viribus pugna "classium"; et omnia media, etiam violentissima, quae eidem favent, eo ipso moralia fiunt.

19. Proprietas privata divitiarum naturalium et mediorum productionis evertenda est.

20. Mulier a servitute matrimonii indissolubilis, curae filiorum et vitae domesticae emancipanda est.

21. Religio non est nisi commentum humanum et "opium," quod a "classibus" dominantibus plebi ignarae opprimendae ministratur.

IV. De totalitarismo

22. Statui competit ius absolutum, directum et immediatum in omnes et in omnia, quae quocumque modo societatem civilem tangunt.

23. Homo et familia iura nativa non habet; sed quidquid iuris privatis competit, unice ex concessione status procedit tum quoad iurium existentiam tum quoad eorum exercitium.

24. Educatio unice et totaliter spectat ad statum.

25. Etiam Ecclesia Catholica statui subiicitur; et nulla sunt ei iura nisi quae a statu conceduntur. Quapropter Ecclesiae nullum competit nativum ius docendi urgendique principia ethica, quibus societatis civilis vita publica et oeconomica regitur.

16. Individuals are to be totally involved, even by compelling them, in common productive work, which takes priority over private goods.
17. Morality is a mere reflex of social conditions.
18. Every effort is to be directed at advancing "class" war; and every means, even the most violent, that favor it become moral by that fact alone.
19. Private possession of natural riches and means of production is to be overturned.
20. Women are to be emancipated from the slavery of indissoluble marriage, the care of children, and housework.
21. Religion is nothing but a human invention and an "opium" that is administered by the ruling "classes" to ignorant commoners in order to oppress them.

IV. On Totalitarianism

22. The state has absolute, direct, and immediate rights over everyone and everything that has to do with civil society in any way.
23. Mankind and the family have no innate rights; the only rights allowed to private persons are granted by the state alone; and this is valid both in the case of rights' existence and in that of their application.
24. Education is the unique and complete preserve of the state.
25. Even the Catholic Church is subject to the state and has no rights except those granted by the state. That is why the Church has no innate right to teach and to urge ethical principles by which the political and economic life of civil society is ruled.

Appendix III

The Holy Office's Comparison Between Its Draft Condemnations and Mit brennender Sorge (1937)

I	II	III
Commisionis Schema de Rassismo	*Commissionis Schema de Hypernationalismo et de Totalitarismo Status*	*Schema litt. Encycl. de conditione Ecclesiae in Germania*

1. Ex "sanguine," quo indoles stirpis continetur, promanant tamquam ex potissimo fonte omnes qualitates hominis intellectuales et morales.

2. Stirpes hominum indole sua nativa et immutabili adeo inter se differunt, ut earum infima magis distet a suprema hominum, quam

SOURCE: ACDF, R.V. 1934, 29; Prot. 3373/34, vol. 4, fasc. 18 (April 1937)

Appendix III

The Holy Office's Comparison Between Its Draft Condemnations and Mit brennender Sorge (1937)

I	II	III
Outline of the Commission on Racism	*Outline of the Commission on Hypernationalism and State Totalitarianism*	*Outline of the Encyclical on the Situation of the Church in the German Reich*

1. From "blood," in which the character of the race is contained, all of mankind's intellectual and moral qualities spring, as if from a mighty fountain.

2. The races of mankind are so different from one another through their innate and unchangeable character that the lowest of them is more different from the

Source: ACDF, R.V. 1934, 29; Prot. 3373/34, vol. 4, fasc. 18 (April 1937)

distat a suprema
brutorum specie.

3. Vigor stirpis et
puritas "sanguinis"
quolibet medio
conservanda et
fovenda sunt;
et medium
quodcumque ad hoc
utile et efficax eo
ipso est honestum et
licitum, quamvis
ipsi legi naturae
adversetur, uti e. gr.
directa innocentis
sterilisatio et abortus
directa procuratio.

9. Natio ipsa sibi est
suprema norma
neque, in bono
proprio prosequendo,
ullum vereri tenetur
ius aliarum
nationum, familiae
hominisque privati.

30. Quodcumque
populo ac rassae
utile est, eo ipso est
moraliter bonum seu
honestum.

4. Finis praecipuus,
nisi unicus,
educationis est
provehere indolem
stirpis, excolendo
corpus idemque
validum et
formosum
efficiendo, atque
inflammare animum
flagranti amore
propriae stirpis,
tamquam summi
boni.

24. Educatio unice et
totaliter spectat ad
Statum.

35. Parentibus non
competit ius
nativum, ipsis
immediate a Deo
datum, statuendi et
exigendi, ut filiorum
institutio et educatio
non fiat nisi
secundum
doctrinam et
praecepta religionis
christianae.

36. Auctoritati
publicae competit
ius parentes vi
minisque cogendi, ut
scholas profanas prae

supreme race of men than from the highest species of animal.

3. The strength of the race and the purity of "blood" are to be preserved and fostered by any means, and every means that is useful and effective for this purpose is, by that fact alone, respectable and permitted; even if in opposition to nature's law—for example, direct sterilization of an innocent person and abortion procured directly.

9. The nation is the supreme standard to itself and, in pursuing its own good, it need not respect any rights of other nations, of the family, or of private individuals.

30. Whatever is useful for a people or a race is, by that fact alone, morally good or honorable.

4. The chief, if not sole, aim of education is to develop the character of the race by taking care of the body and making it strong and handsome, and to fire the mind with burning love of one's own race, as though it were the highest good.

24. Education is the unique and complete preserve of the state.

35. Parents have no innate right, granted to them directly by God, of deciding and demanding that their children's training and education should be conducted only according to the doctrine and precepts of the Christian religion.

36. The public authorities have the

scholis christianis eligant, et ut filios suos modo a religione christiana alieno instrui atque educari sinant. Hic parentum consensus, dicto modo extortus, eos in conscientia et coram Deo ligat.

5. Religio christiana legi stirpis subicitur; quapropter quae in religione christiana ab indole stirpis aliena censentur, auferri aut mutari debent, uti e. gr. doctrina de peccato originali, de redemptione, de cruce christi, de humilitate et mortificatione exercenda.

23. Quae religio christiana docet de peccato originali, concupiscentia rebelli, de generis humani per Christi mortem redemptione, de pugna contra tentationes agenda, de necessitate gratiae, orationis, mortificationis et poenitentiae: non nisi contemptu et ludibrio digna sunt, atque cum hominis nordici mente ac sanguine componi non possunt.

N.B.—Quoad, [*sic*] "religionem" et "Ecclesiam" duo notanda sunt: ex una parte asseclae Rassismi dicunt removendam aut

24. Humilitas christiana et auxilii divini assidua deprecatio sunt sui ipsius indigna

right to compel parents, by force and by threats, to choose secular instead of Christian schools and allow their children to be trained and educated in a manner alien to the Christian religion. This agreement of parents, extracted from them in the way described, is binding on their conscience and before God.

5. The Christian religion is subject to the law of race. For that reason those things in the Christian religion that are considered incompatible with the character of the race should be eliminated or altered—such as, for example, the doctrines of original sin, redemption, Christ's cross, and the practice of humility and mortification.

23. What the Christian religion teaches about original sin, rebellious desire, the redemption of mankind through Christ's death, the battle to be fought against temptations, the necessity of grace, prayer, mortification, and penance: all this is worthy of contempt and ridicule and cannot be reconciled with the way of thinking and the blood of the Nordic man.

N.B.—Concerning "religion" and "the Church," two points

24. Christian humility and

saltem immutandam
religionem et
Ecclesiam
christianam *quae
adest*; ex altera parte
efformanda a iis
statuitur (saltem a
non paucis asseclis
Rassismi) loco
religionis et
Ecclesiae catholicae
nova omnino religio
(stirpea, nationalis,
pantheistica).
Duplex haec
tendentia
sequentibus
propositionibus
describitur, et
proponitur
condemnanda.

6. Enitendum est, ut
religio christiana e
vita publica penitus
elabatur; idcirco e
medio tollendae sunt
catholicae
ephemerides,
scholae,
associationes
quaecumque.

vilificatio et prorsus
alienae a spiritu
heroico stirpis
nordicae.

13. Christus non ex
populo, qui eum
cruci fecit affigi,
naturam humanam
assumpsit.

8. Libri Veteris
Testamenti non ex
integro sunt verbum
Dei.

34. Societati ius est:
externam religionis
christianae
manifestationem et
actionem coartandi,
item quemlibet eius
influxum a vita
publica arcendi et
removendi. Leges
publicae, quae talia
statuunt ligant
subditos in
conscientia.

should be noted: on
the one hand, the
adherents of racism
say that religion
and the Christian
Church, *as it is,*
should be abolished
or at least changed;
on the other hand,
they (or rather a fair
number of racists)
demand that a *new*
religion (of the race,
of the nation, or
pantheistic) should
be founded. This
twofold tendency is
described in the
following
propositions and
proposed for
condemnation.

6. An effort must be
made to eliminate
Christian religion
from public life.
That is why all
Catholic periodicals,
schools, and
associations should
be abolished.

continual invocation
of God's help are an
unworthy lowering
of the self and
wholly alien to the
heroic spirit of the
Nordic race.

13. Christ did not
assume His human
nature from the
people who crucified
Him.

8. The books of the
Old Testament are
not entirely the
Word of God.

34. It is the right
of society to curb
the external
manifestations and
actions of the
Christian religion
and to ward off
and remove any
influence by it on
public life. Public
laws to this effect are
binding on subjects'
consciences.

16. Doctrina, constitutio, regimen atque cultus Ecclesiae ex natura sua non sunt eiusmodi, ut in Ecclesia diversi populi, nationes et rassae secundum naturalem indolem, singulis propriam, vivere se evolvere atque ad plenam perfectionem pervenire valeant.

25. Etiam Ecclesia Catholica statui subiicitur; et nulla sunt ei iura nisi quae a Statu conceduntur. Quapropter Ecclesiae nullum competit nativum ius docendi urgendique principia ethica, quibus societatis civilis vita publica, politica et oeconomica regitur.

17. Fas est egredi e Ecclesia Catholica. Hic egressus est signum et professio genuinae "mentis nordicae," atque constituit obsequium populo ac rassae atque vigenti systemati politico debitum.

18. Non est una pro omnibus populis et nationibus omnium temporum Ecclesia a Christo instituta. Ecclesiae nationales, a Romano Pontifice

16. The teaching, the organization, the government, and the worship of the Church, by their very nature, are not such that different peoples, nations, and races can live and develop to full perfection according to their natural, individual, and particular character.

25. Even the Catholic Church is subject to the state and has no rights except those granted by the state. That is why the Church has no innate right to teach and to enforce ethical principles by which the political and economic life of civil society is regulated.

17. It is permissible to leave the Church. To do so is the mark and affirmation of a true "Nordic way of thinking" and amounts to a due act of obedience to the people, the race, and the current political system.

18. There does not exist one Church founded by Christ for all peoples and nations of all time. National churches, independent of the pope and one

et inter se
independentes, non
offendunt contra
Dei et Christi
voluntatem et
institutionem.

(N.B.—*Nova religio est efformanda.*)

13. Nationi debetur
cultus vere
proprieque
religiosus.

1. Deus concipi
potest universus
mundus; in mundo
Deus fit mundus, et
mundus in Deo fit
Deus. Qui ita de Deo
sentit, Dei verus
cultor vocatur et est.

5. Religio Deusque
Natione et Rassa
circumscribuntur, a
quibus coluntur.

2. Sic dicta
"Providentia divina"
non exsistit.
Quaecumque
accidunt et omnium
hominum sors
"Fato" subsunt
eoque reguntur.

3. Nihil plus valet
quam *Rassa* et
Populus; quidquid
praeter ea valet,
ex iis mensuram
valoris sumit. Rassa
populusque

another, are not contrary to the will and design of God and Christ.

(N.B.—*A new religion is to be founded.*)

13. Religious worship, in the strict sense of the term, is due to the nation.

1. God can be conceived as the universal world; in the world God becomes world, and the world becomes God in God. Those who think about God in this way are called, and are, true worshipers of God.

5. Religion and God are circumscribed by nation and race, by which they are worshiped.

2. So-called "*divine Providence*" does not exist. Everything that happens and the destiny of all men depend on, and are ruled by, "Fate."

3. Nothing has higher worth than the *Race* and the *People*; anything that is of value beyond them is to be

cultu divino digna
sunt.

10. Revelatio divina
neque fuit cum
Christo finita neque
obligat pro semper.
Habentur huius
revelationis
additamenta
posteriora per
homines data;
habentur eius
compensationes et
mutationes
depromptae ex sic
dicto "mytho
sanguinis et rassae."

12. Non tanta est
essendi diversitas
inter Deum et
creaturam, inter
Christum, Deum-
Hominem, et
homines communes,
ut non possit selectus
quidam homo poni
iuxta aut supra aut
contra Christum,
praeditus aequali,
imo potiore iure.

20. Rassae et
sanguinis
"suggestiones," item
emanationes quae ex

measured by their
standard. The race
and the people are
worthy of divine
worship.

10. Divine revelation
neither ended with
Christ nor is it
eternally binding.
Additions to this
revelation are
deemed to have
been made later by
men; they are
supplemented and
altered by the
so-called "myth of
blood and race."

12. There is not such
a difference of being
between God and
creation, between
the God-Man, Christ,
and common men,
that a chosen man
cannot be set beside
or above or against
Christ, endowed
with equal if not
greater power.

20. The "sugges-
tions" of race and
blood, like the facts
that emanate from

rebus gestis historiae procedunt rationem habent revelationis divinae proprie dictae.

21. Firma laetaque in futuram proprii populi fortunam fiducia est fides religiosa vere et proprie dicta.

22. Vera germanaque hominis immortalitas consistit in proprii populi et stirpis perpetuitate, vi cuius, qui e vita cessit, in populo suo vitam continuare censetur et continuat.

7. Fons primus et summa regula universi ordinis iuridici est instinctus stirpis.

10. Bonum Nationis est finis supremus hominis; individui non sunt nisi per nationem et propter nationem.

the events of history, have the effect of divine revelation in the strict sense of the term.

21. A firm and cheerful confidence in the future of one's people is religious faith in the true sense of the word.

22. The true German immortality of man consists in perpetuating one's own people and race, by force of which those who have passed away are considered to continue their lives in the people, as they continue.

7. The prime source and highest principle of all legal organization is the instinct of race.

10. The Good of the Nation is man's supreme aim; individuals do not exist, except through the nation and for the nation.

23. Homo et familia
iura nativa non
habent; sed quidquid
iuris privatis
competit, unice ex
concessione Status
procedit tum quoad
iurium exsistentiam
tum quoad eorum
exercitium.

31. Homo
immediate a Deo
nulla habet iura
nativa. In omnia
hominis iura populo
ac publicae
auctoritati plena et
directa potestas
competit tum quad
[*sic*] eorum
exsistentiam tum
quoad quemlibet
usum et utendi
facultatem.

32. Bonum
commune verum
atque verus societatis
humanae finis
definitivam normam
atque criterium non
habent naturam
hominis, personalem
et socialem.

33. Societas
humana (respublica,
populus, natio,
rassa) ultimatim
est propter se
ipsam; non est
propter hominem
seu personam
humanam.
E contra: homo
ultimatim est
propter societatem.

23. Mankind and the family have no innate rights; the only rights allowed to private persons are granted by the state alone; and this is valid both in the case of laws' existence and in that of their application.

31. Man has no natural rights directly from God. In matters of human rights, full and direct power is in the hands of the people and the public authorities in matters concerning both mankind's existence and any use or ability to make use of it.

32. The true common good and the real aim of human society do not have as their definitive standard and criterion man's personal and social nature.

33. Human society (the state, the people, the nation, the race) exists, in the final analysis, for itself; it does not exist on account of man or the human person. On the contrary: man exists, in the final analysis, for the sake of society.

22. Statui competit
ius absolutum,
directum et
immediatum in
omnes et in omnia,
quae quocumque
modo societatem
civilem tangunt
(totalitarismus,
totalitas status, status
totalis).

8. "Pugna selectiva"
et "vis fortior" si
fuerint fortunatae,
eo ipso victori dant
ius dominandi.

11. Ne illa quidem
expansionismi
nationalis forma
probanda est quae
docet alienas
nationes, vi quoque
et armis adhibitis,
subici earumque
territoria occupari
posse, etiam ad
meram propriae
nationis gloriam et
potestatem
augendam.

12. Cultus belli
fovendus est, et
legitime ad arma
provocatur, etiam eo

22. The state has absolute, direct, and immediate rights over everyone and everything that has to do with civil society in any way (totalitarianism, the totality of the state, the total state).

8. "The battle of selection" and the "stronger force," if successful, give the victor the right to dominate.

11. No condemnation is to be voiced of even that form of national expansionism which teaches that foreign nations can be subjected and their territories occupied by force of arms for the simple purpose of increasing the nation's power and glory.

12. The cult of war is to be encouraged and it is legitimate to provoke armed conflict in order that

tantum, ut natio
heroicae fortitudinis
exercendae et
gloriae militaris
obtinendae
facultatem habeat.

the nation obtain a
possibility of putting
its heroic strength
to trial and of
obtaining military
glory.

Appendix IV

*Pius XI's Instruction to the Rectors of Catholic Universities
and Seminars to Refute "Ridiculous Dogmas" (April 13, 1938)*

In Nativitatis Domini nostri pervigilio, proxime elapso anno, Augustus Pontifex, feliciter regnans, ad Eminentissimos Purpuratos Patres et ad Romanae Curiae Praelatos de gravi, qua Catholica Ecclesia in Germania afficitur, insectatione, ut omnes norunt, moerens allocutus est.

Id vero Beatissimi Patris quam maxime opprimit animum quod ad tantam iniustitiam excusandam impudentes interponunt calumnias atque doctrinas perniciosissimas, falsi nominis scientia fucatas, longe lateque spargentes et mentes pervertere et veram religionem eradicare conantur.

Quae cum ita sint Sacra haec Congregatio Studiorum Universitates Facultatesque Catholicas admonet, ut omnem suam curam atque operam ad veritatem contra grassantes errores defendendam conferant.

Itaque magistri, pro viribus, e biologia, historia, philosophia, apologetica et disciplinis iuridico-moralibus arma sedulo mutuent, ut perabsurda quae sequuntur dogmata valide sciteque refellant:

1. Stirpes humanae indole sua, nativa et immutabili, adeo inter se differunt ut infima ipsarum magis distet a suprema hominum stirpe quam a suprema specie brutorum. *(Cf. Appendix I, 9, and Appendix II, 1)*

2. Stirpis vigor et sanguinis puritas qualibet ratione conservanda et fovenda sunt; quidlibet autem ad hunc finem ducit eo ipso honestum licitumque est. *(Cf. Appendix I, 27, and Appendix II, 2)*

SOURCE: ASV, AES, *Germania* 1938–45 Pos. 736–738, fasc. 354, 50 (April 13, 1938)

Appendix IV

*Pius XI's Instruction to the Rectors of Catholic Universities
and Seminars to Refute "Ridiculous Dogmas" (April 13, 1938)*

On the Christmas Eve of last year, the August Pontiff reigning with success spoke in sorrow to the most eminent cardinals and prelates of the Roman Curia about the grave persecution that afflicts the Catholic Church in Germany, as everyone knows.

What particularly depresses the Holy Father is the fact that, in order to excuse such flagrant injustice, calumnies and most pernicious doctrines, counterfeited with the false name of science, are alleged impudently and diffused far and wide with the purpose of perverting the intelligence and undermining true religion.

In this situation the Sacred Congregation admonishes the Catholic Universities and Faculties to turn all their attention and effort to defending the truth against these raging errors.

And so let the teachers of biology, history, philosophy, apologetics, law, and ethics diligently join forces to refute the following ridiculous dogmas with compelling scholarship:

1. The human races are so different from one another, in their innate and unchangeable nature, that the least of them differs more from the supreme race of men than from the highest species of animals. *(Cf. Appendix I, 9, and Appendix II, 1)*
2. The strength of the race and the purity of blood are to be preserved and nurtured by any means; whatever contributes to this purpose is, by that fact alone, honorable and permissible. *(Cf. Appendix I, 27, and Appendix II, 2)*

SOURCE: ASV, AES, *Germania* 1938–45, Pos. 736–738, fasc. 354, 50 (April 13, 1938)

3. Ex sanguine, quo indoles stirpis continetur, omnes qualitates intellectuales et morales hominis, veluti a purissimo fonte, effluunt. *(Cf. Appendix I, 11, and Appendix II, 3).*

4. Finis praecipuus educationis est indolem stirpis excolere atque animum flagranti amore propriae stirpis, tamquam summi boni, inflammare. (Cf. Appendix I, 24, and Appendix II, 4)

5. Religio legi stirpis subest eique aptanda est. *(Cf. Appendix I, 13, and Appendix II, 5)*

6. Fons prima et summa regula universi ordinis iuridici est instinctus stirpis. *(Cf. Appendix I, 17, and Appendix II, 17)*

7. Non existet nisi Kosmos seu Universum, Ens vivum; res omnes, cum ipso nomine, nihil aliud sunt quam variae formae, per longas aetates succrescentes, *Universi Viventis. (See above, p. 63.)*

8. Singuli homines non sunt nisi per "statum" et propter "statum"; quidquid iuris ad eos pertinet ex status concessione unice derivatur. *(Cf. Appendix I, 40, and Appendix II, 17)*

Quisquis autem his infestissimis placitis alia facile addicere poterit . . . [1]

3. All intellectual and moral qualities stem from blood, in which the nature of the race is contained, as if from the purest fountain. *(Cf. Appendix I, 11, and Appendix II, 3)*

4. The prime aim of education is to develop the character of the race and inflame the mind with ardent love for the race, as if it were the highest good. *(Cf. Appendix I, 24, and Appendix II, 4)*

5. Religion is subject to the law of race and should be adapted to it. *(Cf. Appendix I, 13, and Appendix II, 5)*

6. The chief and paramount standard of all legal organization is the instinct of race. *(Cf. Appendix I, 17, and Appendix II, 17)*

7. Nothing exists except the COSMOS or Universe, a living being: All things with their names are nothing but various forms, developing throughout aeons of time, of the *living universe. (See above, p. 63.)*

8. Individuals do not exist except through the "state" and for the "state"; any legal rights that pertain to them derive solely from a concession by the state. *(Cf. Appendix I, 40, and Appendix II, 17)*

Anyone will be able easily to add further examples to these abominable beliefs . . . [1]

---

[1] This text has been printed, without indication of its sources, in *Actes et documents du Saint-Siège relatifs à la Seconde Guerre Mondiale* 6. *Le Saint-Siège et les victimes de la guerre. Mars 1939—décembre 1940* (Vatican, 1972), 530–31. The translation made by the German bishops in the summer of 1938 is reproduced by K. Repgen, *Judenpogrom, Rassenideologie und katholische Kirche* 1938 (Cologne, 1988), 21–22.

List of Abbreviations in Notes

AAS   Acta Apostolicae Sedis
ACDF   Archivio della Congregazione per la dottrina della fede
AES   Affari Ecclesiastici Straordinari
ASV   Archivio Segreto Vaticano
DBI   Dizionario biografico degli italiani
R.V.   Rerum Variarum
S.O.   Sanctum Officium
VKZ   Veröffentlichung der Kommission für Zeitgeschichte

Index of Primary Sources

ARCHIVIO SEGRETO VATICANO
AES, *Germania* 1932–36, Pos. 632, fasc. 150
AES, *Germania* 1932–36, Pos. 632, fasc. 151
AES, *Germania* 1933–34, Pos. 641–643, fasc. 157
AES, *Germania* 1933–34, Pos. 641–643, fasc. 158
AES, *Germania* 1933–34, Pos. 641–643, fasc. 159
AES, *Germania* 1933–34, Pos. 645, fasc. 163
AES, *Germania* 1933–45, Pos. 645, fasc. 168
AES, *Germania* 1933–36, Pos. 645, fasc. 171
AES, *Germania* 1933–39, Pos. 645–646, fasc. 171
AES, *Germania* 1933–45, Pos. 647, fasc. 172
AES, *Germania* 1934–51, Pos. 661–663, fasc. 210
AES, *Germania* 1934–35, Pos. 666, fasc. 221
AES, *Germania* 1934–35, Pos. 666, fasc. 223
AES, *Germania* 1935–37, Pos. 676, fasc. 245
AES, *Germania* 1935, Pos. 692, fasc. 260
AES, *Germania* 1935–38, Pos. 692, fasc. 263
AES, *Germania* 1935–38, Pos. 692, fasc. 264
AES, *Germania* 1936, Pos. 695, fasc. 267
AES, *Germania* 1936–38, Pos. 719, fasc. 312
AES, *Germania* 1936–38, Pos. 719, fasc. 313
AES, *Germania* 1936–38, Pos. 719, fasc. 314
AES, *Germania* 1936–38, Pos. 719, fasc. 316
AES, *Germania* 1936–38, Pos. 719, fasc. 318
AES, *Germania* 1936–38, Pos. 719, fasc. 319

Notes

INTRODUCTION

1 *Hitler's Table-Talk. Hitler's Conversations recorded by Martin Bormann*, introduced by H. Trevor-Roper (Oxford, 1988), no. 75, 142 ff; *Hitlers Tischgespräche im Führerhauptquartier*, ed. H. Picker (Frankfurt/M., 1993), no. 11, 108 ff.

2 See C.-E. Bärsch, *Die politische Religion des Nationalsozialismus. Die religiösen Dimensionen der NS-Ideologie in den Schriften von Dietrich Eckhart, Joseph Goebbels, Alfred Rosenberg und Adolf Hitler* (Munich, 2002). See further below.

3 J. Cornwell, *Hitler's Pope: the Secret Story of Pius XII* (London, 1999); id., *Pius XII. Der Papst, der geschwiegen hat* (Munich, 1999).

4 D. J. Goldhagen, *A Moral Reckoning: The Role of the Catholic Church in the Holocaust and Its Unfulfilled Duty of Repair* (London, 2002). *Die katholische Kirche und der Holocaust: Eine Untersuchung über Schuld und Sühne* (Berlin, 2002).

CHAPTER 1   UNANSWERED QUESTIONS

1 See now R. Steigmann-Gall, *The Holy Reich. Nazi Conceptions of Christianity 1919–1945* (Cambridge, 2003).

2 Ibid. 27.

3 Ibid. 84 ff.

4 On Hitler's intellectual background, see B. Harmann, *Hitlers Wien. Lehrjahre eines Diktators* (Munich, 1999). For the contrast, see further below.

5 On Gasparri, see below.

6 ASV, Archivio della Nunziatura di Monaco, Pos. 396, fasc. 7, 6–7.

7 Ibid. 75–76.

8 "Konkordate sind völkerrechtliche Vereinbarungen, die eine zwischenstaatliche Bindung bewirken und das Ziel verfolgen, die religiösen und kirchlichen Interessen einerseits und die staatlichen Interessen andererseits in gerechtem Ausgleich so gegeneinander abzuwägen und in einem Vertragswerk festzulegen, dass volle Gegenseitigkeit verbürgt ist." ASV, AES, *Germania* 1933–39, Pos. 645–646, fasc. 171, 15.

9 ASV, AES, *Germania* 1933–34, Pos. 645, fasc. 163, 20.

10 See further below.

11 See L. Volk, *Das Reichskonkordat vom 20. Juli 1933. Von den Ansätzen in der Weimarer Republik bis zur Ratifizierung am 10. September 1933* VKZ B, 5 (Mainz, 1972).

12 Well discussed by H. Hürten, *Deutsche Katholiken 1918–1945* (Paderborn, 1992), 164 ff.

13 See below.

14 Volk, *Reichskonkordat* 14 ff. and see further below.

15 Ibid. 217, n. 20.

16 ASV, AES, *Germania* 1933–45, Pos. 647, fasc. 172, 44 (Pacelli, October 19, 1933).

17 Ibid. 212 ff.

18 ASV, AES, *Germania* 1933–45, Pos. 645, fasc. 168, 41.

19 See L. Volk, *Katholische Kirche und Nationalsozialismus* ed. D. Albrecht VKZ B, 46 (Mainz, 1987), 252 ff.

20 ASV, AES, *Germania* 1933–36, Pos. 645, fasc. 171, 15.

21 Volk, *Katholische Kirche* 201 ff.

22 Kardinal Faulhaber, *Judentum Christentum Germanentum. Adventspredigten gehalten in St. Michael zu München 1933* (München, 1934).

23 See B. Griech-Polelle, *Bishop von Galen: German Catholicism and National Socialism* (Yale, 2002).

CHAPTER 2 TWO ROMES

1 Mussolini, *Opera* XVIII (Florence, 1956), 160 ff, quoted by A. Giardina, "Ritorno al futuro: la romanità fascista," in *Il mito di Roma. Da Carlo Magno a Mussolini* (Bari, 2000) 219. The following paragraphs are indebted to Giardina's excellent study.

2 See E. Gentile, *Il culto del littorio. La sacralizzazione della politica nell' Italia fascista* (Rome, 1993); id. "Die Sakralisierung der Politik" in H. Maier (ed.), *Wege in die Gewalt: Die modernen politischen Religionen* (Frankfurt/M., 2002) 166–82; and Maier, *Politische Religionen: Die totalitären Systeme und das Christentum* (Freiburg, 1995); K. D. Bracher, "Nationalsozialismus, Faschismus und autoritäre Regime" in H. Maier (ed.), *"Totalitarismus" und "Politische Religionen": Konzepte des Diktaturvergleichs* (Paderborn, 1996).

3 *Discorsi di Pio XI ii* (1929–33) 2. ed. D. Bertetto O.S.B. (Vatican, 1985) 18.

4 D. Mack Smith, *Mussolini: A Biography* (New York, 1983), 163, 185, 202.

5 See, e.g., A. Cederna, *Mussolini urbanista: Lo sventramento di Roma negli anni del consenso* (Rome, 1980); M. Calvesi, E. Guidoni, S. Lux (eds.), *E42: Utopia e scenario del regime*, 2 vols (Venice, 1987); R. Marinai, *Fascismo e "città nuove"* (Milan, 1970); M. Rinaldi, "Il volto effemero della città nell' età dell' impero e dell' autarchia" in *La Capitale a Roma: Città e arredo urbano (1870–1945)*, exhibition

catalogue (Rome, 1991), 118–29, and S. Scarrocchia, *Albert Speer e Marcello Piacentini. L'architettura del totalitarismo negli anni trenta* (Milan, 1999).

6 Mack Smith, *Mussolini*, 136–37.

7 On the personality of Pius XI, see the contemporary accounts of F. Charles-Roux, *Huit Ans au Vatican 1932–1940* (Paris, 1947), 9–66, and D. Binchy, *Church and State in Fascist Italy* (Oxford, 1941), 71–99.; for context, see *Achille Ratti, Pape Pie XI*, École française de Rome (Rome, 1996); cf. *Pio XI nel trentesimo della morte (1939–1969) Raccolta di studi e di memorie* (Milan, 1969).

8 *Discorsi* II, 199.

9 P. Kent, *The Pope and the Duce: the International Impact of the Lateran Agreements* (London, 1981), 193.

10 See M. Agostino, *Le pape Pie XI et l'opinion* (Rome, 1991), 445.

11 See K. Repgen in *Handbuch der Kirchengeschichte*, VII: *Die Weltkirche im 20: Jahrhundert*, eds. H. Jedin and K. Repgen (Freiburg, 1979), 51 ff.

12 J. Pollard, *The Vatican and Italian Fascism 1929–32: A Study in Conflict* (Cambridge, 1982), 199.

13 Pollard, *The Vatican...*, 71–72.

14 See M. Galfré, "La disciplina della libertà. Sull' adozione dei testi nella scuola fascista" *Italia contemporanea* 228 (September 2002): 407–38.

15 *Discorsi* II, 214–215.

16 Giardina, "Ritorno al futuro," 256.

17 Quoted by Pollard, *The Vatican...*, 167.

18 See A. Riccardi, "La vita religiosa," in *Roma capitale*, ed. V. Vidotto (Bari, 2002), 303 ff.

19 *Discorsi* II, 1037.

20 *Discorsi* II, 109.

21 *Discorsi* II, 153.

22 *Discorsi* II, 238.

23 *Discorsi* III, 179.

24 On what follows, see the excellent study by G. Miccoli, "Das katholische Italien und der Faschismus," *Quellen und Forschungen aus italienischen Archiven und Bibliotheken* 18 (1998): 539–66.

25 *Discorsi* II, 209.

26 *Discorsi* II, 208.

27 *Discorsi* II, 217.

28 *Discorsi* II, 218.

29 On Rosenberg, see below, p. 48 ff.

CHAPTER 3   INSIDE THE VATICAN

1 A. Hudal, *Missa Papalis. Einführung in die Liturgie der feierlichen Papstmesse* (Rome, 1925), 28 ff.

2 *Acta Apostolicae Sedis* XXI (1929), 300 (paraphrase).

3 A. Ottaviani, *Compendium iuris publici ecclesiastici* (Rome, 1936), 376 ff, 371, 374, 395.

4 F. Ehrle, "Von Benedikt V zu Pius XI," *Stimmen der Zeit* 103 (1922), 16: "der Mann auf dem Stuhle Petri . . . wird selbst den Mächtigen dieser Erde al seine beachtenswerte Macht, als eine weihevolle, ehrfurchtgebietende Erscheinung gelten."

5 E. Pacelli, *Erster Apostolischer Nuntius beim Deutschen Reich, Gesammelte Reden*, ed. L. Kaas (Berlin, 1930), 58 ("Primat des Reichsgedankens . . . Triumph über den düsteren Dämon der Gewalt," "brutaler Machtgedanke . . . milde Imperium des Rechts").

6 Ibid. 88, 119 ff.

7 Ibid. 177–78.

8 See A. Martini, S.J., "Il cardinale Tardini e la seconda Guerra Mondiale," *La Civiltà Cattolica* ii (1968): 3–14.

9 D. Tardini, "San Tommaso d'Aquino e la romanità," *Rivista di filosofia neoscolastica* 39(1937): 14.

10 See O. Chadwick, *A History of the Popes 1830–1914* (Oxford, 1998), 340 ff.

11 Quoted by Chadwick, *History,* 357; on Benigni, see P. Scoppola in *DBI* 8:506–508.

12 ACDF, S.O. 125/28 [R.V. 1928 n. 2], vol. I.

13 D. Sbarretti, *Il primo giubileo dell'opera della preservazione della fede in Roma* (Vatican, 1924), 8–13.

14 A. Riccardi, "La vita religiosa," in *Roma capitale*, ed. Vidotto, 306 ff.

15 G. Pizzardo, *Union internationale des ligues féminines catholiques. IXe conseil international: Deux conférences sur l'Action catholique* (March 29–30, 1934), 19.

16 Id., *Azione cattolica e assistenza religiosa agli operai* (Rome, 1937).

17 C. Salotti, *Le crisi della società contemporanea: Studi apologetici* (Isola del Liri, 1931).

CHAPTER 4 VOICES FROM GERMANY

1 See K. Repgen, *Von der Reformation zur Gegenwart: Beiträge zu Grundfragen der neuzeitlichen Geschichte,* eds. K. Gotto and H. Hockerts (Paderborn, 1968), 155ff.

2 Ibid. 181ff.

3 Ibid. 187.

4 See W. Adolph, *Sie sind nicht vergessen: Gestalten aus der jüngsten Kirchengeschichte* (Berlin, 1972), 15–60, and M. Biffi, *Mons. Cesare Orsenigo: Nunzio Apostolico in Germania (1930–1946)* (Milan, 1997).

5 ASV, AES, *Germania* 1933–34, Pos. 641–643, fasc. 157, 19^r.

6 Ibid. 22^r.

7 Ibid. 32^{r-v} (March 22, 1933).

8 Ibid. 42ff.

9 Ibid. 107^v.

10 Scholder, *Die Kirchen und das Dritte Reich: Vorgeschichte und Zeit der Illusionen 1918–1934* (Munich, 2000), I, 364 ff, especially 371.

11 ASV, AES, *Germania* 1933–34, Pos. 641–643, fasc. 157, 88^r.

12 "Poiché è nelle tradizioni della Santa Sede svolgere la sua universale missione di pace e di carità verso tutti gli uomini, a qualsiasi condizione sociale e religione appartengono, interponendo anche, ove sia necessario, i suoi caritatevoli uffici, il Santo Padre incarica l'Eccellenza Vostra Reverendissima di vedere se e come sia possibile interessarsi nel senso desiderato." ASV, AES, *Germania* 1933–34, Pos. 641–643, fasc. 158, 4^r.

13 Ibid. 5^r.

14 Ibid. 11^r.

15 Ibid. 14^{r}ff. Cf. W. Kaltefleiter, *Zwischen Kreuz und Hakenkreuz* (Wiesbaden, 2003).

16 "Ist nicht diese Vergötzung der Rasse und der Staatsgewalt, die täglich durch Rundfunk den Massen eingehämmert wird, eine offene Häresie? Ist nicht der Vernichtungskampf gegen das jüdische Blut eine Schmähung der allerheiligsten Menschheit unseres Erlösers ...? " Ibid. 17^r.

17 Ibid. 18^r.

18 Ibid. 33^{r-v}.

19 ASV, AES, *Germania* 1933–34, Pos. 641–643, fasc. 159, 122ff (cipher: May 2, 1933).

20 Ibid. 51^{r-v} (August 30, 1933).

21 Ibid. 54^v (October 2, 1933).

22 Ibid. 86^v (August 16, 1934).

23 On Muckermann, see H. Gruber, *Friedrich Muckermann, S. J. 1883–1946: Ein katholischer Publizist in der Auseinandersetzung mit dem Zeitgeist* (Mainz, 1993).

24 "Der Nationalsozialismus ist seinem Wesen nach eine Art Religion ... Der Nationalsozialismus tritt vielmehr das Erbe der Reformation Luthers an, um alles das zu beseitigen, was Luther noch hatte stehen lassen. Wir haben es also mit einer Religion zu tun ... dazu geführt von Männern, die keinerlei religiöse und moralische Hemmungen kennen. Sie arbeitet mit einer revolutionären Dynamik, die sich vor allem an die untermenschlichen Instinkte wendet ... Warum, so fragt das Volk und so fragt bald die ganze Welt, tritt die Kirche gegen den Nationalsozialismus nicht mit der gleichen Energie auf, die sie gegenüber dem Bolschewismus und dem Sozialismus gefunden hat?" ASV, AES, *Germania* 1934–35, Pos. 666, fasc. 221, 5 ff.

25 ASV, AES, *Germania* 1932–36, Pos. 632, fasc. 150, 3–5.

26 Ibid. 6^r, 42^r, 44^r.

27 Ibid. 45^v (July 30, 1933).

28 Ibid. 47^r.

29 Ibid. 49^r–51^r.

30 "Eine grosse Erleichterung für den Episkopat würde es sein, wenn der Heilige Stuhl selbst über die Opportunität einer Stellungnahme Beschluss fassen oder

einen Wink dem Episkopat geben wollte, der wegen der Tragweite dieser Angele-
genheit . . . nicht wird vorgehen können." Ibid. 51^r.

31 Ibid. 56^r (Pacelli to Orsenigo, August 10, 1933).

32 Ibid. 68ff.

33 Ibid. 80^r.

34 ASV, AES, *Germania* 1932–36, Pos. 632, fasc. 151, 15ff.

35 ACDF, S.O. *Germania*—Segretariato di Stato Prot. 1220/1933, R.V. 1933 n. 15.

36 "Mit staatspolizeilichen Gewaltmitteln allein wird die kommunistische
Gefahr nicht beseitigt . . . Das Ziel der Kirche dagegen ist nicht die Vernichtung
der Kommunisten, sondern ihre Belehrung." Ibid. 4^d.

37 "Eine durch Machtziele verratene Kirche hat das deutsche Volk vergiftet . . .
Wo steht dieser Gegner? Die Kirche in Rom," "Wir haben einen tausendjährigen
Feind, den Feind in Rom," "Rom ist schuld am verlorenen Krieg." Basic educational course for female teachers of economics (Erster Schulungskurs für
Wirtschaftslehrerinnen), Mindelburg bei Mindelheim July 8–14, 1934, sent by Father Robert Leiber to Pius XI, ASV, AES, *Germania* 1932–36, Pos. 632, fasc. 151, 44^r
ff, especially 46^r, 53^r.

38 ACDF, S.O. 535/30; R.V. 1934/12.

CHAPTER 5   THE POLITICS OF CONDEMNATION

1 See M. Liebmann, "Bischof Hudal und der Nationalsozialismus," *Geschichte
und Gegenwart* 44 (1988), 263–280, and M. Langer, *Alois Hudal: Bischof zwischen
Kreuz und Hakenkreuz. Versuch einer Biographie* (Ph.D. dissertation, Vienna, 1995).

2 On Hudal's earlier career, see *Jahresbericht der deutschen Nationalstiftung S.
Maria dell'Anima in Rom*, 1925–27, 6.

3 *Soldatenpredigten* (Graz, 1917).

4 "Nichts ist dem Geiste Christi fremder als nationaler Chauvinismus, der die
Gesetze des Blutes über jene der Kultur stellt. Wenn wir ehrlich sein wollen,
müssen wir gestehen, dass der überspannte Nationalismus vieler Kreise unseres
Vaterlandes eine Mitursache dieses grausamen Krieges war. Sie haben die Ver-
wandtschaft des Blutes höher gewertet als die Gemeinsamkeit der Menschen in
Religion, Wissenschaft und Kunst. Es musste der Krieg kommen, um diese Ver-
wirrung des Menschengeistes, diesen Abfall vom Geiste christlicher Liebe, zu
heilen." Ibid. 44–45.

5 "Fahnentreue ist Gottestreue," ibid. 116.

6 *Die serbisch-orthodoxe Nationalkirche* (Graz, 1922), preface.

7 ACDF S.O., 1939/27; R.V. 1927, 18.

8 A. Hudal, *Römische Tagebücher. Lebensbeichte eines alten Bischofs* (Graz,
1976), 41.

9 See F. Engel-Janosi, *Vom Chaos zur Katastrophe. Vatikanische Gespräche
1918–1938* (Vienna, 1971), 73 ff.

10 J. Kremsmaier, *Der Weg zum Österreichischen Konkordat von 1933/34* (Vienna,
1980).

11 *Vom deutschen Schaffen in Rom: Predigten, Ansprachen und Vorträge* (Innsbruck, 1933), 82; 255–257.

12 See above, p. 25.

13 "Die gesamte deutsche Sache, deren Diener und Wegbereiter im Ausland ich immer sein wollte," *Ecclesiae et Nationi. Katholische Gedanken in einer Zeitwende* (Rome, 1934), 9.

14 Ibid., 32.

15 Ibid., 48.

16 Hudal in B. Galletto, *Vita di Dolfuss* (Turin, 1935), v–vii.

17 See J. Prévotat, *Les catholiques et l'Action française: Histoire d'une condamnation 1899–1939* (Paris, 2001).

18 ACDF, S.O. 1413/30 i.

19 See above, p. 40.

20 See P. Godman, *Weltliteratur auf dem Index. Die geheimen Gutachten des Vatikans* (Berlin, 2001).

21 *Indice dei libri proibiti* (Rome, 1930), iii and v.

22 F. Sandmann, *Die Haltung des Vatikans zum Nationalsozialismus im Spiegel des "Osservatore Romano" (von 1929 bis zum Kriegsausbruch)*, diss. Mainz (1965), 31 ff.

23 On Rosenberg, his book, and its reception, see R. Baumgärtner, *Weltanschauungskampf im Dritten Reich: Die Auseinandersetzung der Kirchen mit Alfred Rosenberg*, VKZG. F 22 (Mainz, 1977).

24 ACDF, S.O. 4304, 1933 i (1). On his role in the censure of Rosenberg, see Hudal, *Römische Tagebücher* 119.

25 See B. Hamann, *Hitlers Wien: Lehrjahre eines Diktators* (Munich, 1998), 285ff, especially 333ff.

26 *Hitler's Table-Talk*, no. 148, 315; *Hitlers Tischgespräche*, no. 25, 147.

27 See Bärsch, *Die politische Religion des Nationalsozialismus*, 220ff.

28 Baumgärtner, *Weltanschauungskampf*, 66 ff.

29 E. Bergmann, *Die deutsche Nationalkirche* (Breslau, 1933); ACDF, S.O. 4304, 1933 i (2).

30 Baumgärtner, *Weltanschauungskampf*, 154 ff.

31 Stasiewski, *Akten* I, 540.

32 Hudal, *Römische Tagebücher* 82, 117 ff.

33 See above, p. 11.

34 "Der N[ational-]S[ozialismus] habe, wenn religiös geläutert, nach meiner Überzeugung eine providentielle Aufgabe gegenüber dem Vordrängen des Nihilismus aus dem Osten," *Römische Tagebücher* 118.

35 ACDF, S.O. R.V. 1934, 29, Prot. 3373/34, vol. 1, 1, 2–4.

36 See above, p. 26.

37 ACDF, S.O., R.V. 1934, 29, Prot. 3373/34, vol. 1, 1, 3–4.

CHAPTER 6   THE JESUITS AND THE RACISTS

1 See F. Zippel, *Kirchenkampf in Deutschland 1933–1934: Religionsverfolgung und Selbstbehauptung der Kirchen in der nationalsozialistischen Zeit*, ed. H. Herzfeld (Berlin, 1965), 418 ff (no. 40).

2 M. Burleigh, *Die Zeit des Nationalsozialismus: Eine Gesamtdarstellung* (Frankfurt/Main, 2000), 227 ff.

3 Zippel, *Kirchenkampf* 423–424.

4 A. Tenneson, S.J., "Pie XI et la Compagnie," *Lettres de Jersey* XLIII (1929–30), 309–24.

5 On Ledóchowski, see W. Gramatowski in *Diccionario histórico de la Compañia de Jesus*, eds. E. O'Neil and J. Domínguez, S.J., II (Rome, 2001), 1697ff. and cf. G. Cassiani Ingoni, S.J., *P. Wlodimiro Ledóchowski, XXVI Generale della Compagnia di Gesù (1866–1942)* (Rome, 1945).

6 See Huber, *Friedrich Muckermann*, 306 ff.

7 Ibid. 271 ff, 292 ff, 306 ff.

8 F. Muckermann, *Im Kampf zwischen zwei Epochen: Lebenserinnerungen*, ed. N. Junk (Mainz, 1973), 105 ff, 107 ff.

9 See I. Richter, *Katholizismus und Eugenik in der Weimarer Republik und im Dritten Reich: Zwischen Sittlichkeitsreform und Rassenhygiene*, VKG B 88 (Paderborn, 2001), and M. Burleigh, *Death and Deliverance: "Euthanasia" in Germany c. 1900–1945* (Cambridge, 1994).

10 J. Mayer, *Gesetzliche Unfruchtbarmachung Geisteskranker* (Freiburg, 1927). With ACDF, S.O. 1797/1928 and 1855, 1930.

11 AAS 18 (1926), 523.

12 See Stasiewski (ed.), *Akten* I, 358 ff.

13 On Rabeneck, see M. Colpo, S.J., in *Archivum Historicum Societatis Iesu* XXIX (1960), 526.

14 ACDF, S.O. R.V. 1934, n. 29; Prot. 3373/34, 1, 1–3.

15 Bärsch, *Die politische Religion des Nationalsozialismus*, 271 ff.

16 See above, p. 1.

17 See Y. Congar, *The Catholic Church and the Race Question* (Paris, 1953).

18 Bärsch, *Die politische Religion des Nationalsozialismus*, 305 ff.

19 Ibid. 304, 312, 334 ff.

20 Ibid. 272.

CHAPTER 7   APPEASEMENT AND OPPORTUNISM

1 See J. Cornwell, *Hitler's Pope: The Secret History of Pius XII* (London, 1999).

2 Ibid. 193 ff.

3 None of the diplomatic notes edited by D. Albrecht, *Der Notenwechsel zwischen dem Heiligen Stuhl und der deutschen Reichsregierung* 3 vols. VKZ Q, 1,10,29 (Mainz, 1965-1980) is cited by Cornwell in the original.

4 "Der Heilige Stuhl kann zu seinem Bedauern seine Zustimmung nicht aussprechen, wenn mit vielfach fragwürdiger, vor einer eingehenderen Betrach-

tung nicht standhaltender Schematisierung verschiedenartigster Symptome und Einzelheiten versucht wird, Erklärungen für Zustände zu finden, die von Tag zu Tag unerträglicher werden und deren beschleunigte Überwindung ein unausweichliches Postulat der Billigkeit, Gerechtigkeit, der Staatsautorität und Vertragstreue ist. Ein autoritäres Regime, das sich mit Bewusstsein von den behaupteten Mängeln und Unzulänglichkeiten eines von Massenstimmungen abhängigeren Regimes abwendet und im Führergedanken die Grundvoraussetzung staatlicher Aufbauarbeit sieht, kann weniger als andere Herrschaftsformen seine Aufgabe darin erblicken, vor solchen Stimmungen zu kapitulieren oder sie durch Toleranz indirekt zu begünstigen." Albrecht (ed.), *Notenwechsel* 1, 126.

5 Cornwell, *Hitler's Pope* 165, quoting the document from E. Helmreich, *The German Churches under Hitler: Background, Struggle, and Epilogue* (Detroit, 1979), 268.

6 "Der katholische Volksteil, gleich welcher politischen Richtung er in einer früheren Zeit folgte, ist gleichberechtigter Bestandteil des gesamten deutschen Volkes. Er hat den Anspruch, nicht unter Ausnahmerecht und Ausnahmemisstrauen gestellt zu bleiben . . . Im staatspolitischen Bereich werden die gläubigen Katholiken jeder berechtigten Beanspruchung ihrer Treue und Opferbereitschaft nachkommen. Wenn sie ihre Unterstützung solchen Strömungen verweigern, die unter staatspolitischer Tarnung weltanschaulich-irreligiöse Ziele verfolgen, dann tun sie dies nicht deshalb, weil sie dem Staate nicht geben wollen, was des Staates ist, sondern weil sie den heiligen Imperativ des Schriftwortes vor sich sehen: 'Man muss Gott mehr gehorchen als den Menschen.' " Albrecht (ed.), *Notenwechsel* I, 126–27.

7 "Der Heilige Stuhl kann seine oberstkirchlichen Erwägungen und Urteile nicht von irgendwelchen parteipolitischen Rücksichten beeinflussen lassen. Seine Mission ist das Heil der unsterblichen Seelen." Ibid. 127.

8 See above, p. 22.

9 Albrecht (ed.), *Notenwechsel* I, 128, 130.

10 Ibid. 136.

11 Ibid. 138.

12 Ibid. 145.

13 "Sinnlosigkeit" / "Ungeheuerlichkeit." Ibid. 146.

14 "Der erzieherische Totalitätsanspruch des Staates ist demnach nicht nur in thesi falsch, sondern auch in praxi auf die Dauer selbstmörderisch. Die Geister, die er auf den Wegen einer konfessionsfreien und konfessionsfeindlichen Staatserziehung heranzieht, werden in ihrer religiösen Entbundenheit seine Feinde von Morgen sein. Es gibt keine wahre Volks- und Staatswohlfahrt ohne Religion. Nur zuchtvolle Kraft ist wahren Aufbaus fähig. Zuchtentwöhnte physische Kraft wird in Zerstörung enden. Zucht ist undenkbar ohne Norm. Menschliche Norm ist undenkbar ohne Verankerung im Göttlichen. Diese letzte Verankerung kann nicht liegen in einem gewillkürten 'Göttlichen' der Rasse. Nicht in der Verabsolutierung der Nation. Ein solcher 'Gott' des Blutes und der Rasse wäre weiter nichts als das selbstgeschaffene Widerbild eigener Beschränktheit und Enge. Eine Vergötterung

kollektiven Stolzes, aber nicht das gläubige und demütige Anerkennen eines alles Geschöpfliche überragenden höchsten Seins, in dessen Vaterhand die ganze Menschheit geborgen ist als in ihrem Schöpfer, ihrem Erhalter und Lenker. Die von manchen Kreisen gepredigte Rückkehr zu einer 'Nationalreligion' wäre nicht nur ein 'Sündenfall' im übernatürlichen, sondern auch ein Rückfall im natürlich-kulturellen Sinne. *Die Kirche als Hüterin des Glaubenserbes Christi kann nicht widerstandslos zusehen, wenn der Jugend, der Trägerin der kommenden Generationen, statt der Frohbotschaft der Lehre Christi die Trutz- und Trugbotschaft eines neuen Materialismus der Rasse gepredigt wird und staatliche Institutionen hierzu missbraucht werden.*

Die Kirche weiss um die Rasse als biologische Tatsache und leugnet in gewissen, von unwissenschaftlichen und unhistorischen Übertreibungen sich fernhaltenden Grenzen die Lebenswerte und Kulturantriebe nicht, die in ihr ruhen. Sie weiss aber auch, dass die Verabsolutierung des Rassegedankens und vor allem seine Proklamation als Religionsersatz ein Irrweg ist, dessen Unheilsfrüchte nicht auf sich warten lassen werden. Aus solchen Zielsetzungen wird nie eine Jugend erwachsen können, die den gewaltigen Belastungsproben der schweren Gegenwart und Zukunft gewachsen ist. Solchen irrigen Parolen gegenüber, die von einflussreichen Stellen gerade in die heranwachsende Jugend geworfen werden, ist die Erhaltung und Sicherung einer normalen Erziehungsfunktion der Kirche unter der Jugend als Ausgleich und Korrektive, auch vom wohlverstandenen Staatsinteresse aus gesehen, von lebensnotwendiger Unentbehrlichkeit." Ibid. 146–47.

15 ASV, AES, *Germania* 1934–51, Pos. 661–63, fasc. 210, 23 ff.

16 See Besier, *Die Kirchen und das Dritte Reich*, 122 ff.

17 ASV, AES, *Germania* 1935, Pos. 692, fasc. 260, 4–8, 22, 23, 25, 30.

18 "Bezüglich der kirchlichen Stellungnahme zur Sterilisation in der in Deutschland üblichen Kanzlerverkündigung dürfte ein Schritt des Heiligen Stuhls in dem angeregten Sinne schwer tunlich sein. Bei einem etwaigen negativen Bescheid seitens der Reichsregierung würde die Lage des Episkopates nur noch schwieriger sein. Die Form der Verkündigung kann—Einheitlichkeit vorausgesetzt—dem gewissenhaften Ermessen des Hochwürdigen Episkopates überlassen bleiben . . . Falls die Hochwürdigen Herren Bischöfe glauben, dass ein Akt der Höflichkeit gegenüber der Regierung Ihre Lage erleichtern werde, können sie unmittelbar vor der Verlesung eine entsprechende Mitteilung . . . an die zuständige Stelle gelangen lassen, mit dem Hinweis, dass die erwähnte Verlesung nach Massgabe des Reichskonkordats . . . stattfinden wird." Ibid. 38.

19 Ibid. 51.

20 ASV, AES, *Germania* 1935–38, Pos. 692, fasc. 264, 5.

21 ASV, AES, *Germania* 1934–35, Pos. 666, fasc. 221, 27–28.

22 ASV, AES, *Germania* 1934–35, Pos. 666, fasc. 223, 3 ff.

23 *Deutsches Volk und christliches Abendland* (Innsbruck, 1935).

24 Ibid. 15–16.

25 Ibid. 22–23.

26 "Dem politischen Führer haben religiöse Lehren und Einrichtungen seines Volkes immer unantastbar zu sein, sonst darf er nicht Politiker sei, sondern soll Reformator werden, wenn er das Zeug hierzu besitzt. Eine andere Haltung würde vor allem Deutschland zu einer Katastrophe führen." I (Munich, 1933), 127.

27 *Deutsches Volk*, 24–25.

28 "Rom muss uns mehr sein als eine Rechtsangelegenheit, mehr als eine religiöse Organisation . . . ," *Deutsches Volk* 28.

29 *Der Vatikan und die modernen Staaten* (Innsbruck, 1935).

30 Ibid. 50.

31 Ibid. 59.

32 Ibid. 49.

33 "Der religiöse und sittliche Auswurf des Judentums, der heute von Moskau aus die christlichen Völker Europas in ständiger Unruhe halt, um die Weltherrschaft einer Rasse die Wege zu bereiten, die der Menschheit wertvolle Kulturgüter und hervorragende Persönlichkeiten geschenkt hat, die aber, sobald sie religiös entwurzelt ist, jeden anderen Kulturkreis zersetzen muss." Ibid. 82.

34 E. Pacelli, *Discorsi e panegirici (1937–1938)*² (Vatican, 1956), 430 ff.

35 ASV, AES, *Germania* 1935 "Scatole," fasc. 9a, 32–33.

CHAPTER 8 THREE STRATEGIES

1 See above, pp. 81 and 154.

2 See L. Volk, "Die Fuldaer Bischofskonferenz von Hitlers Machtergreifung bis zur Enzyklika 'Mit brennender Sorge,' " in id. *Katholische Kirche und Nationalsozialismus. Ausgewählte Aufsätze* ed. D. Albrecht (Mainz, 1987), 11–33.

3 See above, p. 33.

4 On Chagnon, see G. Chaussé in *Diccionario histórico de la Compañía de Jesus* I (Rome, 2001), 747–748.

5 *Notenwechsel* I (ed. Albrecht), 309.

6 ACDF, S.O. R.V. 1934, 29; Prot. 3373/1, 3, 16–26.

7 "Der katholischen Kirche liegt es fern, eine Staatsform oder eine staatliche Um- und Neuorganisation als solche abzulehnen. Sie lebt in korrekten und guten Beziehungen zu Staaten der verschiedensten Regierungsformen und der unterschiedlichsten inneren Struktur. Sie hat Konkordate abgeschlossen mit Monarchien und Republiken, mit demokratisch und mit autoritär geleiteten Staaten." *Notenwechsel* I (ed. Albrecht), 69.

8 "Sie beurteilt die einzelnen Staatsformen nach ihrem Nutz- und Erfolgswert für die wahre Wohlfahrt der Völker, welch letztere nie und nimmer in Fremdheit oder gar im Kampf gegen die geoffenbarte christliche Wahrheit . . ." Ibid. 309.

9 See above, p. 15.

10 Cf. H. Trevor-Roper, "Hitlers Kriegsziele." *Vierteljahrshefte für Zeitgeschichte* 13 (1965): 285–337.

11 D. Kertzer, *Unholy War. The Vatican's Role in the Rise of Modern Anti-Semitism* (London, 2001), 275.

12 See above, pp. 25–26.

13 See below, p. 121.

14 See above, p. 73.

15 See below, p. 104.

16 See above, p. 33.

17 ... "Die Menschenrechte sind in Gefahr. Niemand wagt mehr zu sprechen gegen jene Diktatoren, die den Menschen behandeln wie einen Sklaven. Niemand spricht angesichts all der Konzentrationslager, der Morde, der Vergewaltigungen der Freiheit jenes göttliche Wort: Das ist Dir nicht erlaubt! Spräche es die Kirche, erfüllte sie hier ihren hohen Beruf, die Antwort wäre ein begeistertes Echo über die ganze Erde hin!"

18 For background, see V. Lippomarda, *The Jesuits and the Third Reich* (Lampeter, 1989).

19 See Sandmann, *Die Haltung des Vatikans*, 108 ff.

20 "Überaus selten trifft man jemanden, der das Regime aus grundsätzlichen Überzeugungen ablehnt, und niemanden habe ich getroffen, der zur aktiven Opposition bereit wäre ... das tägliche Gift der Verlogenheit und der monotone Optimismus ... wirkt [*sic*] wie Opium auf die Geister, auch auf die, die der Meinung sind, die Dinge zu durchschauen und nichts von dem zu glauben, was täglich aus der Goebbelschen Lügenküche vorgesetzt wird. Niemand, der täglich der Einwirkung dieses Giftes ausgesetzt ist, kann sich auf Dauer seinen den Geist lähmenden Wirkung entziehen," ASV, AES, *Germania* 1935–37, Pos. 676, fasc. 245, 35 ff.

21 "Die Arbeit der katholischen Kirche trägt schon unverkennbare Früchte. Aber es zeichnet sich auch jetzt schon immer deutlicher die Gefahr ab, dass die Anregung, die der Widerstand gegen die weltanschaulichen Experimente der Nazis gibt, nicht bis zu einer aktiven Opposition auf religiösem Gebiet weitergeführt wird, sondern in einem Katakombenchristentum endet ... d.h. dass man auf alle Einwirkung auf das Leben ausserhalb der Kirchenmauern verzichtet," ibid. 37.

22 Ibid. 38.

23 See Y. Congar, *Mon Journal du Concile* II (Paris, 2002), 606 (*s.n.*).

24 A Ottaviani, *Institutiones iuris publici ecclesiastici*, 2 vols. (Vatican, 1935).

25 Ibid. 42 ff.

26 Ibid. 130 ff.

27 *Compendium iuris publici ecclesiastici* (Vatican, 1936), discussed by H. Hürten, *Deutsche Katholiken 1918–1945* (Paderborn, 1992), 370 and n. 36.

CHAPTER 9 THE GRAND DESIGN

1 ACDF, S.O., R.V. 1934, 29, Prot. 3373/34, vol. 2, 4.

2 M. S. Gillet, *L'église catholique et les relations internationales* (Rome, 1932).

3 Id., *Le Pape Pie XI et les hérésies sociales* (Paris, 1939).

4 See above, p. 24.

5 See C. Casula, *Domenico Tardini 1888–1961* (Rome, 1988).

6 D. Tardini, *Pio XII* (Vatican, 1960).

7 Quoted by M. Feldkamp, *Pius XII und Deutschland* (Göttingen, 2000), 132 and n. 371.

8 ACDF, S.O., R.V. 1934, 29, Prot. 3373/34, vol. 2, 4, 7.

9 ACDF, S.O., R.V. 1934, 29, Prot. 3373/34, vol. 2, 4, 9.

10 ACDF, S.O., R.V. 1934, 29, Prot. 3373/34, vol. 2, 5.

11 ACDF, S.O., R.V. 1934, 29, Prot. 3373/34, vol. 2, 6, 2.

12 Gruber, *Friedrich Muckermann*, 308, 317 ff.

13 J. Ledit, *Paradossi del communismo* (Milan, 1938), 79, and cf. id., *La religione e il comunismo* (Milan, 1937).

14 See E. Tokareva, "Le relazioni fra l'URSS e il Vaticano: dalle trattative alla rottura (1922–1929)" in *Santa Sede e Russia da Leone XIII a Pio XI* Atti del simposio organizzato dal Pontificio Comitato di Scienze Storiche e dall'Istituto di Storia Universale dell'Accademia delle Scienze di Mosca (Vatican, 2002), 149–261.

15 See H. Stehle, *Die Ostpolitik des Vaticans 1917–1975* (Munich, 1975), 150 ff.

16 Ibid. 176.

17 ACDF, S.O., R.V. 1934, 29, Prot. 3373/34, vol. 2, 7.

18 See above, p. 77.

19 See R. De Felice, *Mussolini il Duce II: Lo Stato totalitario 1936–1940* (Turin, 1981).

20 ACDF, S.O., R.V. 1934, 29, Prot. 3373/34, vol. 2, 8.

21 ACDF, S.O. 2935/29i.

22 See above, p. 15.

23 See below, Appendix II.

24 ACDF, S.O., R.V. 1934, 29, Prot. 3373/34, vol. 4, 12.

25 ACDF, S.O., R.V. 1934, 29, Prot. 3373/34, vol. 4, 12, 5–6.

26 Ibid.

27 ACDF, S.O., R.V. 1934, 29, Prot. 3373/34, vol. 4, 12–13.

28 ACDF, S.O., R.V. 1934, 29, Prot. 3373/34, vol. 4, 12, 16.

29 *The Catholic Mind* 40 (January 1943), 41–60.

30 ACDF, S.O., R.V. 1934, 29, Prot. 3373/34, vol. 12, 37

CHAPTER 10 OUTBURSTS AND INTRIGUES

1 ASV, AES, *Germania* 1935–38, Pos. 692, fasc. 264, 5.

2 See Besier, *Die Kirchen und das Dritte Reich*, 686 and n. 163.

3 ASV, AES, *Germania* 1935–38, Pos. 692, fasc. 264, 9.

4 "So handeln Freunde nicht. Wir sind in Wahrheit von Schmerz erfüllt und tief unzufrieden." Ibid.

5 Ibid. 10.

6 Ibid. 37.

7 "Neben verbindlichem Dank für ausgesprochene Glückwünsche bedingt Gesamtlage leider Hinweis auf tiefe Beunruhigung, die staatliche Haltung gegenüber katholischer Kirche und soeben eintreffende Nachrichten von Polizei-

massnahmen gegen Priester und katholische Jugendvereinigungen hervorrufen,"
ibid. 38.

8 Ibid. 40 (February 21, 1936, Orsenigo to Pacelli).

9 Ibid. 42 (copy of Neurath's letter to Orsenigo).

10 Ibid. 44 (March 29, 1936).

11 Ibid. 46 (April 24, 1936, Orsenigo to Pacelli).

12 ASV, AES, *Germania* 1936, Pos. 695, fasc. 267, 5–10.

13 Ibid. 13 ff.

14 "Andererseits ist es eine von jedem guten deutschen Staatsbürger als Selbstver-
ständlichkeit angesehene Notwendigkeit, dass der Staat alle jungen Deutschen
ohne Unterschied der Konfessionen zu einem klaren positiven nationalsozialistischen Bekenntnis . . . erzieht, wie es selbstverständlich ist, dass der nationalsozialistische Staat nur jene Jugend nehmen kann, die sich ehrlich und rückhaltlos zur
nationalsozialistischen Weltanschauung bekennt." Ibid. 14.

15 "Wenn ich recht sehe, ist es die Absicht des Ministeriums, diktatorisch zu handeln . . . auf unsere Eingaben gar nicht oder nur kurz ausweichend zu antworten,
aber inzwischen unter Anwendung aller staatlichen Machtmittel aller Mitglieder
katholischer Vereine in die nationalsozialistischen Verbände zu bringen, dagegen
eine gleichzeitige Mitgliedschaft derselben zu katholischen Organisationen als
verderblich für die Volkseinheit und darum als untragbar zu bezeichnen, um so die
Auswirkung des Reichskonkordats indirekt als nicht mehr aktuell zu behandeln."
Ibid. 66.

16 "An führenden Stellen der nationalsozialistischen Partei ist der Geist des
Bolschewismus als Hass gegen das Christentum und speziell gegen die katholische
Kirche so scharf, dass ich schon wiederholt der Regierung vorgehalten habe: die
Publikationen und Abbildungen offizieller Zeitschriften nationalsozialistischer
Organisationen sind noch schlimmer und schmachvoller, als sie in Russland gewe-
sen sind. Wie die Stimmen offizieller Organe ist doch auch der Geist des
Führertums." Ibid. 67[r].

17 "Ein Vernichtungskampf gegen das katholische Glaubensleben." Ibid. 67[v].

18 Ibid. 69.

19 Ibid. 72–74.

20 ASV, AES, *Germania* 1935–38, Pos. 692, fasc. 263, 36 ff = *Bischof Clemens August von Galen, Akten, Briefe und Predigten 1935–1946*, I, ed. P. Löffler, VKZ A, 42
(Paderborn, 1996), no. 164, 367 ff, especially 372.

21 ASV, AES, *Germania* 1936, "Scatola" 12, 29 ff.

22 Ibid. 46.

23 Ibid. 53.

24 Ibid. 103.

25 ASV, AES, *Germania* 1936, "Scatola" 13, 19–20, 35.

26 *Notenwechsel* I (ed. Albrecht), 333 ff.

27 Engel-Janosi, *Vom Chaos zur Katastrophe*, 186.

28 For background, see E. Weinzerl-Fischer, "Österreichs Katholiken und der Na-

tionalsozialismus II," *Wort und Wahrheit* XVIII (1963), 493 ff, and R. Ebneth, *Die Österreichische Wochenschrift "Der Christliche Ständestaat" Deutsche Emigration in Österreich 1933–1938,* VKZ B. 19 (Mainz, 1976), 114 ff.

29 See above, p. 56.

30 *Akten Kardinal Michael von Faulhabers 1917–1945,* II, ed. L. Volk (Mainz, 1978), 196 and n. 4.

31 *Reichspost* 1936, No. 215, 5.8., 1 ff.

32 Ibid. 1936, No. 202, 23.7, 1 ff.

33 *Völkischer Beobachter* 1936, No. 291, 17.10., 1 ff.

34 *Akten zur deutschen auswärtigen Politik 1918–1948, Aus dem Archiv des deutschen Auswärtigen Amtes* I, D (1937–1945), *Von Neurath zu Ribbentrop* (Baden-Baden, 1950), 2070/449771–776.

35 "Diesen Mann für uns kampffähig zu halten." Quoted by Besier, *Die Kirchen und das Dritte Reich* 764 and n. 225.

36 Ibid.

37 Weinzerl-Fischer, "Österreichs Katholiken . . . ," II, 498.

38 Probably an allusion to the policy of religious tolerance pursued toward Catholics by Theodoric (c. 445–526, German: Dietrich), king of the Ostrogoths from 475 and ruler of Italy from 493. From medieval Germanic poetry the name also acquired a heroic aura.

CHAPTER 11   THE COURT THEOLOGIAN OF THE PARTY

1 *Die Grundlagen des Nationalsozialismus: Eine ideengeschichtliche Untersuchung von Katholischer Warte,* 5 ed. (Leipzig, 1937).

2 Ibid. 20.

3 " . . . wäre es nicht möglich, diese grosse Bewegung im Sinne ihres Ursprunges als ein rein politisches Programm auszubauen, das nur Deutschlands Grösse will, aber die religiöse Sphäre der Anhänger als ein unverletzliches Heiligtum unberührt lässt?" ibid. 17.

4 See above, p. 55.

5 See above, p. 56.

6 "Hat der Nationalsozialismus nicht auch gute, wertvolle Anregungen dem deutschen Volke gebracht, so dass schon deshalb eine Unterstützung der Bewegung durch religiös positiv eingestellte Menschen nicht bloss wünschenswert, sondern unbedingt notwendig ist, um die religiöse Klärung, vor allem die Trennung des rein Politischen vom Weltanschaulichen herbeizuführen, die Hitler in seinem Buch 'Mein Kampf' richtunggebend für die Partei mit seinen Gedanken über Religion, Politik, Weltanschauung und Los-von-Rom-Bewegung vorgezeichnet hat." *Grundlagen* 17.

7 *Grundlagen,* 17.

8 Cf. G. Denzler, "Katholische Zugänge zum Nationalsozialismus" in id. and L. Siegele-Wenschkewitz (eds.), *Theologische Wissenschaft im "Dritten Reich": Ein ökumenisches Projekt* (Frankfurt, 2000), 40–67.

9 "über das Ziel dieses Werkes ist es auch [*sic*], den Nationalsozialismus an der kristallhellen Klarheit der katholischen Kirche zu beurteilen." *Grundlagen*, 18.

10 "mit dem Faschismus das feste Bollwerk zu sein gegenüber den Flutwellen des asiatischen Kulturbolschewismus, der heute alle Staaten und Völker in gleicher Weise bedroht." Ibid.

11 See above, p. 54.

12 *Grundlagen*, 26.

13 "Dem politischen Führer haben religiöse Lehren und Einrichtungen seines Volkes immer unantastbar zu sein, sonst darf er nicht Politiker sein, sondern Reformator werden, wenn er das Zeug hierzu besitzt!" *Mein Kampf,* I, 97–101, ed. (Munich, 1934), 126 cf 118 ff.

14 *Grundlagen*, 47. On Hitler's attitude to Schönerer, see Hamann, *Hitlers Wien*, 356 ff.

15 Ibid. 53, 56–57.

16 Ibid. 59.

17 Ibid. 64.

18 Ibid. 72 ff.

19 Ibid. 79–81.

20 See above.

21 *Grundlagen*, 84 ff.

22 "Wir haben als Christen und Katholiken nicht den geringsten Anlass, jenes Judentum zu verteidigen, das nach dem Weltkriege die Führung der Arbeitermassen im Sinne des Marxismus an sich gerissen und reichlich genug für selbstsüchtige Zwecke missbraucht hat." Ibid. 91–92.

23 Ibid. 99.

24 Ibid. 106.

25 Ibid. 109 ff.

26 Ibid. 134 ff.

27 Ibid. 139.

28 "vollständiges Abtreten des weltanschaulichen Gebiets an die Kirche" cited by Besier, *Die Kirchen und das Dritte Reich*, 764 and n. 230.

29 *Grundlagen*, 157.

30 Ibid. 171 ff. and 178.

31 Ibid. 179.

32 Ibid. 196.

33 Ibid. 217.

34 Ibid. 235.

35 Ibid. 240

36 Ibid. 243.

37 "Niemand im katholischen Lager leugnet das Positive, Grosse und Bleibende, das in dieser Bewegung gelegen ist, die neue Probleme berührt und Fragen aufgeworfen hat, mit denen das Christentum sich auseinandersetzen muss, um eine moderne Synthese von Deutschtum und Glaube zu finden." Ibid. 246.

38 "Ist der Nationalsozialismus nur ein politisch-soziales Problem, dann ist kein Grund für die Katholiken, die sich in der Liebe und Treue zu Staat und Nation von niemandem übertreffen lassen, um nicht auch treue vorbehaltlose Anhänger dieser Bewegung zu sein." Ibid. 253.

39 "Der Führer beherrscht die diplomatischen und gesellschaftlichen Formen mehr wie ein geborener Souverän sie beherrscht." *Akten Faulhaber*, I (ed. Volk), 194 (copy of a report sent to Pacelli).

40 "Der Reichskanzler lebt ohne Zweifel im Glauben an Gott. Er anerkennt das Christentum als den Baumeister der abendländischen Kultur … Weniger klar steht das Bild der katholischen Kirche vor seinem Geist als göttliche Stiftung, mit ihrer göttlichen dem Staat gegenüber selbständigen Mission, mit ihren unveränderlichen Dogmen, mit ihrer geschichtlichen und kulturellen Grösse." Ibid.

41 Ibid. 187, 192.

42 Ibid. 187, 189.

43 Ibid. 192.

44 Ibid. 185 ff.

45 Ibid. 187.

46 See above.

47 *Akten Faulhaber*, I.

48 "Sie sind als das Oberhaupt des Deutschen Reiches für uns gottgesetzte Autorität, rechtmässige Obrigkeit, der wir im Gewissen Ehrfurcht und Gehorsam schulden." Ibid. 188.

49 Ibid. 192–193.

50 "Ich will keinen Kuhhandel schlieben. Sie wissen, dass ich ein Feind von Kompromissen bin, aber es soll ein letzter Versuch sein. Die Bischöfe werden also bestimmte Vorschläge machen müssen, sei es in Form eines neuen Hirtenbriefes oder in Form einer neuen Adresse, noch bevor Bischof Hudal zum Hoftheologen der Partei ernannt wird." Ibid. 193.

51 *Akten Faulhaber*, II (ed. Volk), 196 n. 1.

52 "Wir müssen uns täglich mit den harten Wirklichkeiten herumschlagen: Die Geistlichen aus der Schule, die Jugend gegen die Kirche aufgeputscht, die heidnische Bewegung. Jetzt kommt ein Bischof von aussen und spricht aus den Wolken heraus: Der Nationalsozialismus ist ja die Gnade Gottes." Ibid. 196 (November 16, 1936).

53 Engel-Janosi, *Vom Chaos zur Katastrophe*, 188 ff.

54 Hudal, *Römische Tagebücher*, 129.

55 Hudal, *Römische Tagebücher*, 129.

56 *Akten Faulhaber* II (ed. Volk) 198.

57 Ibid. 130–137.

58 Ibid. 131.

59 Ibid. 142.

60 Ibid. 137.

61 Ibid. 131.

62 Ibid. 142.

CHAPTER 12   THE COMMUNISTS AND THE CARDINALS

1 *Römische Tagebücher* 121.

2 "L' "Internazionale" della barbarie nella sua lotta contro la civiltà," *Civiltà Cattolica* 19 (September 1936): 114 ff.

3 J. Coverdale, *Italian Intervention in the Spanish Civil War* (Princeton, 1975), and I. Saz, *Mussolini contra la II República* (Valencia, 1986).

4 See J. Petersen, *Hitler—Mussolini: Die Entstehung der Achse Berlin–Rom 1933–1936* (Tübingen, 1973), and R. De Felice, *Mussolini il duce: II. Lo stato totalitario 1936–1940* (Turin, 1981), 376 ff.

5 G. Bottai, *Diario 1935–1944*, ed. G. Guerri (Milan, 1982), 115.

6 ASV, AES, *Germania* 1936–38, Pos. 719, fasc. 312, 5 ff.

7 See chapter 11, above.

8 ASV, AES, *Germania* 1935, "scatola" 10, 86–91.

9 ASV, AES, *Germania* 1936, "scatola" 15, 48, 53.

10 Ibid. 109^v.

11 *Akten Faulhaber*, II (ed. Volk), 199.

12 Ibid. 212.

13 Ibid. 244 ff.

14 Ibid. 261.

15 "Wenn auch frühere Erfahrungen und neuerdings eingelaufene Informationen leider dazu zwingen, bezüglich der Weiterentwicklung trotz mancher gut klingenden Worte besorgt zu sein und eine Besserung der schweren Lage nicht als nahe zu betrachten, so soll doch kirchlicherseits keine echte Gelegenheit unbenutzt bleiben, um den Weg zu einer verantwortbaren Verständigung zu ebnen." Ibid. 210 (Pacelli to Faulhaber December 1, 1936).

16 *Akten Faulhaber*, II (ed. Volk), 275–77.

17 See P. Lehnert, *"Ich durfte ihm dienen": Erinnerungen an Papst Pius XII* (Würzburg, 1983), 71–72.

18 "Ich gehe jeden Tag wieder hin. Ich liebe Deutschland jetzt mit recht, weil es leiden muss," *Akten Faulhaber*, II (ed. Volk), 276.

19 ASV, AES, *Germania* 1936–38, Pos. 719, fasc. 314, 5 ff.

20 *Akten Faulhaber*, II (ed. Volk), 277–79.

21 "Hudal: Er glaubt uns alle dagegen. Bertram: Aber rein ideologisch, nicht nach der katholischen Literatur und ohne die Schwierigkeiten draussen in Wirklichkeit [*zu kennen*]." Ibid. 278.

22 "Für die Kirche geht es zur Zeit um Leben und Tod: man will direkt ihre Vernichtung," ASV, AES, *Germania* 1936–38, Pos. 719 fasc. 314, 5.

23 *Akten Faulhaber*, II (ed. Volk), 279.

24 See above, p. 52.

25 *Akten Faulhaber*, II (ed. Volk), 278.

26 Cf. Faulhaber's account ibid. 279 ff and Preysing's in W. Adolph, *Kardinal Preysing und zwei Diktaturen. Sein Widerstand gegen die totalitäre Macht* (Berlin, 1971), 73.

27 KARDINAL BERTRAM: "Die gegenwärtige Regierung und die sie stützende Partei sind mit allen Kräften am Werk, um die stufenweise Aushöhlung aller unserer kirchlichen Einrichtungen durchzusetzen. Unsere grösste und brennendste Sorge ist die Jugend. Unvorstellbar gross ist der Mangel an kirchlicher Freiheit. Jeder hat das Recht, die Kirche anzugreifen; die Kirche nicht das Recht, sich zu verteidigen. Die Entkonfessionalisierung des öffentlichen Lebens ist ein wesentlicher Programmpunkt der Regierung. Das will hinaus auf das vollständige Verschwinden der Konfessionen. Die grossen Vorteile, die das Konkordat uns rechtlich gebracht hätte, werden von Tag zu Tag immer mehr durch die Politik der vollendeten Tatsachen ausgehöhlt."

HEILIGER VATER: "Trotz all dem sind die Bischöfe mit dem Konkordat nicht unzufrieden. Schon gleich bei seinem aus sachlichen Gründen erfolgten Abschluss wussten Wir, mit was für Leuten Wir zu tun hatten. Aber ein solches Mass von Untreue gegenüber dem gegebenen Wort hätten wir nicht geglaubt und erwartet. Aber das Konkordat ist auch unter den gegenwärtigen Umständen immer noch von Wert, wenigstens wenn man sich auf den Boden des Rechtes stellt."

KARDINAL BERTRAM: "Die Regierung vernichtet die kirchliche Freiheit. Der erste Brief, den ich in Rom erhielt, war ein Schreiben des Herrn Reichserziehungsministers, wonach es keine katholischen Kindergärten, also keine "katholischen Kinder" mehr geben soll. Die Umdeutung der Begriffe, welche die Folge solcher ein objektives Recht verneinende Politik ist, ist geradezu bedrückend."

HEILIGER VATER: "Wir haben die Leiden Christi nie so gut verstanden wie in dieser jetzigen Zeit. Unser eigenes Leiden hat Uns etwas Kostbares gelehrt, und vor allem anderen das Geheimnis des Leidens Christi. Wir waren gewissermassen Analphabeten in der grossen heiligen Wissenschaft des Leidens und des Schmerzes. Nunmehr hat der so gütige, auch mit uns so gütige Gott, Uns in Seine Leidenschule genommen. Die Arbeit war Unser ganzes Leben lang Uns Freunde und Glück. Jetzt haben wir begonnen, in das Begreifen des Schmerzes einzudringen. Wie viele schmerzhafte Dinge gibt es zur Zeit (Deutschland, Spanien, Russland, Mexiko)! Wer weiss, was das Zusammentreffen Unserer Schmerzen mit diesen vielen grossen Schmerzen bedeutet? Jedenfalls ist es uns Anlass Tag um Tag, unser Vertrauen auf eine bessere Zukunft zu mehren. Wir sagen "Tag um Tag"— weil buchstäblich jeder Tag uns neue tiefe und schwere Leiden verspricht und bringt! Aber unsere Leidensintention ist: pro Germania, pro Russia, pro Hispania, pro Mexico, für alle diejenigen Teile des mystischen Leibes Christi, die mehr leiden als die anderen. Es ist ein wahres solatium mentis et corporis, so denken zu können."

KARDINAL VON FAULHABER: "Wir haben den ersten und schwersten Kampf zu bestehen um die konfessionelle Schule. Wir haben in der Praxis des täglichen Lebens erfahren, welch grosses Geschenk Eure Heiligkeit uns gemacht hat mit dem Reichskonkordat. Ohne dieses Reichskonkordat wären wir vielleicht schon am Ende dieses unseres Kampfes angelangt. Solange wir dieses Reichskonkordat haben, können wir wenigstens mit Aussicht auf die Zustimmung der Gutgesinnten, wenn auch ohne unmittelbaren praktischen Sacherfolg, Protest gegen die Rechtsbeugungen und Rechtsverweigerungen einlegen. Wir haben eine Rechtsbasis unter den Füssen, die mindestens prinzipiell, und in gewissen Auswirkungen auch praktisch, von Bedeutung ist, trotz aller Gewaltmassnahmen."

HEILIGER VATER: "Wir bewahren festes Vertrauen, felsenfestes Vertrauen nicht auf die Menschen, sondern auf Gott. Der gütige Gott, der das alles z. Z. zulässt, hat ganz gewiss besondere Absichten."

KARDINAL VON FAULHABER: "Wir danken auch ehrerbietigst für die machtvollen diplomatischen Noten, die Eminenz P[acelli] in Verteidigung der kirchlichen Rechte und in Unterstützung des Episkopats immerfort an die Regierung richtete. Wir Bischöfe bleiben ohne Antwort auf unsere Vorstellungen. Aber die Noten des Hl. Stuhles können doch nicht ohne Antwort bleiben."

HEILIGER VATER: *gibt seiner väterlichen Zustimmung zu der Arbeit des Kardinalstaatssekretärs mehrfach Ausdruck* ... "Wir gehen Unseren Weg mutvoll und vertrauensvoll weiter. Wir sind nicht pessimistisch. Bringen Sie Bayern Unseren Apostolischen Segen."

KARDINAL SCHULTE: "In Köln und im Rheinland hat man in der letzten Zeit besonders den Kampf gegen die Bekenntnisschule und die Kirchenaustrittsbewegung systematisch begünstigt und vorwärtsgetrieben. Aber trotz aller Verluste ist der Glaube und die Treue der grossen Masse der Katholiken stark. Es herrscht eine grosse und wachsende, wenn auch natürlich unorganisierte und öffentlich sich nicht hervorwagende Unzufriedenheit mit der Regierung. Das ist vielleicht ein Anlass zur Hoffnung. Von den katholischen Jugendführern sind noch drei in Berlin in Haft. Diejenigen Geistlichen, die nach monatelanger Haft zurückgekehrt sind, haben nichts von ihrem Mut verloren. Ein grosser Teil der katholischen Jugend steht noch fest—auch in Organisationen. Man ist noch keineswegs ohne Hoffnung."

BISCHOF VON PREYSING: "In Berlin ist der Druck von Regierung und Partei nicht so stark wie in rein katholischen Gegenden. Die Katholiken sind hier eine Minderheit, die man weniger fürchtet. Die Gegenwart des diplomatischen Corps rät zur Vorsicht."

HEILIGER VATER: "Bischof von Galen, Wir hören viel Glorreiches über Sie."

BISCHOF VON GALEN: "Ich habe ein sehr treues Volk und einen treuen Klerus. Dieser Klerus und sehr grosse Teile dieses Volkes stehen in Festigkeit zur Kirche. Unsere grosse Sorge ist die Entwicklung, welche auf die Dauer die Jugend nehmen wird. Wir haben mit einem Gegner zu tun, der mit uns nicht einmal die Grundbegriffe der Treue und Ehrenhaftigkeit gemeinsam hat. Alles was er sagt und tut, ist Unwahrhaftigkeit und Lüge."

HEILIGER VATER: "Unser ganz besonderer Segen gilt allen unseren tapferen Kämpfern. Unsere Sache wird gewiss siegen. Das ist unsere feste Zuversicht. Unsere Sache ist in den Händen Gottes. Und das ist besser, als wenn sie in den Händen von Menschen aufgehoben wäre. Wir sind demnach in guten und gütigen Händen. Immerhin stehen wir z. Z. in einer sehr trüben und geradezu bedrohlichen Stunde. Aber auch für unsere Zeit und für die Feinde der Kirche in dieser Zeit gilt das ewig wahre Wort: *Non praevalebunt!* Wenn der gütige Gott mit seiner Gnade, seiner Hilfe und seinem Trost bei uns ist, dann kann der endliche Ausgang dieses Ringens nicht so schlecht sein, wie es manchem Kleinmütigen heute scheinen mag. Bringen Sie Unseren väterlichen Segen allen Ihren 'Mitbischöfen', dem Klerus, dem ganzen katholischen Volk Deutschlands, das Wir in treuer Hirtenliebe umfangen und dem Wir von Herzen die Frucht seiner Leiden und seiner Treue wünschen . . ." ASV, AES, *Germania* 1936–38, Pos. 719, fasc. 314, 22 ff.

28 See above, p. 30.

29 See above, p. 19.

CHAPTER 13   WITH BURNING CONCERN

1 See above, p. 103.

2 See above, p. 114.

3 "Bei Tisch fragt Pacelli, ob nicht ein Hirtenbrief Anlass wäre, das Konkordat zu kündigen. Schulte meint ja, das könnte es sein. Ich: Dann wären unsere Hirtenbriefe längst zum Anlab genommen worden. Der Hirtenbrief des Hl. Vaters kann nicht polemisch sein. Nationalsozialismus und Partei überhaupt nicht nennen, sondern dogmatisch, friedlich, aber mit Bezug auf deutsche Verhältnisse." *Akten Faulhaber*, II (ed. Volk), 28.

4 For his contributions, see *Notenwechsel*, I (ed. Albrecht), 404 ff.

5 "einen unvollkommenen und wohl auch ganz unbrauchbaren Entwurf," *Akten Faulhaber* II (ed. Volk), 282.

6 "sehe ich, dass das für einen bischöflichen Hirtenbrief in Deutschland vielleicht geht, aber für ein päpstliches Schreiben nicht würdig ist," ibid.

7 *Notenwechsel*, I (ed. Albrecht), 404–405.

8 Ibid. 410.

9 "Habet acht, dass nicht die Rasse oder der Staat oder andere Werte der Volksgemeinschaft, die wohl in der Ordnung der irdischen Werte einen Ehrenplatz beanspruchen können, überschätzt und mit Götzenkult vergöttert werden," ibid. 410.

10 "Dab nicht der dreimal heilige Gottesname als leere Etikette für irgend ein gedankenloses Gebilde der menschlichen Phantasie gebraucht werde. Unser Gott ist der persönliche, übermenschliche, überweltliche, der allmächtige und unendlich vollkommene Gott," ibid. 410.

11 Ibid. 411.

12 Ibid. 404. The German text of *Mit brennender Sorge* is edited and commentated by A. Fritzek, *Pius XI und Mussolini, Hitler, Stalin: Seine Weltrundschreiben gegen Faschismus, Nationalsozialismus, Kommunismus* (Eichstätt, 1987), 63–152.

13 *Notenwechsel,* I (ed. Albrecht), 405.

14 ASV, AES, *Germania* 1936–38, Pos. 719, fasc. 312, 9 (author's italics).

15 See above, p. 30.

16 "Trotz mancher schwerer Bedenken haben Wir daher Uns damals den Entschluss abgerungen, Unsere Zustimmung nicht zu versagen," *Notenwechsel,* I (ed. Albrecht), 405–406.

17 Ibid. 407–408.

18 "Wer in pantheistischer Verschwommenheit Gott mit dem Weltall gleichsetzt, Gott in der Welt verweltlicht und die Welt in Gott vergöttlicht, gehört nicht zu den Gläubigen," ibid. 409.

19 "weit von wahrem Gottesglauben und einer solchem Glauben entsprechenden Lebensauffassung entfernt," ibid. 410.

20 Ibid. 411.

21 Ibid. 424.

22 Ibid. 424–25.

23 Ibid. 416.

24 Ibid. 443.

25 ASV, AES, *Germania* 1936–38, Pos. 719, fasc. 313, 43.

26 F. Muckermann, *Im Kampf zwischen zwei Epochen. Lebenserinnerungen,* ed. N. Junk VKZ. A, 15 (Mainz, 1973), 636.

27 ASV, AES, *Germania* 1936–38, Pos. 719, fasc. 316, 4 ff.

28 "Wir wollten . . . dieses kirchengeschichtliche Dokument für die Rettung des katholischen Glaubens in Deutschland nutzbar machen," ibid. 18.

29 ASV, AES, *Germania* 1936–38, Pos. 719, fasc. 319, 41, 62 ff, 67; fasc. 320, 4, 8, 40, 57, 60; fasc. 321, 3 ff, 17 ff, 23.

30 ASV, AES, *Germania* 1936–39, Pos. 719, fasc. 316, 22 ff.

31 Ibid. 28–29.

32 ASV, AES, *Germania* 1937–38, Pos. 720, fasc. 329, 11–13.

33 ASV, AES, *Germania* 1936–38, Pos. 719, fasc. 321, 29.

34 Ibid. 34.

35 ASV, AES, *Germania* 1937–38, Pos. 720, fasc. 329, 40.

36 Ibid. 43.

37 Ed. Fritzek, *Pius XI und Mussolini, Hitler, Stalin,* 153–218.

38 See above, p. 129.

39 ACDF, R.V. 1934, 29, Prot. 3373/34, vol. 4, fasc. 16.

40 ACDF, R.V. 1934, 29, Prot. 3373/34, vol. 4, fasc. 18.

41 ACDF, R.V. 1934, 29, Prot. 3373/34, vol. 4, fasc. 19.

42 See above, p. 103.

43 See above, p. 124.

44 ASV, AES, *Germania* 1937–38, Pos. 720, fasc. 329, 22 (Magistrati to Pacelli March 19, 1938).

45 "Nationalsozialismus ist nach seinem Ziel und seiner Methode nichts anderes als der Bolschewismus. Ich würde das dem Herrn Hitler sagen," *Akten Faulhaber,* II (ed. Volk), 284.

46 ASV, AES, Germania 1937–38, Pos. 720, fasc. 329, 23.

47 See Besier, *Die Kirchen und das Dritte Reich,* 799 ff.

48 ASV, AES, *Germania* 1937–38, Pos. 720, fasc. 326, 42.

49 ASV, AES, *Germania* 1937–38, Pos. 720, fasc. 328, 50 (Cicognani to Pacelli, June 1, 1937).

50 Ibid. 45.

51 ASV, AES, *Germania* 1937–38, Pos. 720, fasc. 329, 15.

52 G. Cogni, *Il razzismo* (Milan, 1937).

53 *Sa Sainteté Pie XII. Discours et panégyriques 1931–1938* (Paris, 1939), 351, 382.

54 See epigraph.

CHAPTER 14   THE EXCOMMUNICATION OF HITLER

1 ASV, AES, *Germania* 1937–38, Pos. 720, fasc. 329, 31.

2 The expression is De Felice's, *Mussolini il duce,* II: *Lo stato totalitario,* 131.

3 See Pollard, *The Vatican and Italian Fascism,* 190.

4 De Felice, *Mussolini il duce,* II: *Lo stato totalitario,* 141 ff and 148–50.

5 Ibid. 142–44.

6 G. Bottai, *Diario 1935–1945,* ed. G. Guerri (Milan, 1982).

7 Ibid. 137.

8 G. Ciano, *Diarii 1937–43,* ed. R. De Felice (Milan, 1994).

9 ASV, AES, *Germania* 1937–38, Pos. 735, fasc. 353, 4.

10 Ibid. 7.

11 Ciano, *Diarii 1937–43,* 134.

12 Ibid. 25 ff (May 3, 1938).

13 See above, p. 152.

14 ASV, AES, *Germania* 1937–38, Pos. 720, fasc. 329, 25.

15 Ibid. 27ʳ⁻ᵛ.

16 De Felice, *Mussolini il Duce,* II, 489.

17 See above, p. 154.

18 See A. Acerbi, "L'insegnamento di Pio XI sull'educazione cristiana" in *Chiesa, cultura e educazione in Italia tra le due guerre,* ed. L. Pazzaglia (Brescia, 2003), 27–53.

19 *Actes et documents du Saint-Siège relatifs à la Seconde Guerre Mondiale,* 6. *Le Saint-Siège et les victimes de la guerre: Mars 1939–décembre 1940* (Vatican, 1972), 529 ff.

20 Ibid. 530.

21 See Appendix IV with the sources listed beside each point.

22 ACDF R.V. 1934/29; Prot. 3373/34, vol. 4, 12.

23 See above, p. 104.

24 See R. Moro, "Propagandisti cattolici del razzismo antisemita in Italia (1937–1941) in *Les racines chrétiennes de l'antisémitisme politique (fin XIV–XX siècle)*, eds. C. Brice and G. Miccoli, Collection de l'École française de Rome 306 (Rome, 2003), 275–345, and G. Miccoli, "Santa Sede e Chiesa italiana di fronte alle leggi antiebraiche del 1938," in *La legislazione anti-ebraica in Italia e in Europa* Atti del Convegno nel cinquantenario delle leggi razziali, Rome, October 17–18, 1988 (Rome, 1989), 188 ff.; cf. R. De Felice, *Mussolini il Duce*, II: *Lo stato totalitario*, 489 ff, and S. Zuccotti, *The Italians and the Holocaust: Persecutions, Rescue, and Survival* (Lincoln, 1987).

25 See, best, the lucid study of G. Miccoli, *I dilemmi e i silenzi di Pio XII. Vaticano, Seconda Guerra Mondiale e Shoah* (Milan, 2000), 308 ff.

26 Quoted by Miccoli, ibid. 309.

27 Cf. S. Zuccotti, *Il Vaticano e l'Olocausto in Italia* (Milan, 2001), 11 ff.

28 See Hürten, *Deutsche Katholiken* 427 and K. Repgen, *Judenpogrom, Rassenideologie und katholische Kirche 1938* (Cologne, 1988), 22 ff.

29 ASV, AES, *Germania* 1938–45, Pos. 736–38, fasc. 354, 50.

30 *Actes et documents* 6, 530.

31 ASV, AES, *Germania* 1938–45, Pos. 736–38, fasc. 354, 54 ff (*Der Weltkampf*).

32 See *Wider den Rassismus. Entwurf einer nicht erschienenen Enzyklika (1938). Texte aus dem Nachlass von Gustav Gundlach SJ,* ed. A. Rauscher (Paderborn, 2001), and G. Passelecq and B. Suchecky, *L'encyclique cachée de Pie XI: Une occasion manquée de L'Église face à l'anti-sémitisme* (Paris, 1995), with J. Schwarte, *Gustav Gundlach S.J. (1892–1963). Massgeblicher Repräsentant der katholischen Soziallehre während der Pontifikate Pius' XI und Pius' XII* (Munich, 1975), 75–105, and G. Miccoli, "L'enciclica mancata di Pio XI sul razzismo e l'antisemitismo," *Passato e presente* 15 (1997): 35–54.

33 See Miccoli, "L'enciclica mancata . . . ," 54 and n. 71.

34 ASV, AES, *Germania* 1938, Pos. 742, fasc. 354, 40 ff.

35 "Wenn die Regierung die Beziehungen abbricht, gut—es wäre aber nicht klug, wenn wir von unserer Seite abbrächen." ASV, AES, *Germania* 1934–44, "scatole" 50, 75 ff.

36 "Wir haben das Beste getan und jede Möglichkeit zur Verbesserung der Dinge versucht . . . Wir wollen sehen, einen Versuch wagen. Wenn sie einen Kampf wollen, fürchten wir uns nicht . . . Die Welt soll sehen, dass wir alles versucht haben, um in Frieden mit Deutschland zu leben," ibid. 64–65.

37 " . . . die zweite Gelegenheit wäre eine Enzyklika. Aber dazu braucht man viel Zeit," ibid. 64. Cf. *Actes et documents du Saint-Siège relatifs à la Seconde Guerre Mondiale*, 2: *Lettres de Pie XII aux Évêques allemands* (Vatican, 1967), 413.

38 Quoted by Bouthillon, *La naissance* 299, and by J. Sánchez, *Pius XII and the Holocaust. Understanding the Controversy* (Washington, 2002), 151 (from *The Tablet*, April 4, 1964, 389).

39 Sánchez, *Pius XII . . .* 153, 154.

40   See O. Chadwick, *Britain and the Vatican During the Second World War* (Cambridge, 1986), 86 ff.

41   O. Chadwick, "Pius XII: The Legends and the Truth," *The Tablet*, March 28, 1998, 401.

42   *Inviti all'eroismo*, 3 vols. (Rome, 1941).

43   ASV, AES, *Germania* 1938, Pos. 720, fasc. 336, 39 ff.

44   Ibid. 41.

45   Ibid. 50.

46   Ibid. 54 ff.

47   Ibid. 56.

48   Ibid. 59.

49   Ibid. 60.

50   Ibid. 62.

51   Ibid. 66 ff.

52   Ibid. 70 ff.

53   *Goebbels Tagebücher aus den Jahren 1942–1943*, ed. L. Lochner (Zürich, 1948), 2116.

54   See H. Stehle, "Bischof Hudal und SS-Führer Meyer: Ein kirchenpolitischer Friedensversuch 1942/43," *Vierteljahreshefte für Zeitgeschichte* 37(1989), 298–322.

55   Hudal, *Römische Tagebücher*, 213.

56   Ibid. 215 and *Actes et documents du Saint-Siège relatifs à la Seconde Guerre Mondiale*, 9: *Le Saint-Siège et les victimes de la guerre janvier–décembre 1943* (Vatican, 1975), no. 373; 509–10.

57   Cf. M. Aarons and J. Loftus, *Unholy Alliance. The Vatican, the Nazis and the Swiss Banks* (New York, 1998), 29 ff.

58   See M. Phayer, *The Catholic Church and the Holocaust 1930–1965* (Indiana, 2000), 169. Phayer's grasp of Vatican realities appears shaky. He claims, for example (ibid. 11–12), that "in spite of his appreciation of Nazism, Hudal won an appointment as the rector of the Collegia [*sic*] del [*sic*] Anima in Rome" (cf. ibid. 166), although Hudal had not written a word about the Nazis at the time of that appointment.

59   See S. Stehle, *Geheimdiplomatie im Vatikan: Die Päpste und die Kommunisten* (Zürich, 1993), 203.

60   Hudal, *Römische Tagebücher*, 162–63, and cf. id., "Die katholische Caritas in einer Zeitenwende," *Anima-Stimmen* (1951), 26.

Select Bibliography

Aarons, M., and J. Loftus. *Unholy Alliance. The Vatican, the Nazis and the Swiss Banks* (New York, 1998).

———. *Unholy Trinity* (New York, 1991).

Acerbi, A. "L'insegnamento di Pio XI sull'educazione cristiana" in *Chiesa, cultura e educazione in Italia tra le due guerre*, ed. L. Pazzaglia (Brescia, 2003).

Achille Ratti, Pape Pie XI, École française de Rome (Rome, 1996).

Acta Apostolicae Sedis XIX, XXI–XXIX (Rome, 1922; 1929–37).

Actes et documents du Saint Siège relatifs à la Seconde Guerre mondiale, eds. P. Blet S.J., B. Schneider, S.J., A. Martini, S.J., and R. Graham (Vatican City, 1965–81).

Adolph, W. (ed.) *Geheime Aufzeichnungen aus dem nationalsozialistischen Kirchenkampf 1935–1943 VKZG.A* 28. Ed. U. von Hehl (Mainz, ⁴1987).

———. *Hirtenamt und Hitler-Diktatur* (West Berlin, 1965).

———. *Kardinal Preysing und zwei Diktaturen: Sein Widerstand gegen die totalitäre Macht* (West Berlin, 1971).

———. *Sie sind nicht vergessen: Gestalten aus der jüngsten Kirchengeschichte* (Berlin, 1972).

Agostino, M. *Le pape Pie XI et l'opinion* (Rome, 1991).

Akten zur Deutschen Auswärtigen Politik 1918 bis 1945. Aus dem Archiv des Auswärtigen Amtes, Serie C: 1933–1937. *Das Dritte Reich: Die ersten Jahre*, vol. III/1: *14. Juni bis 31. Oktober 1934;* vol. III/2: *1. November 1934 bis 30. März 1935* (Göttingen, 1973); vol. IV/1: *1. April bis 13. September 1935;* vol. IV/2: *16. September 1935 bis 4. März 1936,* (ibid., 1975); vol. V/2: *26. Mai bis 31. Oktober 1936* (ibid., 1977); vol. VI/1: *1. November 1936 bis 15. März 1937;* vol. VI/2: *16. März bis 14. November 1937* (ibid., 1981); Serie D, vol. 1: 1937–1941. *Von Neurath zu Ribbentrop* (ibid., 1950); vol. 3: 1937–1941. *Deutschland und der spanische Bürgerkrieg* (ibid., 1951).

Albrecht, D. (ed.) *Der Notenwechsel zwischen dem Heiligen Stuhl und der deutschen Reichsregierung*, vol. I: *Von der Ratifizierung des Reichskonkordats bis zur Enzyklika "Mit brennender Sorge"* VKZG.Q 1 (Mainz, 1965); vol. II: *1937–1945,*

VKZG.Q 10 (ibid., 1969); vol. III: *Der Notenwechsel und die Demarchen des Nuntius Orsenigo 1933–1945*, VKZG.Q 29 (ibid. 1980).

———. *Katholische Kirche im Dritten Reich. Eine Aufsatzsammlung zum Verhältnis von Papsttum, Episkopat und deutschen Katholiken zum Nationalsozialismus 1933–1945* (Mainz, 1976).

Altgeld, W. "Katholisches Christentum im faschistischen Italien 1922 bis 1943 und in der Zeit der Resistenz" in: Doering-Manteuffel, A./Mehlhausen, J. (eds.), *Christliches Ethos und der Widerstand gegen den Nationalsozialismus in Europa* KoGe 9 (Stuttgart-Berlin-Cologne-Mainz, 1995).

Altmeyer, K. A. *Katholische Presse unter NS-Diktatur. Die katholischen Zeitungen und Zeitschriften Deutschlands in den Jahren 1933 bis 1945. Dokumentation* (West Berlin, 1962).

Aretz, J. "Die katholische Arbeiterbewegung (KAB) im Dritten Reich" in: Gotto, K./Repgen, K. (eds.), *Die Katholiken und das Dritte Reich* (Mainz, ³1990), 119–33.

Arnold, C. *Katholizismus als Kulturmacht. Der Freiburger Theologe Joseph Sauer (1872–1949) und das Erbe des Franz Xaver Kraus* VKZG.F 86 (Paderborn, 1999).

Bankier, D., *Die öffentliche Meinung im Hitler-Staat. Die "Endlösung" und die Deutschen. Eine Berichtigung* (Berlin, 1995).

Bärsch, C.-E. "Alfred Rosenberg's 'Mythus des 20. Jahrhunderts' als politische Religion. Das 'Himmelreich in uns' als Grund völkisch-rassischer Identität der Deutschen," in H. Maier, M. Schäfer (eds.), *"Totalitarismus" und "politische Religionen,"* vol. II (Paderborn-Munich-Vienna-Zurich, 1997), 227–48.

———. *Die politische Religion des Nationalsozialismus. Die religiöse Dimension der NS-Ideologie in den Schriften von Dietrich Eckart, Joseph Goebbels, Alfred Rosenberg und Adolf Hitler* (Munich, 1998).

Baumgärtner, R. *Weltanschauungskampf im Dritten Reich: Die Auseinandersetzung der Kirchen mit Alfred Rosenberg*, VKZG.F 22 (Mainz, 1977).

Becker, H. "Liturgie im Dienst der Macht: Nationalsozialistischer Totenkult als säkularisierte christliche Paschafeier" in Maier, H. /Schäfer, M. (eds.), *"Totalitarismus" und "politische Religionen,"* vol. II (Paderborn-Munich-Vienna-Zurich, 1997), 37–65.

Behrenbeck, S. *Der Kult um die toten Helden: Nationalsozialistische Mythen, Riten und Symbole 1923–1945*, Kölner Beiträge zur Nationsforschung 2 (Vierow, 1996).

Bergmann, E. *Die deutsche Nationalkirche* (Breslau, 1933).

Bertetto, D., O.S.B. (ed.) *Discorsi di Pio XI* ii (1929–1933) (Vatican, 1985).

Besier, G. "Begeisterung, Ernüchterung, Resistenz und Verinnerlichung in der NS-Zeit (1933 bis 1945)," in G. Heinrich, (ed.), *Tausend Jahre Kirche in Berlin-Brandenburg* (Berlin, 1999), 703–61.

———. *Die Kirchen und das Dritte Reich: Spaltungen und Abwehrkampfe 1937* (Munich, 2001).

Biesinger, J. A. "The Reich Concordat of 1933: The Church Struggle Against Nazi

Germany," in F. J. Coppa, (ed.), *Controversial Concordats. The Vatican's Relations with Napoleon, Mussolini, and Hitler* (Washington, D.C., 1999), 120–81.

Biffi, M. *Mons. Cesare Orsenigo: Nunzio Apostolico in Germania (1930–1946)* (Milan, 1997).

Binchy, D. *Church and State in Fascist Italy* (Oxford, 1941).

Bleistein, R. "Abt Alban Schachleiter OSB. Zwischen Kirchentreue und Hitlerkult" *Historisches Jahrbuch* 115 (1995), 170–87.

Boberach, H. *Berichte des SD und der Gestapo über Kirchen und Kirchenvolk in Deutschland 1934–1944*, VKZG.Q 12 (Mainz, 1971).

Bollmus, R. *Das Amt Rosenberg und seine Gegner: Studien zum Machtkampf im nationalsozialistischen Herrschaftssystem*, Studien zur Zeitgeschichte 1 (Stuttgart, 1970).

Bottai, G. *Diario 1935–1944*, ed. G. Guerri (Milan, 1982).

Bracher, K. D. "Nationalsozialismus, Faschismus und autoritäre Regime," in H. Maier, (ed.), *'Totalitarismus' und 'Politische Religionen': Konzepte des Diktaturvergleichs* (Paderborn, 1996).

Bracher, K. D., Mikat, P., et al. (eds.) *Staat und Parteien. Festschrift Rudolf Morsey zum 65. Geburtstag* (Berlin, 1992).

Breuning, K. *Die Vision des Reiches: Deutscher Katholizismus zwischen Demokratie und Diktatur (1929–1934)* (Munich, 1969).

Brunotte, H. /Wolf, E. (eds.) *Zur Geschichte des Kirchenkampfs: Gesammelte Aufsätze*, II AGK 26 (Göttingen, 1971).

Brzoska, E. (ed.) *Ein Tedeum für Kardinal Bertram. Adolf Kardinal Bertram. Vorsitzender der Deutschen Bischofskonferenz im Bündnis mit dem Heiligen Stuhl während des Kirchenkampfs 1933–1945* (Cologne, 1981).

Burleigh, M. *Death and Deliverance. Euthanasia in Germany c. 1900–1945* (Cambridge, 1995).

———. *Die Zeit des Nationalsozialismus. Eine Gesamtdarstellung* (Frankfurt/M., 2000).

Calvesi, M., Guidoni, E., and Lux, S. (eds.) *E42: Utopia e scenario del regime*, 2 vols. (Venice, 1987).

Cassiani Ingoni, G., S.J. *P. Wlodimiro Ledóchowski XXVI Generale della Compagnia di Gesù (1866–1942)* (Rome, 1945).

Casula, C. *Domenico Tardini 1888–1961* (Rome, 1988).

Cecil, R. *The Myth of the Master Race: Alfred Rosenberg and Nazi Ideology* (London, 1972).

Cederna, A. *Mussolini urbanista: Lo sventramento di Roma negli anni del consenso* (Rome, 1980).

Chadwick, O. *A History of the Popes 1830–1914* (Oxford, 1998).

———. *Britain and the Vatican During the Second World War* (Cambridge, 1986).

———. "Pius XII: The Legends and the Truth," *The Tablet* (March 28, 1998), 400–401.

————. "The English Bishops and the Nazis," *Annual Report 1973 of the Friends of Lambeth Palace Library* (London, 1973), 9–28.

————. "The Papacy and World War II," *Journal of Ecclesiastical History* 18, no. 1 (April 1967): 71–79.

————. "The Pope and the Jews in 1942," in *Persecution and Toleration*, ed. W. J. Sheils (London, 1984).

————. "Weizsäcker, the Vatican, and the Jews of Rome," *Journal of Ecclesiastical History* 28, no. 2 (April 1977): 179–99.

Charles-Roux, F. *Huit Ans au Vatican 1932–1940* (Paris, 1947).

Ciano, G. *Diarii 1937–1943*, ed. R. De Felice (Milan, 1994).

Cogni, G. *Il razzismo* (Milan, 1937).

Cohn, N. *Das Ringen um das Tausendjährige Reich: Revolutionärer Messianismus im Mittelalter und ein Fortleben in den modernen totalitären Bewegungen* (Bern-Munich, 1961).

Congar, Y. *The Catholic Church and the Race Question* (Paris, 1953).

Conrad, W. *Der Kampf um die Kanzeln. Erinnerungen und Dokumente aus der Hitlerzeit* (West Berlin, 1957).

Conway, J. S. *Die nationalsozialistische Kirchenpolitik 1933–1945: Ihre Ziele, Widersprüche und Fehlschläge* (Munich, 1969).

————. *The Nazi Persecution of the Churches* (New York, 1968).

————. "The Silence of Pope Pius XII," *Review of Politics* 27, no. 1 (January 1965): 105–31.

————. "The Vatican and the Holocaust: A Reappraisal," *Miscellanea Historiae Ecclesiasticae* 9 (1984): 475–89.

————. "The Vatican, Germany, and the Holocaust," in *Papal Diplomacy in the Modern Age*, eds. P. Kent and J. F. Pollard (Westport, Conn., 1994).

Conzemius, V. *Eglises chrétiennes et totalitarisme national-socialiste: un bilan historiographique* (Louvain, 1969).

————. "Joseph Lorz—ein Kirchenhistoriker als Brückenbauer," *Geschichte und Gegenwart: Vierteljahreshefte für Zeitgeschichte, Gesellschaftsanalyse und politische Bildung* 9 (1990), 247–78.

Cooney, J. *The American Pope: The Life and Times of Francis Cardinal Spellman* (New York, 1984).

Coppa, F. J. (ed.) *Controversial Concordats: The Vatican's Relations with Napoleon, Mussolini, and Hitler* (Washington, D.C., 1999).

————. "The Hidden Encyclical of Pius XI against Racism and Anti-Semitism Uncovered—Once Again!" *Catholic Historical Review* 84, no. 1 (January 1998): 63–72.

Cornwell, J. *Hitler's Pope: The Secret Story of Pius XII* (London, 1999); *Pius XII: Der Papst, der geschwiegen hat* (München, ²2000).

Corsten, W. (ed.) *Kölner Aktenstücke zur Lage der katholischen Kirche in Deutschland 1933–1945* (Cologne, ²1948).

Coverdale, J. *Italian Intervention in the Spanish Civil War* (Princeton, 1975).

Crivellin, E. W. "Pio XI e la guerra di Spagna" in G. Campanini (ed.), *I cattolici italiani e la guerra di Spagna*. Studi e ricerche. Biblioteca di storia contemporanea (Brescia, 1987), 41–59.

De Felice, R. *Mussolini il duce: Lo stato totalitario 1936–1940* (Turin, 1981).

Denzler, G. "Katholische Zugänge zum Nationalsozialismus," in G. Denzler and L. Siegele-Wenschkewitz, (eds.), *Theologische Wissenschaft im "Dritten Reich": Ein ökumenisches Projekt* (Frankfurt/M., 2000), 40–67.

Denzler, G., and Fabricius, V. *Die Kirchen im Dritten Reich: Christen und Nazis Hand in Hand?* (Frankfurt/M. 1984).

Denzler, G., and Siegele-Wenschkewitz, L. (eds.) *Theologische Wissenschaft im "Dritten Reich": Ein ökumenisches Projekt* (Frankfurt/M., 2000).

Dietrich, D. J. *Catholic Citizens in the Third Reich: Psycho-Social Principles and Moral Reasoning* (New Brunswick–Oxford, 1988).

———. "Catholic Resistance to Biological and Racist Eugenics in the Third Reich," in F. Nicosia and L. D. Stokes (eds.), *Germans Against Nazism: Nonconformity, Opposition and Resistance in the Third Reich: Essays in Honour of Peter Hoffmann* (Oxford, 1990), 137–155.

Domarus, M. *Hitler: Reden und Proklamationen 1932–1945: Kommentiert von einem deutschen Zeitgenossen*, vol. I: *Triumph:* Erster Halbband (1932–34); Zweiter Halbband (1935–38); vol. II: *Untergang:* Erster Halbband (1939–40); Zweiter Halbband (1941–45) (Munich, 1965).

Ebneth, R. *Die Österreichische Wochenschrift "Der Christliche Ständestaat": Deutsche Emigration in Österreich 1933–1938*, VKZ B. 19 (Mainz, 1976).

Ehrle, P. "Von Benedikt XV zu Pius XI," *Stimmen der Zeit* 103 (1922).

Engel-Janosi, F. *Vom Chaos zur Katastrophe: Vatikanische Gespräche 1918–1938: Vornehmlich auf Grund der Berichte der österreichischen Gesandten beim Heiligen Stuhl* (Vienna-Munich, 1971).

Falconi, C. *The Silence of Pius XII* (Boston, 1970).

Fattorini, E. *Germania e Santa Sede: Le nunziature de Pacelli tra la Grande Guerra e la Repubblica di Weimar* (Bologna, 1992).

Kardinal Faulhaber. *Judentum Christentum Germanentum: Adventspredigten gehalten in St. Michael zu München 1933* (München, 1934).

Feldkamp, M. F. *Pius XII and Deutschland* (Göttingen, 2000).

Friedländer, S. *Nazi Germany and the Jews: The Years of Persecution 1933–1939* (New York, 1997); *Das Dritte Reich und die Juden*, vol. 1: *Die Jahre der Verfolgung 1933 bis 1939* (Munich, 1998).

———. *Pius XII and the Third Reich: A Documentation* (New York, 1966).

Fritzek, A. *Pius XI und Mussolini, Hitler, Stalin: Seine Weltrundschreiben gegen Faschismus, Nationalsozialismus, Kommunismus* (Eichstätt, 1987).

Fröhlich, E. (ed.) *Die Tagebücher von Joseph Goebbels: Sämtliche Fragmente*. Teil I: *Aufzeichnungen* 1924–1941, vol. 2: 1.1.1931–31.12.1936 (Munich–New York–London–Paris, 1987); Teil I: *Aufzeichnungen* 1923–1941, vol. III/2: März 1936–Februar 1937 (Munich, 2001); vol. I/4: März–November 1937 (ibid., 2000).

Galfré, M. "La disciplina della libertà. Sull' adozione dei testi nella scuola fascista," *Italia contemporanea* 228 (September 2002):407–38.

Galletto, B. *Vita di Dolfuss* (Turin, 1935).

Gamm, H.-J. *Der braune Kult: Das Dritte Reich und seine Ersatzreligion: Ein Beitrag zur politischen Bildung* (Hamburg, 1962).

Gariboldi, G. A. *Il Vaticano nella Seconda Guerra Mondiale* (Milan, 1992).

Gellately, R. *Backing Hitler—Consent and Coercion in Nazi Germany* (Oxford, 2001).

Gentile, E. *Il culto del littorio: La sacralizzazione della politica nell' Italia fascista* (Rome, 1993).

———. "Die Sakralisierung der Politik," in H. Maier (ed.), *Wege in die Gewalt: Die modernen politischen Religionen* (Frankfurt/M., 2002).

Giardina, A. "Ritorno al futuro: la romanità fascista," *Il mito di Roma: Da Carlo Magno a Mussolini* (Bari, 2000), 219.

Gillet, M. S. *L'église catholique et les relations internationales* (Rome, 1932).

———. *Le Pape Pie XI et les hérésies sociales* (Paris, 1939).

Godman, P., *Weltliteratur auf dem Index: Die geheimen Gutachten des Vatikans* (Berlin, 2001).

Goebbels Tagebücher aus den Jahren 1942–1943, ed. L. Lochner (Zürich, 1948).

Goldhagen, D. J. *A Moral Reckoning: The Role of the Catholic Church in the Holocaust and Its Unfulfilled Duty of Repair* (London, 2002); *Die katholische Kirche und der Holocaust: Eine Untersuchung über Schuld und Sühne* (Berlin, 2002).

Gotto, K., and Repgen, K. (eds.) *Die Katholiken und das Dritte Reich* (Mainz, ³1990).

Gramatowski, W. "Ledóchowski, Wlodomir" in *Diccionario histórico de la Compañia de Jesus*, eds. E. O'Neil and J. Domínguez, S.J., II (Rome, 2001), 1697–1690.

Griech-Polelle, B. *Bishop von Galen: German Catholicism and National Socialism* (Yale, 2002).

Gruber, H. *Friedrich Muckermann, S.J. 1883–1946: Ein katholischer Publizist in der Auseinandersetzung mit dem Zeitgeist* (Mainz, 1993).

Günther, W. *Frömmigkeit nordischer Artung* (Jena, 1934).

Hamann, B. *Hitlers Wien: Lehrjahre eines Diktators* (Munich, ³2000).

Hehl, U. von (ed.) *Priester unter Hitlers Terror: Eine biographische und statistische Erhebung*, VKZG.Q 37, ed. U. von Hehl, C. Kösters, P. Stenz-Maur, und E. Zimmermann, 2 vols. (Paderborn-Munich-Vienna-Zurich, ⁴1998).

Helmreich, E. *The German Churches Under Hitler: Background, Struggle, and Epilogue* (Detroit, 1979).

Hitler, A. *Mein Kampf* (Munich, 1937).

Hitler's Table-Talk: Hitler's Conversations recorded by Martin Bormann, introduced by H. Trevor-Roper (Oxford, 1988), no. 75, 142 ff; *Hitlers Tischgespräche im Führerhauptquartier*, ed. H. Picker, (Frankfurt/M., 1993).

Hudal, A. "Der 11: Juli von katholischer Warte," in *Reichspost*, July 23, 1936.

————. *Missa Papalis: Einführung in die Liturgie der feierlichen Papstmesse* (Rome, 1925).

————. *Der Vatikan und die modernen Staaten* (Innsbruck, 1935).

————. *Deutsches Volk und christliches Abendland* (Innsbruck, 1935).

————. *Die Grundlagen des Nationalsozialismus: Eine ideengeschichtliche Untersuchung von katholischer Warte* (Leipzig, 1937).

————. *Die serbisch-orthodoxe Nationalkirche* (Graz, 1922).

————. "Nochmals: Der 11. Juli von katholischer Warte" in *Reichspost,* August 5, 1936.

————. *Ecclesiae et Nationi: Katholische Gedanken in einer Zeitwende* (Rome, 1934).

————. *Römische Tagebücher: Lebensbeichte eines alten Bischofs* (Graz, 1976).

————. *Soldatenpredigten* (Graz, 1917).

————. "Die katholische Caritas in einer Zeitenwende," *Anima-Stimmen* (1951), 26.

————. *Vom deutschen Schaffen in Rom: Predigten, Ansprachen und Vorträge* (Innsbruck, 1933).

Hürten, H. *Deutsche Katholiken 1918–1945* (Paderborn, 1992).

————. *Kurze Geschichte des deutschen Katholizismus 1800–1960* (Mainz, 1986).

————. *Waldemar Gurian: Ein Zeuge der Krise unserer Welt in der ersten Hälfte des 20. Jahrhunderts,* VKZG.F 11 (Mainz, 1972).

Iber, H. *Christlicher Glaube oder rassischer Mythus. Die Auseinandersetzung der Bekennenden Kirche mit Alfred Rosenbergs "Der Mythus des 20. Jahrhunderts"* (Frankfurt/M.–Bern–New York–Paris, 1987).

Indice dei libri proibiti (Rome, 1930), iii and v.

Jahresbericht der deutschen Nationalstiftung S. Maria dell'Anima in Rom, 1925–27.

Jedin, H., and Repgen, K. (eds.) *Handbuch der Kirchengeschichte,* vol. VII: *Die Weltkirche im 20. Jahrhundert* (Freiburg-Basle-Vienna, 1979).

Jenner, H., and Klieme, J. (eds.) *Nationalsozialistische Euthanasieverbrechen und Einrichtungen der Inneren Mission: Eine Übersicht* (Reutlingen-Stuttgart, 1997).

Jochmann, W. (ed.) *Adolf Hitler: Monologe im Führerhauptquartier 1941–1944: Die Aufzeichnungen Heinrich Heims* (Hamburg, 1980).

Kaas, L. (ed.) *E. Pacelli, Erster Apostolischer Nuntius beim Deutschen Reich, Gesammelte Reden* (Berlin, 1930).

Kaiser, J.-C., Nowak, K., and Schwartz, M. (eds.) *Eugenik, Sterilisation, "Euthanasie": Politische Biologie in Deutschland 1895–1945: Eine Dokumentation* (Berlin, 1992).

Kaltefleiter, W. *Zwischen Kreuz und Hakenkreuz* (Wiesbaden, 2003).

Keller, E. *Conrad Gröber 1872–1948 Erzbischof in schwerer Zeit* (Freiburg-Basle-Vienna, 1991).

Kent, P. *The Pope and the Duce: The International Impact of the Lateran Agreements* (London, 1981).

Kershaw, I. *Der Hitler-Mythos. Führerkult und Volksmeinung* (Stuttgart, 1999).

————. *Hitler 1889–1936* (Stuttgart, 1998).

————. *Hitler 1936–1945* (Stuttgart, ⁴2000).

Kertzer, D. *Unholy War: The Vatican's Role in the Rise of Modern Anti-Semitism* (London, 2001).

Klöss, E. (ed.) *Reden des Führers: Politik und Propaganda Adolf Hitlers 1922–1945* (Munich, 1967).

Knauft, W. *Konrad von Preysing—Anwalt des Rechts: Der erste Berliner Kardinal und seine Zeit* (Berlin, 1998).

Koch, D. (ed.) "Karl Barth. Offene Briefe 1909–1935," in *Karl Barth Gesamtausgabe*, V (Zurich, 2001).

————. "Karl Barth: Offene Briefe 1935–1942," in *Karl Barth Gesamtausgabe*, V (Zurich, 2001).

Kremers, H. "Nationalsozialismus und Protestantismus," *Volksschriften des Evangelischen Bundes* 35 (Berlin, ⁵1933).

Kremsmaier, J. *Der Weg zum Österreichischen Konkordat von 1933/34* (Vienna, 1980).

Kretschmar, G., and Nicolaisen, C. (eds.) *Dokumente zur Kirchenpolitik des Dritten Reiches*, vol. I: *Das Jahr 1933* (Munich, 1971); vol. II: 1934/35. *Vom Beginn des Jahres 1934 bis zur Errichtung des Reichsministeriums für die kirchlichen Angelegenheiten am 16. Juli 1935* (ibid., 1975).

Kreutzer, H. "Das Reichskirchenministerium im Gefüge der nationalsozialistischen Herrschaft," *Schriften des Bundesarchivs*, 56 (Düsseldorf, 2000).

Kringels-Kemen, M./Lemhöfer, L. (eds.) *Katholische Kirche und NS-Staat: Aus der Vergangenheit lernen?* (Frankfurt/M., 1981).

Kroll, F.-L. *Utopie als Ideologie: Geschichtsdenken und politisches Handeln im Dritten Reich* (Paderborn-Munich-Vienna-Zurich, 1998).

Kühl, S. *The Nazi Connection: Eugenics, American Racism and German National Socialism* (New York, 1994).

Kulka, O. D. "Die Nürnberger Rassegesetze und die deutsche Bevölkerung im Lichte geheimer NS-Lage- und Stimmungsberichte," *Vierteljahrschrift für Zeitgeschichte* 32 (1984): 582–624

Künneth, W. *Antwort auf den Mythus: Die Entscheidung zwischen dem nordischen Mythus und dem biblischen Christus* (Berlin, 1936).

Kuropka, J. (ed.) *Clemens August Graf von Galen: Menschenrechte—Widerstand—Euthanasie—Neubeginn* (Münster, 1998).

————. (ed.) *Clemens August Graf von Galen: Neue Forschungen zum Leben und Wirken des Bischofs von Münster* (Münster, 1992).

Ledit, J. *Paradossi del communismo* (Milan, 1938).

————. *La religione e il comunismo* (Milan, 1937).

Lehnert, P. *"Ich durfte ihm dienen": Erinnerungen an Papst Pius XII* (Würzburg, 1982).

Ley, M. *"Zum Schutze des Deutschen Blutes...": "Rassenschandegesetze" im Nationalsozialismus* (Bodenheim bei Mainz, 1997).

Lieber, R., S.J. "Der Papst und die Verfolgung der Juden," *Summa Iniuria oder Durfte der Papst schweigen?*, ed. F. J. Raddatz (Hamburg, 1964).

———. "Pius as I Knew Him," *The Catholic Mind* 57 (1959): 292–304.

———. "Pius XII +" *Stimmen der Zeit* 163 (1958–59): 81–100.

Liebmann, M. "Bischof Hudal und der Nationalsozialismus," *Geschichte und Gegenwart* 44 (1988): 263–280.

Lippomarda, V. A. *The Jesuits and the Third Reich* (Lewiston–New York, 1989).

Löffler, P. (ed.) *Bischof Clemens August Graf von Galen: Akten, Briefe und Predigten 1933–1946*, vol. 1: *1933–1939;* vol. 2: *1939–1946*, VZG.F 42 (Mainz, 1988).

L'osservatore romano. Città del Vaticano, 1935–38.

Mack Smith, D. *Mussolini: A Biography* (New York, 1983).

Maier, H. *Politische Religionen: Die totalitären Regime und das Christentum* (Freiburg-Basle-Vienna, 1995).

———. "Politische Religionen": Ein Konzept des Diktaturvergleichs, in H. Lübbe (ed.), *Heilserwartung und Terror: Politische Religionen des 20. Jahrhunderts* (Düsseldorf, 1995), 94–112.

———. 'Politische Religionen': Möglichkeiten und Grenzen eines Begriffs, in H. Maier and M. Schäfer (eds.) *"Totalitarismus" und "Politische Religionen,"* vol. 2 (Paderborn-Munich-Vienna-Zurich, 1997), 299–310.

———. " 'Totalitarismus' und 'Politische Religionen': Konzepte des Diktaturvergleichs," *Politik- und kommunikationswissenschaftliche Veröffentlichungen der Görres-Gesellschaft* 16 (Paderborn-Munich-Vienna-Zurich, 1996); vol. II: H. Maier and M. Schäfer (eds.), *Politik- und kommunikationswissenschaftliche Veröffentlichungen der Görres-Gesellschaft* 17 (ibid., 1997).

Marinai, R. *Fascismo e "città nuove"* (Milan, 1970).

Marschall, W. (ed.) *Adolf Kardinal Bertram: Hirtenbriefe und Hirtenworte* (Cologne-Weimar-Vienna, 2000).

Martini, A. "Il Cardinale Faulhaber e l'Enciclica di Pio XI. contro il nazismo," *Civiltà Cattolica* CXVII (1966), 421–32.

———. *Studi sulla questione romana e la conciliazione*, Collana di storia del movimento cattolico (Rome, 1963).

May, G. *Kirchenkampf oder Katholikenverfolgung? Ein Beitrag zu dem gegenseitigen Verhältnis von Nationalsozialismus und christlichen Bekenntnissen* (Stein am Rhein, 1991),

Mayer, J. *Gesetzliche Unfruchtbarmachung Geisteskranker* (Freiburg, 1927).

McLaughlin, T. P. (ed.) *The Church and the Reconstruction of the Modern World: The Social Encyclicals of Pope Pius XI* (New York, 1957).

Meier, K. *Der evangelische Kirchenkampf*, 3 vols. (Halle/Saale-Göttingen, 1976–1984).

————. *Die theologischen Fakultäten im Dritten Reich* (Berlin, 1996).

Miccoli, G. "Das katholische Italien und der Faschismus," *Quellen und Forschungen aus italienischen Archiven und Bibliotheken* 18 (1998): 539–66.

————. *I dilemmi e i silenzi di Pio XII: Vaticano, Seconda guerra mondiale e Shoah* (Milan, 2000).

————. "L'enciclica mancata di Pio XI sul razzismo e l'antisemitismo," *Passato e presente* 15 (1997).

————. "Santa Sede e Chiesa italiana di fronte alle leggi antiebraiche del 1938," in *La legislazione anti-ebraiche in Italia e in Europa*, Atti del Convegno nel cinquantenario delle leggi razziali, Rome, October 17–18, 1988 (Rome, 1989).

Micklem, N. *National Socialism and the Roman Catholic Church: Being an Account of the Conflict Between the National Socialist Government of Germany and the Roman Catholic Church, 1933–1938* (London, 1939). [Reprint of the 1939 edition: London–New York, 1981.]

Molau, A. *Alfred Rosenberg: Der Ideologe des Nationalsozialismus: Eine politische Biographie* (Koblenz, 1993).

Moro, R. "Propagandisti cattolici del razzismo antisemita in Italia" (1937–1941) in *Les racines chrétiennes de l'antisémitisme politique (fin XIV–XX siècle)*, eds. C. Brice and G. Miccoli, Collection de l'École française de Rome 306 (Rome, 2003), 275–345.

Mosse, G. L. *Die völkische Revolution: Über die geistigen Wurzeln des National-sozialismus* (Frankfurt/M., ²1991).

Muckermann, F. *Im Kampf zwischen zwei Epochen. Lebenserinnerungen,* ed. N. Junk (Mainz, 1973).

Müller, H. (ed.) *Katholische Kirche und Nationalsozialismus* (Munich, 1965).

————. *Katholische Kirche und Nationalsozialismus: Dokumente 1930–1935* (Munich, 1963).

Mussolini, B. *Opera* XVIII (Florence, 1956).

Neuhäusler, J. *Kreuz und Hakenkreuz: Der Kampf des Nationalsozialismus gegen die katholische Kirche und der kirchliche Widerstand,* Teil I: *Der Kampf des Na-tionalsozialismus gegen die katholische Kirche;* Teil II: *Der Widerstand der katholischen Kirche gegen den Nationalsozialismus* (Munich, ²1946).

Nowak, K. *"Euthanasie" und Sterilisierung im 'Dritten Reich': Die Konfrontation der evangelischen und katholischen Kirche mit dem 'Gesetz zur Verhütung erbkranken Nachwuchses' und der 'Euthanasie'-Aktion* (Göttingen, ³1984).

Ottaviani, A. *Compendium iuris publici ecclesiastici* (Rome, 1936).

————. *Institutiones iuris publici ecclesiastici,* 2 vols. (Vatican, 1935).

Pacelli, E. *Discorsi e panegirici (1937–1938)²* (Vatican, 1956).

Passelecq, G., and Suchecky, B. *L'encyclique cachée de Pie XI: Une occasion manquée de L'Église face à l'anti-sémitisme* (Paris, 1995).

Petersen, J. *Hitler—Mussolini: Die Entstehung der Achse Berlin–Rom 1933–1936* (Tübingen, 1973).

Phayer, M. *Protestant and Catholic Women in Nazi Germany* (Detroit, 1990).

————. *The Catholic Church and the Holocaust, 1930–1965* (Indiana, 2000).

Pio XI nel trentesimo della morte (1939–1969), Raccolta di studi e di memorie (Milan, 1969).

Pius XI. *Rundschreiben über den atheistischen Kommunismus: Authentische deutsche Übertragung* (Berlin, 1937).

————. *Inviti all'eroismo*, 3 vols. (Rome, 1941).

Pizzardo, G. *Union internationale des ligues féminines catholiques. IXe conseil international: Deux conférences sur l'Action catholique* (March, 29–30, 1934).

————. *Azione cattolica e assistenza religiosa agli operai* (Rome, 1937).

Pollard, J. *The Vatican and Italian Fascism 1929–32: A Study in Conflict* (Cambridge, 1982).

Prévotat, J. *Les catholiques et l'Action française: Histoire d'une condamnation 1899–1939* (Paris, 2001).

Prolingheuer, H. *Der Fall Karl Barth 1934–1935. Chronographie einer Vertreibung* (Neukirchen-Vluyn, ²1984).

Raem, H.-A. *Pius XI. und der Nationalsozialismus: Die Enzyklika "Mit brennender Sorge" vom 14. März 1937* (Paderborn-Munich-Vienna-Zurich, 1979).

Rauscher, A. (ed.) *Wider den Rassismus: Entwurf einer nicht erschienenen Enzyklika (1938) aus dem Nachlass von Gustav Gundlach SJ* (Paderborn-Munich-Vienna-Zurich, 2001).

Recker, K. A. *"Wem wollt Ihr glauben?" Bischof Berning im Dritten Reich* (Paderborn, 1998).

Repgen, K. *Von der Reformation zur Gegenwart. Beiträge zu Grundfragen der neuzeitlichen Geschichte* (eds. K. Gotto and H. Hockerts) (Paderborn, 1968), 155ff.

Rhodes, A. *The Vatican in the Age of the Dictators (1922–1945)* (New York, 1973).

Riccardi, A. "La vita religiosa" in V. Vidotto, (ed.) *Roma capitale* (Bari, 2002).

Richter, Alfred (i.e., Roth, Joseph). "Das Verhältnis zwischen dem Staat und der römischen Kirche, römisch-katholisch, geschichtlich und nationalsozialistisch gesehen. Eine Stellungnahme zu dem Werk von Alfredo Ottaviani. Grundlinien des Kirchenrechts," *Deutschlands Erneuerung* 20 (1936): 736–40.

Richter, I. "Der deutsche Episkopat zur Eugenetik, Zwangssterilisation und 'Euthanasie' im NS-Regime" in J. Kuropka (ed.), *Clemens August Graf von Galen. Menschenrechte—Widerstand—Euthanasie—Neubeginn* (Münster, 1998), 185–203.

————. *Katholizismus und Eugenetik in der Weimarer Republik und im Dritten Reich: Zwischen Sittlichkeitsreform und Rassenhygiene*, VKZG.F 88 (Paderborn-Munich-Vienna-Zurich, 2001).

Rinaldi, M. "Il volto effemero della città nell' età dell' impero e dell' autarchia" in *La Capitale a Roma: Città e arredo urbano (1870–1945)*, exhibition catalogue (Rome, 1991).

Rosa, E., S.J. "L'Internazionale' della barbarie nella sua lotta contro la Civiltà," *Civiltà Cattolica*, September 19, 1936, 114 ff.

Salotti, C. *Le crisi della società contemporanea: Studi apologetici* (Isola del Liri, 1931).

Sánchez, J. *Pius XII and the Holocaust: Understanding the Controversy* (Washington, 2002).

Sandmann, F. *Die Haltung des Vatikans zum Nationalsozialismus im Spiegel des "Osservatore Romano" (von 1929 bis zum Kriegsausbruch)*, diss. (Mainz, 1965).

Sa Sainteté Pie XII: Discours et panégyriques 1931–1938 (Paris, 1939).

Saz, I. *Mussolini contra la II República* (Valencia, 1986).

Sbarretti, D. *Il primo giubileo dell'opera della preservazione della fede in Roma* (Vatican, 1924).

Scarrocchia, S. *Albert Speer e Marcello Piacentini: L'architettura del totalitarismo negli anni trenta* (Milan, 1999).

Schellenberger, B. *Katholische Jugend und Drittes Reich: Eine Geschichte des Katholischen Jungmännerverbandes 1933–1939 unter besonderer Berücksichtigung der Rheinprovinz*, VKZG B 17 (Mainz, 1975).

Scherffig, W. *Junge Theologen im "Dritten Reich": Dokumente, Briefe, Erfahrungen*, vol. 1: *Es begann mit einem Nein!* 1933–1935 (Neukirchen-Vluyn, 1989); vol. 2: Im *Bannkreis politischer Verführung.* 1936–1937 (ibid., 1989).

Schmuhl, H.-W. *Rassenhygiene, Nationalsozialismus, Euthanasie. Von der Verhütung zur Vernichtung "lebensunwerten Lebens" 1890–1945*, Kritische Studien zur Geschichtswissenschaft 75 (Göttingen, ²1992).

Schneider, B. (ed.) *Die Briefe Pius' XII. an die deutschen Bischöfe 1939–1944*, VKZG.Q 4 (Mainz, 1966).

Scholder, K. *Die Kirchen und das Dritte Reich*, vol. 1: *Vorgeschichte und Zeit der Illusion 1918–1934* (Frankfurt/M.-Berlin, ³2000); vol. 2: *Das Jahr der Ernüchterung 1934: Barmen und Rom* (ibid., ³2000).

———. "Politik und Kirchenpolitik im Dritten Reich: Die kirchenpolitische Wende in Deutschland 1936/37," in K. Scholder, *Die Kirchen zwischen Republik und Gewaltherrschaft.* Gesammelte Aufsätze, ed. G. Besier (West-Berlin, 1988), 213–227.

Schwaiger, G. (ed.) *Das Erzbistum München und Freising im 19. und 20. Jahrhundert*, vol. 1 (Munich-Zurich, 1984), vol. 2 (Munich, 1989), vol. 3 (ibid., 1989).

———. *Papsttum und Päpste im 20. Jahrhundert. Von Leo XIII. zu Johannes Paul II.* (Munich, 1999).

Schwalbach, B. *Erzbischof Conrad Gröber und die nationalsozialistische Diktatur: Eine Studie zum Episkopat des Metropoliten der Oberrheinischen Kirchenprovinz während des Dritten Reiches* (Karlsruhe, 1985).

Schwarte, J. *Gustav Gundlach S.J. (1892–1963): Massgeblicher Repräsentant der katholischen Soziallehre während der Pontifikate Pius' XI und Pius' XII* (Munich, 1975).

Siegele-Wenschkewitz, L. *Nationalsozialismus und Kirchen: Religionspolitik von Partei und Staat bis 1935* Tübinger Schriften zur Sozial- und Zeitgeschichte 5 (Düsseldorf, 1974).

Stasiewski, B. (ed.) *Adolf Kardinal Bertram: Sein Leben und Wirken auf dem Hintergrund der Geschichte seiner Zeit*, Teil I: *"Beiträge"* (Cologne-Weimar-Vienna, 1992); Teil II: *"Schrifttum"* (ibid., 1994).

———. *Akten deutscher Bischöfe über die Lage der Kirche 1933 bis 1945*, vol. I: 1933–1934, *VKZG.Q* 5 (Mainz, 1965); vol. II: 1934–1935, *VKZG.Q* 20 (ibid., 1976); Bd. III: 1935–1936, *VKZG.Q* 25 (ibid. 1979).

Stehle, H. *Die Ostpolitik des Vaticans 1917–1975* (Munich, 1975).

———. "Bischof Hudal und SS-Führer Meyer: Ein kirchenpolitischer Friedensversuch 1942/43," *Vierteljahreshefte für Zeitgeschichte* (1989), 298–322.

———. *Geheimdiplomatie im Vatikan: Die Päpste und die Kommunisten* (Zürich, 1993).

Steigmann-Gall, R. *The Holy Reich: Nazi Conceptions of Christianity 1919–1945* (Cambridge, 2003).

Tardini, D. "San Tommaso d'Aquino e la romanità," *Rivista di filosofia neoscolastica* 39 (1937).

Tardini, P. *Pio XII* (Vatican, 1960).

Tenneson, A., S.J. "Pie XI et la Compagnie," *Lettres de Jersey* XLIII (1929–1930).

Tokareva, E. "Le relazioni fra l'URSS e il Vaticano: dalle trattative alla rottura (1922–1929)" in *Santa Sede e Russia da Leone XIII a Pio XI.* Atti del simposio organizzato dal Pontificio Comitato di Scienze Storiche e dall'Istituto di Storia Universale dell'Accademia delle Scienze di Mosca (Vatican, 2002), 149–261.

Trevor-Roper, H. "Hitlers Kriegsziele," *Vierteljahrshefte für Zeitgeschichte* 13 (1965) 285–337.

Vieler, E. H. *The Ideological Roots of German National Socialism* (New York et al., 1999).

Volk, L. *Akten deutscher Bischöfe über die Lage der Kirche 1933–1945*, vol. IV: 1936–1939, VKZG.Q 30 (Mainz, 1981).

———. *Akten Kardinal Michael von Faulhabers 1917–1945*, vol. I: 1917–1934, *VKZG.Q* 17 (Mainz, 1975); vol. II: 1935–1945, VKZG.Q 26 (ibid., 1978).

———. "Die Enzyklika 'Mit brennender Sorge': Zum hundertsten Geburtstag Kardinal Michael v. Faulhabers am 5. März 1569" in L. Volk, *Katholische Kirche im Dritten Reich* [Ort und Jahr recherchieren], 34–65.

———. "Die Fuldaer Bischofskonferenz von Hitlers Machtergreifung bis zur Enzyklika 'Mit brennender Sorge' " in L. Volk, *Katholische Kirche und Nationalsozialismus: Ausgewählte Aufsätze*, VKZG.F 46, ed. D. Albrecht (Mainz, 1987), 11–33.

———. *Katholische Kirche und Nationalsozialismus: Ausgewählte Aufsätze*, VKZG.F 46, ed. D. Albrecht (Mainz, 1987), 11–33.

———. "Nationalsozialistischer Kirchenkampf und deutscher Episkopat" in K. Gotto and K. Repgen (eds.), *Die Katholiken und das Dritte Reich* (Mainz, ⁵1990), 49–91.

————. Das Reichskonkordat vom 20. Juli 1933. *Von den Ansätzen in der Weimarer Republik bis zur Ratifizierung am 10. September 1933*, VKZ B, 5 (Mainz, 1972).

Vondung, K. " 'Gläubigkeit' im Nationalsozialismus" in H. Maier and M. Schäfer (eds.), *"Totalitarismus" und "Politische Religion,"* vol. II (Paderborn-Munich-Vienna-Zurich, 1997), 15–28.

Walker, L. D. *Hitler Youth and Catholic Youth, 1935–1936: A Study in Totalitarian Conquest* (Washington, D.C., 1970).

Weinzierl-Fischer, E. "Österreichs Katholiken und der Nationalsozialismus," Teil I: 1918–1933; Teil II: 1933–1945 *Wort und Wahrheit* 18 (1963), 417–439; 493–526.

Weiss, K. "Lothar Kreyssig—Prophet der Versöhnung," *Zeugen der Zeit* (Gerlingen, 1998).

Zippel, F. *Kirchenkampf in Deutschland 1933–1934. Religionsverfolgung und Selbstbehauptung der Kirchen in der nationalsozialistischen Zeit*, ed. H. Herzfeld (Berlin, 1965).

Zuccotti, S. *Under His Very Windows: The Vatican and the Holocaust in Italy* (New Haven–London, 2000); *Il Vaticano e l'Olocausto in Italia* (Milan, 2001).

————. *The Italians and the Holocaust: Persecutions, Rescue, and Survival* (Lincoln, 1987).

Acknowledgments

IN 1990, WHEN I WENT TO TEACH in a united Germany, I did not understand what a society that I admired and liked had to do with the barbarities of the Third Reich. I began to read contemporary history. Although the text of this book emphasizes primary sources, I should wish to think that I have learned from the lessons taught by many excellent German historians, my debt to whom is registered inadequately in the notes.

After several years of research on the history of the Holy Office, in 2002 I went to teach at Rome. There a number of colleagues have helped and encouraged my research, chief among them that best of friends, Roberto Antonelli. For access to previously unknown sources, I thank the prefect of the Vatican Secret Archives, Father Sergio Pagano, and—in particular—the director of the archives of the former Holy Office, Monsignor Alejandro Cifres.

Jens Brandt has made a fundamental contribution to this book and I thank him for his assistance and companionship. Thanks are also due to Klaus Fricke, Roman Hocke, Bruce Nichols, and Rafe Sagalyn.

My hope is that this book will help readers to understand the options available to Rome on the eve of the Second World War and to appreciate the ways in which the leadership of the Catholic Church thought and operated. And if this work attributes fallibility to the Vatican, the same applies to the author. He is, however, in no doubt about his gratitude to the dear friends to whom it is dedicated.

Index

About the Author

PETER GODMAN is an authority on the Inquisition and the history of the Catholic Church, who teaches at the University of Rome. His numerous publications, reaching from the Middle Ages and Renaissance to the twentieth century, have been internationally acclaimed.